PEACEABLE
KINGDOM
LOST

"Peaceable Kingdom." The Quaker artist Edward Hicks (1780–1849) produced more than 100 versions of this allegorical painting based on a passage from Isaiah 11:6–9: "The wolf also shall dwell with the lamb, and the leopard shall lie down with the kid; and the calf and the young lion and the fatling together; and a little child shall lead them." Hicks interpreted Pennsylvania's early history through this biblical allegory, including in most versions of the painting a vignette of William Penn's legendary meeting with the Delawares at Shackamaxon in 1682, adapted from a popular work by Benjamin West (see page 18). Oil on canvas, 29-5/16 × 35-1/2 in., 1834. Gift of Edgar William and Bernice Chrysler Garbisch. Courtesy National Gallery.

PEACEABLE KINGDOM LOST

The Paxton Boys and the
Destruction of William Penn's
Holy Experiment

KEVIN KENNY

OXFORD
UNIVERSITY PRESS

2009

OXFORD
UNIVERSITY PRESS

Oxford University Press, Inc., publishes works that further
Oxford University's objective of excellence
in research, scholarship, and education.

Oxford   New York
Auckland   Cape Town   Dar es Salaam   Hong Kong   Karachi
Kuala Lumpur   Madrid   Melbourne   Mexico City   Nairobi
New Delhi   Shanghai   Taipei   Toronto

With offices in
Argentina   Austria   Brazil   Chile   Czech Republic   France   Greece
Guatemala   Hungary   Italy   Japan   Poland   Portugal   Singapore
South Korea   Switzerland   Thailand   Turkey   Ukraine   Vietnam

Published by Oxford University Press, Inc.
198 Madison Avenue, New York, NY 10016

www.oup.com

Oxford is a registered trademark of Oxford University Press

Library of Congress Cataloging-in-Publication Data
Kenny, Kevin, 1960–
Peaceable kingdom lost : the Paxton Boys and the destruction of
William Penn's holy experiment / Kevin Kenny.
p.   cm.
Includes bibliographical references and index.
ISBN 978-0-19-533150-9
1. Pennsylvania—History—Colonial period, ca. 1600–1775.
2. Paxton Boys. 3. Pennsylvania—Race relations—History—18th century.
4. Vigilantes—Pennsylvania—History—18th century.
5. Indians of North America—Pennsylvania—History—18th century.
6. Culture conflict—Pennsylvania—History.
7. Penn, William, 1644–1718—Philosophy. I. Title.
F152.K29 2009
323.1197074809'033—dc22
2008038445

1 3 5 7 9 8 6 4 2

Printed in the United States of America
on acid-free paper

For Owen

CONTENTS

PEACEABLE
KINGDOM
LOST

INTRODUCTION

The Paxton Boys struck Conestoga Indiantown at dawn on December 14, 1763. "Fifty-seven Men, from some of our Frontier Townships, who had projected the Destruction of this little Commonwealth," Benjamin Franklin wrote in his *Narrative of the Late Massacres in Lancaster County*, "came, all well-mounted, and armed with Firelocks, Hangers [a kind of short sword] and Hatchets, having travelled through the Country in the Night, to *Conestogoe* Manor." Only six Indians were in the town at the time, "the rest being out among the neighbouring White People, some to sell the Baskets, Brooms and Bowls they manufactured." The Paxton Boys, frontier militiamen on an unauthorized expedition, killed these six and burned their settlement to the ground.[1]

The Conestoga Indians lived on a 500-acre tract near the town of Lancaster, which William Penn had set aside for them seventy years earlier. By 1763 only twenty Conestogas were living there—seven men, five women, and eight children. They survived by raising a little corn, begging at local farms, soliciting food and clothing from the provincial government, and selling their homemade brooms and baskets. Rhoda Barber, born three years after the Paxton Boy massacres, recalled in old age what her family had told her about the Conestogas. They "were entirely peaceable," she wrote, "and seem'd as much afraid of the other Indians as the whites were." Her older brother and sisters used to spend whole days with them and were "so attached to them they could not bear to hear them refus'd anything they ask'd for." The Indians "often spent the night by the kitchen fire of the farms round about" and were "much attached to the white people, calling their children after their favorite neighbours."[2]

Local magistrates removed the remaining fourteen Conestoga Indians to the Lancaster workhouse for their safety, but on December 27 the Paxton Boys rode into that town and finished the job they had started two weeks earlier.

Fifty men, "armed as before, dismounting, went directly to the Work-house and by Violence broke open the Door," Franklin observed, "and entered with the utmost Fury in their Countenances." Within a matter of minutes they had slaughtered the fourteen Indians sheltering inside, including the eight children. After the massacres, the Paxton Boys claimed that Conestoga Indiantown was theirs by right of conquest. Some of them tried to settle on the site of the abandoned town, but provincial officials tore down their cabins and drove them off. The Paxton Boys did not succeed in their goal of seizing land, but by annihilating the Conestoga Indians they repudiated the utopian vision laid down by William Penn when he founded Pennsylvania eighty years before.[3]

Inspired by Quaker principles of compassion and tolerance, Penn saw his colony as a "holy experiment" in which Christians and Indians could live together in harmony. He referred to this ideal society as the "Peaceable Kingdom." The nineteenth-century Quaker artist Edward Hicks produced a series of allegorical paintings of the Peaceable Kingdom, juxtaposing a theme from the Book of Isaiah with Penn's meetings with the Delaware Indians. In pursuit of this harmonious vision, Penn treated the Indians in his province with unusual respect and decency. The Conestogas called him "Onas" and the Delawares knew him as "Miquon"; both words mean "feather," referring to the mysterious new quill pen wielded at treaty negotiations. The Conestogas conferred the name Onas on Penn's children and grandchildren as well, in the hope that they might embody his benign spirit.[4]

Yet for all Penn's decency, his holy experiment rested firmly on colonialist foundations. There would have been no Pennsylvania, after all, had he not received a gift of 29 million acres from Charles II in 1681—a gift that made him the largest individual landlord in the British Empire. Within his immense charter, Penn purchased land from Indians fairly and openly. But he did not do so simply out of benevolence. He needed to free the land of prior titles so that he could sell it to settlers and begin to recoup the vast expenses incurred in setting up his colony. As an English landlord, Penn naturally believed that land could be privately owned by individuals and that its occupants could permanently relinquish their title in return for money or goods. This idea ran counter to the ethos of Pennsylvania's Indians, who held their land in tribal trusts rather than as individuals and used it to sustain life rather than to make a profit. Indians often sold the same piece of land on multiple occasions, transferring rights of use and occupancy rather than absolute ownership. Penn wanted harmony with Indians, but he also needed to own their land outright. His holy experiment, therefore, never properly took root. But it left an enduring legacy: Pennsylvania did not fight its first war against Indians until the 1750s, when the Delawares and Shawnees, driven ever westward as they lost their land, launched devastating attacks on the province.[5]

William Penn's holy experiment, already in decline by the time of his death in 1718, disintegrated gradually over the next few decades and collapsed during the Indian wars of the 1750s and 1760s. His son Thomas reverted to Anglicanism, casting off the Quaker faith that sustained his father's humane benevolence. Thomas Penn and his brothers continued to negotiate with Indians, but, unhampered by religious scruples, they did not hesitate to use fraud and intimidation. In 1737 they swindled the Delawares out of a tract of land almost as big as Rhode Island in a sordid transaction known as the "Walking Purchase." Although William Penn's legacy ensured that relations with Indians were at first more harmonious in Pennsylvania than in other American colonies, the eventual outcome was everywhere the same: expropriation, conquest, and extermination. The colony moved from the false dawn of Penn's holy experiment, through the avarice and subterfuge of his sons, to the carnage of the French and Indian War and the ruthless brutality of the Paxton Boys. By the end of 1763, with the annihilation of the Conestoga Indians, what was left of the Peaceable Kingdom had broken down entirely.[6]

The Paxton Boys were Pennsylvania's most aggressive colonialists. Very little is known about them as individuals, but their general profile is clear. They lived in the hill country of northwestern Lancaster County and across the Susquehanna River in Cumberland County. Contemporaries referred to the region as the "frontier," and it was the first to be attacked during Indian wars. Some of the Paxton Boys were squatters, others farmed small plots of low-quality land; all of them hated Indians, and they detested the provincial government for failing to protect them during wartime. Those who were American-born—the great majority—were the children of settlers who came to Pennsylvania from the northern Irish province of Ulster. Contemporary accounts agree that all of them were Presbyterians.[7]

On both sides of the Atlantic, Ulster Presbyterians served as a military and cultural buffer between zones of perceived civility and barbarity, separating Anglicans from Catholics in Ireland and eastern elites from Indians in the American colonies. What they wanted above all else was personal security and land to call their own. Ulster settlers began to arrive in Pennsylvania at the beginning of the eighteenth century, intruding on unpurchased Indian lands as squatters, to the consternation of the provincial government. As squatters they immediately came into conflict with the Penn family, who were simultaneously the rulers and landlords of the province. As early as 1730, a generation before the Paxton Boys, a group of Ulster squatters temporarily occupied Conestoga Manor, declaring that it was "against the Laws of God and Nature that so much Land Should lie idle while so many Christians wanted it to labour on and raise their Bread."[8]

Idle land, hungry Christians, and the "Laws of God and Nature"—these were the words used to justify the dispossession of Indians in the eighteenth century. Together they gave rise to a powerful argument on the relationship between private property and colonialism. The English political philosopher John Locke stated the case cogently in 1690. God had given the earth "to mankind in common," Locke believed, but private property emerged when men applied their labor to nature. By rendering land more productive they gave it value, which properly belonged to the individuals who did the work. Making land productive was not just an opportunity for individual enrichment; it was also a religious obligation. "God, when he gave the world in common to all mankind, commanded man also to labour, and the penury of his condition required it of him," Locke explained. "God and his reason commanded him to subdue the earth, *i.e.* improve it for the benefit of life, and therein lay out something upon it that was his own, his labour."[9]

But what about those who did not wish to "subdue" the land and did not see it as a commodity to be exploited? What, in other words, of the Indians in the "wild woods and uncultivated waste of *America*," as Locke put it, "left to nature, without any improvement, tillage or husbandry"? European settlers had the opportunity to seize this "waste" land for themselves; indeed, they were morally obliged to do so, provided they respected the property rights of other colonists. William Penn found this idea anathema. He had too much respect for Indians to treat them in this way, and he protected their interests as well as his own by decreeing that settlers could acquire land only through his government rather than by direct purchase or seizure. For the Paxton Boys, on the other hand, the idea of seizing Indian land made perfect sense. They were not in the habit of reading John Locke in their spare time; their actions were driven not by political theory but by a desperate desire for land and safety during wartime. They scorned the property rights of other colonists, from the proprietary government downward.[10]

The Paxton Boys used violence as their sole tactic. Locke, by contrast, had argued that violence toward Indians was unnecessary because English claims to American land already rested on impregnable economic and religious grounds. For the same reason, Indians deserved no compensation for idle land lost to industrious settlers. In practice this model of peaceful dispossession never worked; it was a smokescreen for forcing Indians off the land. The Paxton Boys pushed the logic of displacement to its most brutal extreme. Nobody was arrested or prosecuted after the massacres, which encouraged other settlers to behave in similar ways. The result was wave after wave of violence on the frontier, culminating in total war against Indians during the American Revolution. The Paxton Boys' brutality was anomalous as late as 1763, in Pennsylvania at least; by the time of the American Revolution, it had become commonplace.[11]

During the Revolution waging total war against Indians became an act of patriotism. The anti-Indian campaigns of the Revolutionary War enacted the brutal logic of the Paxton Boys on a devastating scale. Now the violence was systematic rather than sporadic. In 1779 General John Sullivan led an expedition up the Susquehanna River to Iroquoia, where he waged a scorched-earth campaign against the Six Nations, destroying forty Iroquois villages, including the sacred ceremonial center of Onondaga. Pennsylvania militiamen similarly devastated the Ohio country. At the end of the war Britain transferred to the United States most of North America east of the Mississippi and south of Canada. Because four of the Iroquois nations had fought on the British side the Iroquois confederacy forfeited all territory to which it laid claim. The United States assumed sovereignty over this vast expanse of Indian land by right of conquest.[12]

A few years before the Revolution the Penn family gave exclusive use of the farm at Conestoga Indiantown to an Anglican minister named Thomas Barton as a reward for his years of service to the proprietary interest. Barton had outspokenly defended the Paxton Boys in a pamphlet published directly after the massacres, yet he had no sympathy for the idea that Conestoga Indiantown rightfully belonged to them. The Paxton Boys, he noted, "took possession of this Farm—built Cabbins and settled upon it under the ridiculous notion of a *right by Conquest*." Yet this "ridiculous notion" was fast becoming ubiquitous on the frontier even as Barton wrote. When the newly founded *Pennsylvania Magazine of History and Biography* published his letter in 1880, the editors noted that the Paxton Boys had believed "they stood in the same position of a nation who conquered its neighbors and enemies by force of arms." The editors also observed that "only a few years later this idea was carried to a successful conclusion by our patriotic forefathers." This statement was not intended ironically or critically. The Paxton Boys did more than declare an end to Pennsylvania's Peaceable Kingdom. They ushered in the new order that reached fruition during the American Revolution.[13]

This book tells the story of how William Penn's Peaceable Kingdom disintegrated over the course of the eighteenth century under the pressure of colonial expansion. Beginning with Penn's benevolent but flawed holy experiment and ending with the turmoil of the American Revolution, the story unfolds chronologically in five parts. The first part, "False Dawn," examines Penn's utopian vision and how it was undermined by his own land policy, the aggression of European settlers, and the duplicitous policies of his sons. In the opening decades of the eighteenth century Pennsylvania forged an alliance with the powerful Iroquois confederacy, which claimed the small Indian nations of Pennsylvania as "tributaries" by right of conquest. The Iroquois invariably claimed to have defeated the ancestors of the subordinate nations in battle; although details of a decisive military victory were often lacking, they backed up the claim with elaborate diplomacy and the threat of force. The Iroquois sometimes required the subject nations to pay a tribute in the form of wampum (beads made from polished shells, woven onto strings or belts and used for currency and ceremonial purposes) or other gifts. More important, they denied their tributaries two fundamental rights: the power to buy or sell land and the power to go to war. Pennsylvania's emerging alliance with the Iroquois, which gave both parties leverage against the colony of New York, hastened the dispossession of the Delaware Indians, most of whom moved across the Susquehanna River to the Ohio country.

The second part of the book, "Theatre of Bloodshed and Rapine," tells the story of the French and Indian War in the west, set against the backdrop of the larger imperial conflict that engulfed North America between 1754 and 1763. The conflict originated in the Ohio country, triggered in part by Virginian adventurers led by George Washington. When a British expedition under General Edward Braddock suffered catastrophic defeat near the French stronghold of Fort Duquesne in 1755, the western Delawares, led by three remarkable brothers, Shingas, Pisquetomen, and Tamaqua, went to war against Pennsylvania. By the end of the year Teedyuscung, the self-styled king of the eastern Delawares, had joined the campaign. In 1756 Pennsylvania took the fateful step of going to war for the first time in its history. The declaration of war, which included scalp bounties for Indians, signaled the collapse of the Peaceable Kingdom and provoked a crisis among Pennsylvania's small but influential faction of strict pacifist Quakers, led by Israel Pemberton Jr., who supported the Delawares' efforts to negotiate a peace with Pennsylvania. The treaty negotiations, combined with the conquest of Fort Duquesne, brought the fighting in Pennsylvania to an end in 1758. But memories of the French and Indian War died hard among frontier settlers, who blamed the Quakers for failing to provide adequate defense and harbored deep suspicions about local Indians, including the Conestogas.

No sooner had the French and Indian War ended with the first Peace of Paris in 1763 than the great Indian uprising known as Pontiac's War began. Against this background the third part of the book, "Zealots," tells the story of the Paxton Boys. After the massacres at Conestoga Indiantown and Lancaster, several hundred Paxton Boys marched on Philadelphia, threatening to sack the city. Due in large part to the efforts of Benjamin Franklin, the rebels chose to write down their grievances rather than proceed with their march. They submitted two documents, the *Declaration* and the *Remonstrance*, castigating the provincial government for its policies regarding Indians during wartime. Only one of their grievances was redressed before the American Revolution: the restoration in 1764 of scalp bounties for Indians killed or captured during wartime, which had been discontinued in 1758, when the Pennsylvania phase of the French and Indian War ended. But the Paxton Boys won a larger victory, escaping unpunished after exterminating a group of Indians who lived under the protection of the government.[14]

The Paxton crisis unleashed an extraordinary exchange of pamphlets in Philadelphia, "A War of Words" that forms the subject of part four of the book. The debate went beyond the massacres and the march on Philadelphia to address the fundamental question of how Pennsylvania ought to be governed. The Penn family, as proprietary governors of the province, controlled the executive branch; the Quaker party dominated the Assembly. From the mid-1750s onward the two branches were locked in disagreement, especially when it came to funding military defense. From the perspective of frontier settlers, the government seemed callously indifferent. In the political crisis triggered by the Paxton Boys, the Quaker party and its supporters squared off against an uneasy coalition of Presbyterians and Anglicans, who rallied to the proprietary interest. Franklin's *Narrative of the Late Massacres*, attacking the Paxton Boys, Presbyterianism, and the Penn family, triggered a pamphlet war in 1764 that culminated in his ill-conceived proposal for royal government in Pennsylvania. Only twelve years later Franklin was at the forefront of the patriotic movement to rid the American colonies of monarchy. Yet he was consistent throughout this period in his contempt for archaic forms of power and privilege; he merely broadened his focus by 1776 to include George III as well as the Penns.[15]

The final part of the book, "Unraveling," follows the Paxton Boys through the period of colonial Pennsylvania's disintegration, from the aftermath of the pamphlet war to the American Revolution. After the Conestoga massacres the frontier descended into anarchy. John Penn's Quaker critics insisted that his failure to pursue the Paxton Boys had undermined the reputation of the provincial government and given carte blanche to like-minded frontier settlers, thereby threatening to provoke another Indian war. When the Fort Stanwix Treaty of 1768 cleared the way for large-scale settlement in Pennsylvania west of the Allegheny mountains, violent seizure of Indian land became the norm rather than the exception. Having disappeared from view for almost six years after the Conestoga massacres, the Paxton Boys reemerged in 1769. They offered their services as mercenaries to the Susquehannah Company, a Connecticut land speculation venture intent on planting a colony in the Wyoming Valley of northern Pennsylvania.

Lazarus Stewart, who led the attack on the Lancaster workhouse in 1763, brought a group of Paxton Boys into the Wyoming Valley, where they finally acquired the land they had long been fighting for. As the American Revolution approached the Paxton Boys cast themselves as Yankee patriots doing battle against the arch-Tory Thomas Penn. They fought their last battle in July 1778, when an army of loyalists and Iroquois Indians invaded the Wyoming Valley. The Paxton Boys died as patriots—of a sort—fighting Indians over land. The Indians won the fight that day, but they could not hope to prosper in the world the Paxton Boys had helped create. Wholesale destruction of Indian culture came later in the Peaceable Kingdom than in other American colonies, but Pennsylvania was the gateway to the west—and hence to the future.

ONE

FALSE DAWN

CHAPTER 1
NEWCOMERS

In April 1701 forty Indians from the lower Susquehanna Valley came to Philadelphia to make a treaty with William Penn. They were led by Connoodaghtoh, the "King of the Indians inhabiting upon and about the River Susquehannah." About ten years earlier Connoodaghtoh had led a group of his Susquehannock Indians from Maryland back to their homelands on the Susquehanna River. They settled along Conestoga Creek, where they became known as the "Conestogas." The Shawnees were represented in Philadelphia by their king, Opessah, who, like Connoodaghtoh, had recently returned from Maryland to Pennsylvania. Also at the conference was the Onondaga chief Ahookasoongh to represent the Iroquois confederacy, which claimed the Indian nations of the Susquehanna Valley as tributaries by right of conquest.[1]

The treaty signed in Philadelphia on April 23, 1701—the only surviving Indian treaty negotiated by William Penn—reiterated Pennsylvania's commitment to nurture good relations with the Indians living in the province. Thus far in Pennsylvania's history, the treaty stated, "there hath always been a Good Understanding & Neighbourhood" between Penn "and the several Nations of Indians." Henceforth there would be "a firm & lasting Peace" between "the said William Penn, his Heirs & Successors, & all the English & other Christian Inhabitants of the said province . . . & all the severall People of the Nations of Indians aforesaid." Pennsylvania's Christians and Indians would "for ever hereafter be as one head & one heart, & live in true Friendship and Amity as one People." Neither side would "hurt, Injure or Defraud" the other, nor commit "any Act of Hostility or Violence, Wrong or Injury." Pennsylvania's Indians would "have the full & free priviliges & Immunities of all the said Laws as any other Inhabitants." All that was required of them was to acknowledge and live by "the Authority of the Crown of England and Government of this Province."[2]

The Conestoga Indians who negotiated with Penn were descendants of the once mighty Susquehannocks, the dominant Indian nation in the lower Susquehanna Valley in the seventeenth century. In 1675, weakened by disease and threatened by the Iroquois confederacy, the Susquehannocks had resettled in Maryland at the invitation of that colony. Harassed by militias from both Virginia and Maryland, they fought back, triggering Bacon's Rebellion in 1676 and suffering catastrophic defeat. In the wake of Bacon's Rebellion, Governor Edmund Andros of New York invited the surviving Susquehannocks to settle in his province under the protection of the Iroquois, with whom he had just forged a powerful alliance known as the "Covenant Chain."[3]

By inviting the Susquehannock Indians to New York, Governor Andros hoped to secure control of their homeland in the Susquehanna Valley. Some Susquehannocks took up the invitation, scattering among the Iroquois nations, but many decided to join Pennsylvania's Lenape Indians along the Delaware River instead. Connoodaghtoh led a third group back to the lower Susquehanna Valley. Sometime around 1690 William Penn gave these Indians a 500-acre tract on Conestoga Creek. About four miles from the town they abandoned when they left for Maryland, they founded a new one, which became known as Conestoga Indiantown. Thus, in a convoluted process, the Conestogas regained control of some of their lost territory in the lower Susquehanna Valley.

The Iroquois continued to claim the valley's Indians as tributaries, but the Conestogas, aware that Iroquoia lay 300 miles to the north, looked instead to William Penn as their protector. He willingly assumed this role as it helped him counter the ambitions of both the Iroquois and New York in the Susquehanna Valley. Governor Thomas Dongan of New York had purchased the valley from the Iroquois in 1683 on behalf of his master, the Duke of York. But in 1697, out of office and resident in London, Dongan sold the region to William Penn for the token sum of £100. Two Conestoga negotiators executed a deed confirming their approval of this purchase in September 1700, and it was written into the Philadelphia treaty in April 1701.[4]

Although Penn's central concern in 1701 was land, military defense was also a pressing issue. Quaker Pennsylvania had no militia, and Penn needed to ensure that local Indians would not turn against him. Iroquois oversight of the tributary nations would help in this regard. But given the risk of Pennsylvania's Indians gravitating toward the French in future military conflicts, Penn knew that good diplomacy was even more important. The treaty of 1701 made a significant diplomatic concession to the Susquehanna Valley Indians by granting their request that the Conoys of the Potomac region, over which Pennsylvania

THE DELAWARE AND SUSQUEHANNA VALLEYS

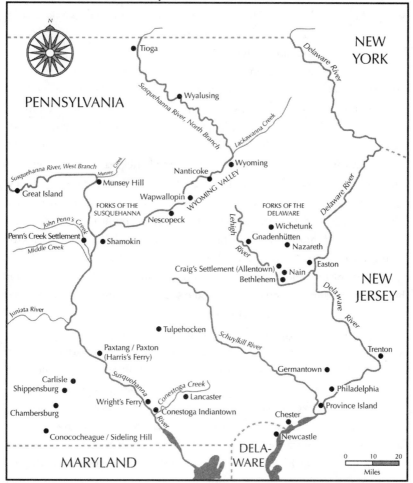

claimed jurisdiction in a boundary dispute with Maryland, would have "free Leave" to settle in the lower valley.[5]

Penn's other main goal in 1701 was to foster trade between Indians and Philadelphia's merchants, to the mutual benefit—as he saw it—of both parties. The Indians had an abundant supply of animal pelts, coveted in Philadelphia and Europe. In exchange for these furs merchants provided a variety of imported goods, including guns and ammunition, which were much in demand among Indian hunters. Under the treaty of 1701, Pennsylvania pledged to prevent the "Abuses that are too frequently put upon the said Indians" by requiring all who engaged in the Indian trade to be licensed by the government. The Indians were to do business only with licensed traders. As a quid pro quo Penn and "his heirs & Successors" promised to "take care to have them the said Indians, duely furnished with all sorts of necessary goods for their use, at Reasonable Rates."[6]

All parties to the conference of 1701 could derive satisfaction from the outcome. By treating Pennsylvania's Indians respectfully, Penn laid the basis for a lasting peace while consolidating his colonial control over the lower Susquehanna Valley, including its lucrative Indian trade. The Iroquois, with their interests in the Susquehanna Valley threatened by the rise of Pennsylvania, successfully cast themselves in the role of intermediaries between Penn and the small Indian nations in his province. They thereby created the potential for a new alliance with Pennsylvania that might serve as a counterweight to their alliance with New York. The year 1701 was a turning point in the diplomatic history of the Iroquois more generally; they also struck separate deals with the French at Montréal and the English at Albany. On the basis of the "Great Settlement" of 1701 the Iroquois carved out a position of neutrality between the French and English empires, which allowed them to influence the balance of power during much of the half-century to come.[7]

The Indians of the lower Susquehanna Valley, even though they were negotiating from a position of weakness, also made some important gains in Philadelphia. Other than the Conestogas, the most significant group in the lower valley were the Shawnees (or Shawanese). An Algonquian-speaking nation originally from the Ohio country, they had migrated to the Carolinas and present-day Alabama and Georgia in the seventeenth century. After settling along the Savannah River, from which they probably derived their name, they migrated north to the Potomac River and in the 1690s began to move into Pennsylvania. One group of Shawnees, led by Opessah, moved to the lower Susquehanna Valley around 1697, settling along Conestoga and Pequea Creeks.[8]

The Conestogas and Shawnees were prepared to help William Penn if they could achieve some of their own ends by doing so. In return for recognizing Penn's ownership of the Susquehanna Valley they extracted an assurance that they could continue to live there with the same rights "as any other Inhabitant." Moreover, they were able to counter the Iroquois claim of overlordship by turning to Penn as their champion. Two months after the treaty of 1701 Penn visited Conestoga Indiantown. No record of this visit survives, but he presumably met Connoodaghtoh and other local chiefs, and he may have inspected the lower Susquehanna River with a view to building a city there as a western counterpart to Philadelphia.[9]

Penn decided not to pursue this idea, and by the autumn he was preparing to return to England. Learning of his departure, Connoodaghtoh and Opessah led a delegation of Indians to Philadelphia, where they presented an appreciative farewell address in which "the Kings and Sachems of the Ancient Nations of the Sasquehannah and Shavanah [i.e., Shawnee] Indians" paid homage to their "Loving and good Friend and Brother William Penn." The Indians expressed their appreciation to Penn for protecting them from "any Wrong from any of the People under his Government." Invoking the recently signed treaty, they expressed their earnest hope "That we and our Children and People will be well used and be encouraged to continue to live among the Christians according to the Agreement that he and We have solemnly made for us and our Posterity as long as the Sun and the Moon shall endure, One head, One Mouth, and one Heart."[10]

For the next sixty years the Conestoga Indians continued to live peacefully under the agreement signed with William Penn. The treaty parchment was among their most cherished possessions. They carried it with them to several subsequent conferences in Philadelphia, and it was found among the charred remains of Conestoga Indiantown on December 14, 1763.[11]

The treaty conference of 1701 came toward the end of William Penn's second and final visit to his colony. As proprietary governor, Penn was both political ruler and principal landlord of Pennsylvania. He lived there for only two brief periods, in 1682–1684 and again in 1699–1701. After he was incapacitated by a stroke in 1712 his second wife, Hannah, managed the province. Before his stroke he had laid down a policy on land and Indians based on Quaker principles of tolerance and pacifism. Inspired by a spirit of providential mission, Penn envisioned his colony as a "holy experiment."[12]

Treating Indians humanely was an essential part of Penn's vision. The spirit of Quaker tolerance did not yet extend to African slaves, of whom Penn acquired several, but his policy toward Indians was notably enlightened by the standards of the time. Shortly after his arrival in 1682 he reportedly met with leaders of the Lenni Lenape (Delaware) Indians at Shackamaxon in present-day Philadelphia. The record of this conference survives on both sides only in oral tradition and in nineteenth-century paintings by Benjamin West and Edward Hicks, who glorified Penn's pacifist egalitarianism. In all likelihood there was a series of meetings rather than one.[13]

In 1701 there were probably no more than 5,000 Indians in Pennsylvania. The largest and most powerful Indian nation in the province was the Lenni

William Penn (1644–1718). Lithograph on title page of Augustus Loumey, *Bicentennial March, 1682–1882: William Penn's March* (Philadelphia: Lee & Walker, 1882). Keffer Collection of Sheet Music. Courtesy of University of Pennsylvania Library.

Lenapes ("original people"). At the time of their contact with Dutch traders in the 1620s they were living along the Atlantic coast from Delaware Bay to Manhattan Island, on the west bank of the lower Hudson River, and in the lands drained by the Delaware River that later became Pennsylvania and New Jersey. In English they came to be known as the Delaware Indians. By 1701 English and German colonists were displacing them from their homelands in southeastern Pennsylvania. Many resettled in the fertile lands of the Forks of the Delaware, where the Lehigh and Delaware Rivers met. Others moved west into the Susquehanna Valley.[14]

Hannah Penn (1671–1726). Society portrait. Courtesy of Historical Society of Pennsylvania.

Although the Delawares were the most powerful Indian nation in Pennsylvania, the Iroquois claimed them as a subject nation who, like the Conestogas, had no right to make war or own land. Meeting with Pennsylvania's lieutenant governor Charles Gookin in Philadelphia in May 1712, the Delaware leader Sassoonan formally acknowledged this status, admitting that his people were "many years ago" made tributaries to the Iroquois. Sassoonan told Gookin that a delegation of Delawares was about to visit the Iroquois bearing a calumet (Indian pipe) and thirty-two belts of wampum. Yet the Delawares too had a bond with William Penn, dating back to the legendary meeting at Shackamaxon in 1682. They paid formal obeisance to the Iroquois, but they too looked to Philadelphia for friendship and protection.[15]

Penn's Treaty with the Indians at Shackamaxon, 1682. Portrait by Benjamin West, 1771. Gift of Mrs. Sarah Harrison. The Joseph Harrison Jr. Collection. Courtesy of the Pennsylvania Academy of the Fine Arts, Philadelphia.

Although Penn treated Indians respectfully, he also needed to turn a profit from his colony. He purchased rather than seized Indian land partly for humane reasons, but also because he needed to clear it of prior titles in order to sell it to settlers. Penn was a benevolent colonialist, but a colonialist nonetheless. Although he failed to make a profit in Pennsylvania and died in debt, his land policy proved effective over the long term. He appointed commissioners of property, a surveyor general with deputies for each county, an official to record deeds and mortgages, and a receiver general to manage accounts. Together these men constituted the land office, which managed all land transactions in Pennsylvania.[16]

Penn divided the vast territory within his charter into three categories. The first consisted of land purchased from Indians and made available to settlers. Only the proprietary government could purchase land in this way; settlers could not deal directly with Indians. Settlement on land not yet legitimately purchased by the government was prohibited. Once the land had been purchased it was surveyed, divided into lots, and made available for sale. The second category consisted of proprietary manors reserved for the Penn family's use, typically one-tenth of the best land in tracts opened for sale. The third category was the proprietary family's personal estates, which included William Penn's country home, Pennsbury, situated on the Delaware River in Bucks County.[17]

Penn originally envisioned a series of English-style agricultural villages with individual holdings radiating outward from Philadelphia. Quaker settlers and land speculators, however, sought out the best land rather than forming tight-knit rural communities. The result was a pattern of widely dispersed individual farms, in contrast to the well-regulated nucleated villages of New England. Townships in Pennsylvania, especially in the west, emerged in a comparatively haphazard manner. Speculators purchased land or received grants from the provincial government, surveyed it, and sold or rented it to smaller settlers. Squatters set themselves up on unpurchased Indian land, staking their claims by right of occupancy.[18]

Pennsylvania's landholding system retained certain feudal characteristics that distinguished it sharply from New England, where title to legitimately purchased land was absolute and purchasers were free not only from prior encumbrances but also from future impositions. In Pennsylvania land purchases came with annual quitrents payable to the Penn family in perpetuity. In medieval times quitrents rendered the payer "quit and free" of feudal service. Settlers in Pennsylvania were not coerced into performing labor or military service for the Penn family, but they did have to pay a yearly fee. Medieval lords had based their entitlement on the protection they provided to the poor; the Penns claimed quitrents as compensation for the expense of clearing land of prior Indian titles. Yet clearing land of encumbrances in this way might be seen as the obligation of any seller, and doing so was certainly in the Penns' interest as they could not sell the land otherwise. The proprietary family therefore pointed out, as a further justification for quitrents, that Pennsylvania's residents were required to pay no other taxes directly to the provincial government. Counties and townships did impose taxes on land, animals, servants, and slaves, but these were local rather than provincial impositions. Not until Pennsylvania went to war in the 1750s did the province impose a general tax on property.[19]

Quitrents were a source of revenue, yet they also had symbolic importance. The annual fee might amount to several shillings per 100 acres of good land. But it could consist of a token payment, such as a peppercorn, a red rose, an Indian arrow, a deer's foot, a beaver skin, or a bushel of wheat. Whether real or nominal, quitrents signified that the Penn family exercised ultimate control over land ownership as well as political authority in Pennsylvania. Quitrents were much resented, however, especially after Thomas Penn raised the rates and tried to enforce collection more rigorously. Settlers neglected to honor their quitrents whenever possible, especially in the west, and squatters had none to pay.[20]

The Susquehanna Valley was home not just to Conestoga and Shawnee Indians but also to increasing numbers of Delawares displaced from eastern Pennsylvania. Through the valley ran the mighty Susquehanna River, whose name meant "long crooked river" in Iroquois and "muddy river" in Algonquian. The river's western and northern branches converged at the Forks of the Susquehanna, a site of great strategic and diplomatic importance, with its main branch then flowing down to Chesapeake Bay.

Among those who moved to the Susquehanna Valley was Sassoonan, leader of the powerful Unami ("Turtle") Lenapes, who were favored by William Penn. Sassoonan relocated from the upper Schuylkill River watershed some time shortly after the turn of the eighteenth century. By 1709 he was living in a town recently founded by Delaware and Shawnee Indians on the Susquehanna about forty-five miles north of Conestoga Indiantown. The Shawnee leader Opessah joined Sassoonan at this tranquil place in 1711.

The Delawares called the place Peshtank, meaning "where the waters stand," which in English became Paxtang. Here the Susquehanna reached its shallowest point, making Paxtang an ideal location for the transportation of people and commodities across the river. The town was situated along the Iroquois diplomatic and commercial trails running south from Onondaga through the Susquehanna Valley to the Chesapeake and Delaware Bays. Located at the point where the piedmont merged into the Alleghenies, Paxtang marked what European settlers referred to as the "frontier." Just north of Paxtang were the Kittatinny mountains; to the west, over the Alleghenies, was the sparsely populated Ohio country. The Shawnee Indians had lived there before their southern migration, and they were beginning to resettle the region at this time, moving across the Susquehanna River with Delaware Indians displaced from eastern Pennsylvania. Because of its location Paxtang was an important crossroads of commerce, migration, and cultural exchange, first as an Indian town and then as a European settlement.

Land-hungry settlers from the northern Irish province of Ulster began to drive out Paxtang's Indians in the 1710s. Sassoonan and the last of the Delawares left for Shamokin some time before 1728. The principal Indian town east of the Susquehanna until its abandonment at the beginning of the French and Indian War, Shamokin was located fifty miles upriver from Paxtang at the Forks of the Susquehanna. At around the time Sassoonan left for Shamokin, an English immigrant named John Harris founded a trading post in Paxtang. In 1733 the provincial government granted him exclusive rights to run a ferry crossing there. Henceforth the town was known as Harris's Ferry as well as Paxtang or, more commonly, Paxton. John Harris Jr. inherited most of his father's estate in 1749 and took over the ferry rights. He later laid out the city of Harrisburg on the site of Paxton town.[21]

The residents of Conestoga Indiantown also found themselves surrounded by growing numbers of European settlers by the second decade of the eighteenth century. German and Swiss Mennonites arrived in the area as early as 1709. Followers of Menno Simon, a religious leader in the German Palatinate during the Reformation, they resembled the early Quakers in several respects, advocating pacifism, compassion, modesty, and simple dress. The Ulster Presbyterians who began settling in the area in the 1710s could not have been more different. They showed no scruple in seizing land belonging to or reserved for others. Believing that "idle" Indians had no right to occupy land needed by industrious Christians, they embodied a rapacious form of colonialism that threatened the shaky foundations of William Penn's Peaceable Kingdom.[22]

In an effort to impose order on the settlers moving into the Conestoga region, the provincial secretary James Logan laid out a new manor of 16,000 acres for the exclusive use of the Penn family in 1718. Conestoga Manor extended northward from the mouth of Conestoga Creek along the Susquehanna River and then eastward to the area that later became Lancaster town. The manor included the 500 acres Penn had set aside for the Conestoga Indians. Alarmed by the influx of European settlers and the creation of Conestoga Manor, a delegation of Conestogas, led now by Captain Civility (Tagotolessa) instead of Connoodaghtoh, came to Philadelphia to meet Lieutenant Governor William Keith in June 1718. The provincial government had good reasons for retaining friendly relations with the residents of Conestoga Indiantown, which remained a significant trading and diplomatic center until the 1730s.[23]

Keith reassured Civility that the creation of the new proprietary manor would work to the Conestogas' advantage. The fence recently erected around their cornfields was designed to keep squatters, intruders, and stray animals out, thereby securing the protection guaranteed in the treaty of 1701. Keith also promised to take measures against "Loose Idle fellows bringing Quantities of Rum amongst them to their Great Injury" and authorized a local English farmer and fur trader named John Cartlidge, a business associate of James Logan, to supervise the protection of the Conestoga Indians. Civility presented Keith with a selection of deer skins at the beginning of the conference, which the province valued at £8 6 s. Exchanging presents in this way was an essential part of Indian diplomacy. In return, Keith authorized the presentation of gifts worth slightly more—including coats, powder, lead, stockings, tobacco, and pipes—along with all "necessarys During their stay & for their Journey on their return home." Equipped with these presents, Civility and his people went home to Conestoga Manor. A few weeks later, on July 30, 1718, Onas passed away in England, his holy experiment already in decline.[24]

CHAPTER 2

SETTLERS AND SQUATTERS

When William Penn died, none of his three sons with Hannah Callowhill Penn—John "the American," Thomas, and Richard—had reached twenty-one, the age of inheritance. Hannah had been running Pennsylvania since her husband's incapacitation in 1712, and she continued to do so until her death in 1726. She bequeathed half of Pennsylvania to John and a quarter each to Thomas and Richard. The inheritance, however, was contested. William Penn had an older son, almost twenty years John Penn's senior, from his first marriage. William Penn Jr. received land in Ireland from his father's will but nothing in Pennsylvania, which he believed was rightfully his. He disputed the inheritance until his death in 1720, and his son Springett continued the dispute until he died in 1731. Springett's brother, William Penn III, then executed a release of his claims on Pennsylvania, and the case was finally resolved in favor of the Callowhill Penns.[1]

During this chaotic period the dominant figure in Pennsylvania was James Logan, who served as secretary of the province from 1701 to 1732. Logan was a native of Ulster, but as a Quaker he had a dismal opinion of the Presbyterians who made up the majority of Irish migrants to Pennsylvania at this time. Born in 1674 into a family of Quaker converts, he first met William Penn in the English port city of Bristol, a Quaker stronghold, when he was head of a local school for which Penn was on the oversight committee. Meeting Penn was the turning point in Logan's life. He came to Pennsylvania as Penn's secretary in 1699 and lived there until his death half a century later. Before returning to England Penn appointed him clerk of the Council, secretary of the province, receiver general, and commissioner of property. Logan managed land purchases, Indian affairs, and other business dealings for the Penn family, amassing a fortune for himself. He also acquired a near monopoly over the fur trade, importing goods from England and selling them on credit to traders

James Logan (1674–1751). Portrait by Thomas Sully (after Gustavus Hesselius), 1831. Courtesy of the Library Company of Philadelphia.

who exchanged the goods for Indian pelts. The traders then sold these pelts to Logan, repaying their debt with interest. Logan exported the pelts to Europe and imported more goods for sale to the Indians.[2]

The thirteen-year interval between William Penn's death and the settlement of his inheritance paralyzed the land office. This period coincided with the first large-scale non-English migration into Pennsylvania, with settlers arriving from the northern Irish province of Ulster and a region in southern Germany known as the Rhineland-Palatinate. As the notoriously slow-moving Chancery Court deliberated in London on which branch of the Penn family owned Pennsylvania, title to lands bought and sold in the province remained unclear. Indians were reluctant to sell land to Hannah Penn and her sons; settlers were reluctant to purchase. Ulster migrants, and to a lesser extent Germans, took advantage of the confusion to set themselves up as squatters on land not yet purchased from Indians. An ongoing boundary dispute between Pennsylvania and Maryland, which led to sustained violence in the form of "Cresap's War" in the 1730s, gave settlers in southern Pennsylvania a further excuse to squat rather than purchase title.[3]

James Logan disliked Ulster Presbyterians, but he was also suspicious of Germans. "Just now," he wrote in September 1727, "one large Ship has brought above 400 of them & we are assured there are no less than three more at sea whose arrival is daily expected." Instead of the "three Ships of Palatines," he later noted, six had arrived, bringing "above 1200 of these Foreigners." Logan warned John Penn that "many of them are a surley people, divers Papists amongst them, & yᵉ men generally well arm'd." The result, he feared, would be a Germanic invasion, resulting in "a German Colony here & perhaps such an one as Britain once recd. from Saxony in the 5ᵗʰ Century."[4]

The people classified as German in eighteenth-century Pennsylvania made up the largest element of the province's population. Dr. William Smith, the Anglican provost of the College of Philadelphia, estimated Pennsylvania's non-Indian population in 1759 at 250,000, of whom about 25,000 were Anglicans, 50,000 Quakers, 55,000 Presbyterians, and 10,000 Catholics. According to Smith the remainder of the population, just under 45 percent, consisted of Germans: Lutherans, Calvinists, and "quietists" (Anabaptists and Mennonites) in about equal measure, along with 5,000 or so Moravians and "Dunkers." In reality the European population of Pennsylvania when Smith wrote was closer to 220,000, of whom about one-third were German.[5]

The first Germans to arrive in Pennsylvania were Mennonite pacifists invited by William Penn. During the 1680s they established a settlement about six miles north of Philadelphia, where they were joined by German Quakers. This settlement came to be known as Germantown. The great majority of Germans, however, settled not in towns but in the countryside, either on isolated farms or in tight-knit rural communities. Independent farmers prospered in the Schuylkill Valley and the lower Lehigh Valley and on the rich and fertile soil of Lancaster Plain. Only a handful of Germans moved west across the Susquehanna River before the American Revolution. Much more than migrants from Ulster, Germans arrived with the financial resources to settle on better land east of the river. A significant number came to Pennsylvania as indentured servants, but this practice was much more common among Ulster migrants (about half of whom were servants in the middle decades of the eighteenth century). Even when they arrived with sufficient resources, Ulster settlers rarely had the experience appropriate for the relatively large-scale intensive agriculture practiced in the central parts of Lancaster County. Germans were much more likely to establish themselves on prosperous family farms in the most fertile regions of the province.[6]

In addition to setting up as independent farmers, a significant number of Germans established self-contained agricultural communities to preserve their distinctive customs and beliefs. Among the first of these communities were the Mennonites who settled near Conestoga Indiantown in the first decade of the eighteenth century. "Hooker Mennonites," so named for their use of hooks instead of buttons to fasten their clothing, commenced settlement in the 1720s. Followers of the seventeenth-century Swiss Mennonite preacher Jacob Aman, they became known as the Amish. Another small community were the New Baptists or Dunkers, who derived their name from the habit of full-immersion baptism. In 1732 a Dunker faction founded a monastery at Ephrata, about fifteen miles from present-day Lancaster town. The members of Ephrata Kloster (Cloister) wore triangular or round linen caps of white or gray, ate no meat, drank no liquor, and used no tobacco; the men grew long beards; men and women slept in separate quarters and remained celibate.[7]

Another set of German-speaking communities was established by the Moravian Brotherhood, who were best known for their missionary work with Pennsylvania's Delaware Indians. Formally known as the Unitas Fratrum, or United Brethren, the Moravians traced their origins to the fifteenth-century Hussite movement in Moravia and Bohemia. Their first settlement in Pennsylvania was Nazareth, which they established in 1740 near the intersection of the Lehigh and Delaware Rivers. They went on to found several more missions in this region, including Nain, Wichetunk, and Gnadenhütten.[8]

Despite their desire to be left alone, German settlers caused much concern to highly placed Anglo-Pennsylvanians. James Logan's fears about the influx of the 1720s were matched a generation later by Benjamin Franklin, in a brief but classic statement of American nativism. In his pamphlet *Observations Concerning the Increase of Mankind* Franklin demanded to know, "[Why] should the *Palatine Boors* be suffered to swarm into our Settlements, and by herding together, establish their Language and Manners to the Exclusion of ours?" Pennsylvania, he pointed out, was "founded by the English." Why, then, should it "become a Colony of Aliens, who will shortly be so numerous as to Germanize us instead of our Anglifying them, and will never adopt our Language or Customs, any more than they can acquire our Complexion"? These were words Franklin would come to regret.[9]

Compared to the Germans, migrants from Ulster were united by much tighter bonds of religion, culture, and history. Germans came from a wide variety of geographical, religious, and cultural backgrounds. Even those who shared principles of pacifism and austerity, such as the Amish and the Mennonites, lived in isolation from other Germans as well as from English-speaking Pennsylvanians and Indians. The more successful these sects were in building their communities, the more fractured became any overall sense of Germanness in Pennsylvania. The Ulster Irish, by contrast, originated in a single compact province. They shared common ancestors, the Scottish planters who colonized

Ulster in the seventeenth century. Rather than a profusion of dialects they spoke one regional version of English. As Presbyterians they adhered to a single Protestant faith. They settled on widely scattered farms or squats, but instead of diluting their sense of identity their isolation reinforced their familiar role as a buffer between what they saw as savagery and civilization.

Presbyterians began to leave Ulster for America in large numbers at the turn of the eighteenth century. They left in pursuit of land and religious toleration, the two goals that had brought their Scottish forefathers to Ulster over the previous three generations. The majority of those who left Ulster were tenant farmers rather than independent landowners. They hoped that land would be cheaper and more abundant in the American colonies. As Protestants who dissented from the doctrines of the established Anglican Church, they also hoped that America would provide a haven of religious tolerance. Dissenters had endured outright persecution in England and Scotland as well as Ireland until the late seventeenth century. Under legislation passed in 1703, all officeholders in Ireland were required to take communion according to the ritual of the Anglican Church, a measure that excluded Presbyterians as well as Catholics. Dissenters' marriages were deemed irregular unless performed by an Anglican minister. And Presbyterians, like Catholics, were required to pay tithes to the established Church of Ireland. From 1719 onward Presbyterians were permitted to conduct their own services without fear of ecclesiastical prosecution, but they suffered daily reminders of their inferior status and lived in fear of renewed persecution.

This climate of intolerance, on its own, would not have led to mass emigration. But when combined with crop failures, the renewal of leases at high rents (often by auction), and repeated crises in the linen industry, it helped trigger a wave of migration that reached periodic peaks over the rest of the century. Hugh Boulter, the Anglican archbishop of Armagh and lord primate of Ireland, reviewed the origins of Ulster migration in the 1720s. Presbyterians, he wrote, resented the principle of tithes and their enforcement by ecclesiastical courts. More important, a succession of three bad harvests had "made oatmeal, which is their great subsistence, much dearer than ordinary." For several years, moreover, "some agents from the colonies in America, and several masters of ships" had been traveling the country "and deluded the people with stories of great plenty, and estates to be had for going for [sic], in those parts of the world; and they have been the better able to seduce people, by reason of the necessities of the poor of late." According to Benjamin Franklin, one-third of Pennsylvania's population, about 100,000 people, were of Ulster descent by the time of the Revolution (though one-quarter would be closer to the mark).[10]

The first Ulster Presbyterians to cross the Atlantic chose Boston as their destination. They did not receive a warm welcome from their fellow Protestant dissenters, the Puritans, quarreling with them over theology and alarming them by their poverty and manners. As early as 1700 the Puritan divine Cotton Mather denounced proposals to bring Ulster colonists to Boston as "formidable attempts of Satan and his Sons to Unsettle us." Unwelcome in Boston, Ulster migrants began moving to more western and northern parts of New England. But Pennsylvania soon replaced New England as their principal area of settlement. Belfast merchants had extensive links with the Delaware ports, which helped determine the direction of migration. Although no vessels at this time catered exclusively to the emigrant trade, passengers traveled in the holds of cargo ships returning to America after delivering their freight in England. These ships landed in the ports just below Philadelphia.[11]

Ulster Presbyterians knew that, because of William Penn's legacy, Pennsylvania was the most religiously tolerant place in the Atlantic world. They had no intention of setting up a city on a hill; instead they wanted to be left alone to live their lives as they saw fit. In pursuit of this goal, however, they had no compunction about appropriating Indian land. Whereas William Penn had insisted on legitimate land purchase from Indians, Ulster migrants regarded the interior of Pennsylvania as theirs for the taking.

Presbyterian ministers exerted an extraordinary degree of authority among Ulster settlers in Pennsylvania. In an emerging frontier society where civil jurisdiction was at a minimum they often provided the only stable source of authority. On both sides of the Susquehanna River churches were erected and congregations recognized long before townships and counties were marked out. Individual Presbyterian sessions not only governed their own internal religious and secular affairs, but they regulated morality in their communities and adjudicated arguments between church members, investigating marital disputes, illicit sexual relations, domestic violence, dishonest or questionable business dealings, and cases of dishonesty, drunkenness, and swearing. The sessions took evidence from witnesses, ruled on guilt or innocence, and doled out punishments, the most onerous being exclusion from worship and the sacraments. The capacity of the Presbyterian Church to function as both moral arbiter and court of law meant that it not only formed the basis of community, but was initially the only effective form of government on the frontier.[12]

Presbyterian congregations consisted of a minister, lay rulers known as elders, and the lay membership. Ministers held authority over spiritual matters, and elders (including deacons and trustees) governed certain temporal affairs, chiefly financial. Each congregation had a governing body known as a session, consisting of the minister and a group of elders. Ministers and elders from several congregations came together to form presbyteries, which licensed and assigned ministers and adjudicated on moral and theological disputes. These presbyteries, in turn, came under the jurisdiction of a synod. Francis Makemie, a native of Ulster known as the "Father of American Presbyterianism," founded the first American presbytery with a group of ministers in Philadelphia in 1706. A second presbytery was founded in Newcastle, Delaware, ten years later. With two presbyteries now established in the Philadelphia area, Presbyterians organized the Synod of Philadelphia in 1716, the first such body in the American colonies. In 1732 the Presbytery of Donegal was established to govern affairs among Ulster settlers in the Susquehanna Valley.[13]

As soon as they had cleared some forest ground and erected cabins to live in, frontier settlers typically set to work building a church. They erected a temporary log building first, followed by a permanent structure several years later. In the meantime the new community of worship requested formal recognition as a congregation from the Presbytery in Newcastle or Donegal. The Ulster Presbyterian settlers who drove the Delawares and Shawnees out of Paxtang had built their first church there by 1716. This congregation won official recognition from Newcastle Presbytery in 1732 and erected a permanent building in 1740, Paxton Presbyterian Church. Nearby Old Derry Church and Donegal Church both had functioning churches by about 1720, several years before their formal recognition as congregations. Their Irish place names reflected the heavy presence of Ulster settlers in the region at this time.[14]

Presbyterian ministers were in short supply in the American colonies, in part because they had to meet exacting standards in theology, Latin, Greek, and Hebrew. Those who had not been trained in Scotland before coming to Pennsylvania returned to attend Glasgow or Edinburgh universities to be educated. The first ministers on the Pennsylvania frontier invariably divided their time among several congregations. The Rev. James Anderson, a graduate of Edinburgh University and a charter member of Donegal Presbytery, ministered to Paxton and Derry as well as Donegal from 1726 to 1732. His successor, William Bertram, also a graduate of Edinburgh and a charter member of Donegal Presbytery, supplied Paxton until 1736 and Derry until his death ten years later. A third Edinburgh graduate, the Rev. John Elder, served Paxton full time from 1738 until 1791. For more than fifty years he was the dominant Presbyterian figure on the Pennsylvania frontier east of the Susquehanna River.[15]

Despite their authority in frontier communities, Presbyterian ministers did little to restrain squatters. Nor could they have done much even if they had been inclined to do so. The congregations of Derry, Paxton, and Donegal were located in the "upper end" of what later became Lancaster County, northwest of Lancaster Plain. Ulster migrants also settled in the "lower end," which was disputed by the Penns and the Baltimores (who owned Maryland) until the 1760s. The provincial government had little authority in either region, and large numbers of squatters established themselves there. From the upper end they spread out onto nearby Indian lands not yet purchased by the government. In the lower end they took advantage of the boundary dispute by refusing to make purchases from either Pennsylvania or Maryland. In 1726 the land office estimated that as many as 100,000 people were settled illegally in Pennsylvania, a figure that was unrealistically high but captured the extent of official anxiety.[16]

James Logan repeatedly expressed his concerns to the Penn family. He wrote to the three brothers in 1728 informing them of the "vast Numbers of Newcomers & Incroachers" who were squatting on most of the "Vacant Lands that are of any Value." In the lower end, he warned the following year, the squatters refused to pay the Penns for land "before your Dispute is issued." Although settlers were refusing to pay rent or purchase money to Maryland as well, Lord Baltimore held the advantage because he was not charging them quitrents. The principal source of the problem, Logan explained, was the "difference arising in the family" over the inheritance of Pennsylvania, which happened to coincide with the first large-scale migration from Ulster.[17]

Logan had mixed feelings about the Ulster influx into the upper end. Although he despised the newcomers' manners and religion and was alarmed by their violation of land policy, he saw clear advantages in directing them toward outlying areas between the province's German and Indian populations. Logan advised that "it might be wise to plant a Settlem^t. of Such Men as those who formerly had so bravely defended Derry and Inniskillen as a frontier in case of any Disturbance," recollecting the Irish phase of the Glorious Revolution in 1688–1689. Yet Logan could not help concluding that Ulster settlers caused more problems than they solved. The only hope of a solution, he concluded, was "to induce John Penn himself to come over." The boundary dispute with Maryland could not be addressed in Penn's absence and land could not be properly bought or sold. "The Indians all expect him next Spring," Logan noted in 1729, "every body expects him and tis in vain for him to expect that others will doe his business for him."[18]

CHAPTER 3

EXPANSION

Most western settlers were farmers of one kind or another. On Lancaster Plain, German and English farmers cultivated grain and raised animals, initially for subsistence and eventually for the market. The more prosperous among them sometimes owned one or two slaves. Further west and north, where the hillside soil was thinner, Ulster settlers cleared brush and forest to plant a few acres with oats and other grain and grow some beans, peas, or turnips to feed their families. They also grew hemp and flax, which women spun to make clothing. Once settled most families kept pigs, cattle, or sheep, which foraged in the woods. On substantial farms oxen were used for plowing and horses for human transportation. As the number of settlers grew, one farmer in a given area might set up a grist mill to grind his own and his neighbors' wheat, corn, and rye into flour and meal. Another might set up a distillery to produce liquor from corn, barley, and rye for commercial use, though most farmers also kept their own personal stills.[1]

Although rural settlers in the original eastern counties sometimes built houses of brick or stone, log cabins were nearly universal on the frontier. The further west one went in Pennsylvania, the more isolated the farms and cabins became. On the frontier, Ulster settlers often built single-room houses without finished floors or roofs. These rudimentary structures were intended as temporary dwellings by squatters who had no title to the land; even when they rented or owned land legally they usually did not intend to stay long. Taking advantage of the absence of government on the frontier, they claimed title to their land by "tomahawk right," cutting their initials into the barks of trees to demarcate their territory.

On arrival these settlers made a clearing in the forest to grow crops for a season. Instead of cutting down trees the way German settlers did, they favored the Indian practice of "girdling." Removing a ring of bark interrupted the sap flow, killing the trees but leaving their dead trunks in place. This practice, combined with burning the underbrush, allowed sufficient sunlight to penetrate through gaps in the forest to grow crops. Critics of the Ulster Irish, confronted with a charred landscape pockmarked with the stumps and trunks of dead trees, frowned on their "slash-and-burn" agriculture, but the practice was well suited to life in heavily wooded areas. Ulster settlers also adopted Indian practices of free-range pasture, wore moccasins, and dressed in animal pelts as well as yarn-spun clothing.[2]

Throughout the American colonies Ulster settlers developed a reputation for slovenly and wasteful agriculture, especially when compared to the Germans. Contemporaries invariably commented that Germans lived more frugally, kept neater farms, cleared the land of tree stumps, built higher fences, and looked after their animals better. German farms, they claimed, could be distinguished by the size of their barns, plain but compact houses, tall fences, rich orchards, fertile fields, luxuriant meadows, and "a general appearance of plenty and neatness in everything that belongs to them." Contemporary descriptions of Ulster settlers stood at the opposite extreme. Charles Woodmason, an English-born Anglican itinerant minister, observed while traveling through the Carolinas that although the land was excellent, it was "occupied by a Sett of the most lowest vilest Crew breathing—Scotch Irish Presbyterians from the North of Ireland."[3]

In Pennsylvania James Logan complained that Ulster settlers "sitt frequently down on any spott of vacant Land they can find, without asking questions." They also "settle generally towd^s Maryland," he reported to John Penn, "where no lands can honestly be sold, till ye Dispute wth Ld Balt. is decided." In December 1730, as he informed Thomas Penn, a "panel of Disorderly People" from Donegal and Swatara, two heavily Ulster communities close to Paxton, moved south and "possess'd themselves of all Conestogoe Mannor." Logan warned Penn that a speedy response was imperative. "This is the most audacious attack that has ever yet been offer'd," he wrote. "They are of Scotch-Irish (so called here) of whom J Steel tells me you seem'd to have a pretty good Opinion but it is more than I can have tho' their Country man." What had inspired this "audacious attack"? These Ulster settlers, Logan explained to Penn, believed that "it was against the Laws of God and Nature" to leave land "idle" when it was needed by hungry Christians.[4]

Logan enlisted the support of the Rev. James Anderson, the Presbyterian minister at Donegal Church, in removing the "audaciously impudent" squatters from Conestoga Manor. The government intended to suppress the invasion of Conestoga by force if necessary, he told Anderson, and "to declare these men Rebels & Outlaws and to treat them as such by which they will be putt out of all Protection from the Law." To prevent this bloody scenario Logan asked the pastor to "advise and prevail with these unhappy People to Desist in time & obey the Magistrates who have now strict Orders from the Gove^mt. to proceed immediately against them." With the assistance of volunteers recruited by Anderson, the sheriff and magistrates of Lancaster County evicted the squatters and burned about thirty of their cabins.[5]

Evicting squatters was a good way of bolstering the shaky authority of the provincial government on the frontier. By illegally seizing the land of "idle" Indians, Ulster settlers threatened the sovereignty as well as the financial interest of the Penn family. In places where the Penns already had clear title to the land, such as Conestoga Manor, evictions sent a message to squatters about the sanctity of the law and private property. On land the proprietary family had not yet purchased evictions conveyed a similar message not only to squatters, but also to the land's Indian occupants. The policy of evicting squatters reinforced William Penn's promise that Pennsylvania would protect its Indians and purchase their land through fair and open transactions. But it also demonstrated to the Indians that Pennsylvania claimed ownership over all land in the province, which it intended eventually to control.

The evictions on Conestoga Manor in December 1730 were at best a temporary solution to a larger problem. Some of the evicted families returned to Donegal and Swatara or moved into the hill country further north; others set up new squats in the lower end; a few moved west across the Susquehanna River. By 1733 irate Ulster settlers were resisting efforts to survey land around Donegal and Paxton Townships. Once again the authorities responded by evicting squatters and burning their cabins. The evictions of the 1730s must have left galling memories on the frontier, especially because Indians continued to live under government protection while Ulster families were forcibly ejected.[6]

Evictions were a crude and limited instrument, but the provincial government had more fundamental powers at its disposal to control the west. Chief among these was the ability to establish new counties and determine their political representation. Authority on this matter lay with the Quaker-dominated Assembly, a unicameral legislative body whose members served one-year terms. In the early eighteenth century Pennsylvania consisted of three counties—Philadelphia, Bucks, and Chester—each of which had eight representatives in the Assembly. Five new counties were established between 1729 and 1752, but the maximum number of seats in the Assembly was thirty-six, leaving only ten for the new counties.

Like most oligarchies, the Quakers who controlled the Assembly sought to perpetuate their rule. They did so in part by reducing the voting power of two groups: residents of Philadelphia and western settlers. The electorate in Pennsylvania consisted of freemen who had lived in their counties for two years and owned either fifty acres or £50 worth of real or personal property. The city of Philadelphia received only two seats in the Assembly, and the £50 property qualification restricted the vote to wealthier residents; it was much more difficult for the urban poor to accumulate this amount of property than for rural dwellers to accumulate fifty acres. But, although westerners could vote in larger numbers, the Quaker party checked their power by sharply limiting the amount of seats allocated to their counties in the Assembly.[7]

Of the three eastern counties, Bucks and Philadelphia had clearly defined borders, but Chester covered all the remaining territory in William Penn's charter, the great majority of which had not yet been purchased from Indians. Theoretically the county extended all the way to the Ohio River, though in practice it extended only as far west as the vanguard of European settlement, which had yet to cross the Susquehanna River. As the European population expanded in the 1720s settlers began to petition the provincial government to create a separate western county with its own administrative, fiscal, and judicial apparatus. The petitioners complained that they lived too far from the town of Chester, where courts were held and elections took place. They lamented the long delays in creating new townships and the neglect of roads and bridges. Pointing to the dearth of local magistrates and jails, they warned that law and order might collapse, a persuasive point given Maryland's designs on the region.[8]

The Assembly approved the creation of Lancaster County in 1729. The county was named after Lancashire, the birthplace of the English Quaker settler John Wright, who ran a ferry service on the Susquehanna River near Conestoga Indiantown. Lancaster County initially embraced all of Pennsylvania north and west of Octoraro Creek, the new boundary of Chester County. With European settlers beginning to cross the Susquehanna for the first time, Lancaster's jurisdiction extended west of the river. Despite its great size, however, Lancaster received only four seats in the Assembly.[9]

Lancaster consisted of seventeen townships, some originally part of Chester County and others established in 1729. Conestoga Township, created in 1712, included Conestoga Indiantown. Paxton, the northernmost township in Lancaster County, was bounded by the Susquehanna River to the west and the Kittatinny Mountains to the north. Its principal settlement was Paxton town, also known as Harris's Ferry. The names of four other townships reflected the high degree of Ulster settlement in the region: Derry and Donegal in the upper end and Drumore and Martock in the lower end.

To function as a county, Lancaster needed an administrative center. The site chosen as county seat lay about eighty miles west of Philadelphia, forty miles south of Paxton town, and five miles northeast of Conestoga Indiantown. William Penn would have found the choice of location peculiar. Penn had dreamed of a second city on the Susquehanna, but Lancaster was erected ten miles from the river and a mile from Conestoga Creek. The reason for this choice was that the land belonged to Andrew Hamilton, a close associate of Thomas Penn's who surveyed and laid out Lancaster town in 1730. Hamilton is best known for his defense of John Peter Zenger on libel charges in New York City five years later, which helped establish freedom of the press in America.[10]

In 1734 Andrew Hamilton sold the Lancaster tract to his son James, who developed the town of Lancaster on the grid plan William Penn had devised for Philadelphia. The first buildings included a courthouse and a workhouse that also functioned as a jail. By 1763 Lancaster had 2,800 inhabitants, which made it the largest inland town in the thirteen American colonies. About 70 percent of the residents were of German and Swiss Mennonite origin.[11]

The establishment of Lancaster County significantly enhanced the authority of the provincial government in the west. As western settlement intensified,

PENNSYLVANIA COUNTIES

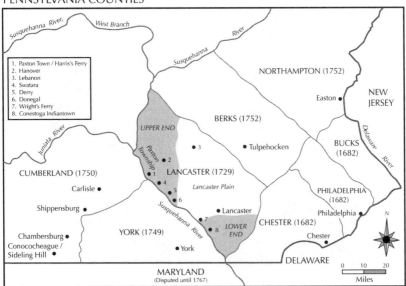

additional counties were founded, including York in 1749, Cumberland in 1750, and Berks and Northampton in 1752. These four counties received only six seats in the Assembly altogether, which meant Lancaster was the only western county with political influence. James Hamilton left Lancaster shortly after developing the town, returning to his political career in Philadelphia, where he went on to serve three terms as lieutenant governor. Edward Shippen replaced him as the principal representative of the proprietary interest in Lancaster County. A member of one of Pennsylvania's most prominent merchant families, Shippen settled permanently in Lancaster town in 1752. As chief magistrate of Lancaster town, he was answerable for the events that unfolded there on December 27, 1763.[12]

Of William Penn's three sons with Hannah Penn, it was the second son, Thomas, who became the dominant figure in Pennsylvania history. Thomas

Thomas Penn (1702–1775). Society portrait. Courtesy of Historical Society of Pennsylvania.

trained as a textile dealer in Bristol before inheriting one-quarter of Pennsylvania from his mother. After the death of his older brother, John, in 1746, he controlled three-quarters of the province. Thomas Penn ruled as an imperious absentee landlord for the next thirty years. Casting off Quakerism in favor of Anglicanism, he retained none of his father's humanitarianism; he wanted only to make a profit from the family colony, and, although he continued to pay Indians for their land, he had no scruples about defrauding them.

Thomas Penn lived in Pennsylvania from 1732 until 1741, his only stay in the province. He arrived intent on evicting squatters, raising land prices and quitrents, and collecting arrears in rents. He demanded that quitrents be paid in English pounds or in local paper money adjusted for depreciation against sterling. The Assembly, protecting its right to control monetary policy, continued to issue currency as legal tender, which could be used to pay quitrents at face value. Penn responded by instructing his lieutenant governors not to sign the Assembly's money bills. A compromise was reached when the Assembly agreed to indemnify Penn against lost rental income, but this agreement would break down in the 1750s during the French and Indian War.[13]

The conflict over monetary policy set the stage for a struggle between the executive and legislative branches that endured for three decades. Until 1701 the Assembly had been authorized merely to vote on laws presented by the executive, but under the Charter of Privileges introduced by William Penn that year it was allowed to initiate its own legislation. Thereafter the Assembly gradually assumed a range of functions originally intended for the executive, including the power to distribute gifts to Indians, determine Indian policy, and regulate the conduct of judges, as well as the right to issue paper money. By midcentury it was the most powerful legislature in the American colonies.[14]

To counter the Assembly's growing power Thomas Penn reorganized the executive branch of government. In place of James Logan he appointed the Anglican clergyman Richard Peters as provincial secretary and secretary of the land office. Peters also became clerk of the Council, which allowed him to keep a close eye on the lieutenant governors. Penn's most trusted confidante in Pennsylvania, Peters retained all three offices until his retirement in 1762. Logan continued to advise the Penn family on land purchases and Indian policy, but his political power was broken. Penn rewarded him for his years of service by allowing him to retain the chief justiceship of Pennsylvania's supreme court, a lucrative but undemanding position. He died in 1751.[15]

After Logan's removal Penn relied on a tight-knit group of political appointees known as the "proprietary party" or "gentlemen's party" to support his

William Allen (1704–1780). Portrait. Record ID 20040326001. Courtesy of Collections of the University of Pennsylvania Archives.

Andrew Hamilton (ca. 1676–1741). Portrait by Adolf Wertmuller from an original now lost. Society portrait. Courtesy of Historical Society of Pennsylvania.

James Hamilton (1710–1783). Portrait. Record ID 20040426007. Courtesy of Collections of the University of Pennsylvania Archives.

Richard Peters (1704–1776). Portrait by John Wollaston (attrib.), ca. 1758. Gift of Mrs. Maria L. M. Peters. Courtesy of the Pennsylvania Academy of the Fine Arts, Philadelphia.

Thomas Barton (ca. 1730–1780). Autographed portrait engraving. Record ID 20040830002. Courtesy of Collections of the University of Pennsylvania Archives.

William Smith (1727–1803). Portrait by Edward D. Marchant after an original oil painting by Gilbert Stuart. Courtesy of the University of Pennsylvania Art Collection. Reprinted by permission of the Office of the Curator.

executive authority and advance his financial interests. Richard Peters and James Hamilton were foremost among them. Also very influential was the Presbyterian businessman William Allen, reputed to be the richest man in Pennsylvania, who inherited a substantial legacy from his Ulster-born father and made a fortune through trade, privateering, and investment in land, copper mining, and the emerging iron industry. A cousin of Edward Shippen, Allen was married to James Hamilton's sister; their daughter Anne married Lieutenant Governor John Penn in 1766. Allen served as chief justice of the Pennsylvania Supreme Court from 1750 to 1774.[16]

Anglican ministers played a central role in Thomas Penn's inner circle. In addition to Richard Peters, the two most important were William Smith and Thomas Barton, who owed their careers to the Penn family and repaid the debt by lobbying for the proprietary interest. A native of Scotland, Smith won Thomas Penn's patronage while on a return visit from Philadelphia to England for his ordination. From 1755 to 1770 he served as provost of the College of Philadelphia. Barton, a native of Ulster, worked as a tutor to the young mathematician and astronomer David Rittenhouse, whose sister Ellen he married. William Smith provided Barton with an introduction to the Penn family when he too journeyed to England for his ordination. With their patronage he became a missionary for the Society for the Propagation of the Faith in Pennsylvania, traveling between the widely distant western congregations of York, Carlisle, and Huntingdon.[17]

The final architect of proprietary policy in Pennsylvania was Conrad Weiser, who moved from Germany to England with his family in 1709 and settled in upper New York the following year. Weiser's father sent him to live with the Mohawk Indians to learn their language and customs. In 1729 he moved to Tulpehocken, in Lancaster County, joining other members of his family. Weiser entered Ephrata Kloster, the Dunker monastery near Lancaster, as a lay brother in 1735. He returned to his wife and family permanently in 1741 and rejoined the Lutheran Church. Because of his command of Indian languages he had already been appointed Pennsylvania's official Indian interpreter, for, as Richard Peters observed, Weiser "must be supposed to know the Minds of the Indians the best." Peters and the other members of the proprietary party needed to know Indian minds well at this time, for Pennsylvania was seeking to build an alliance with the powerful Iroquois confederacy.[18]

CHAPTER 4
FRAUD

In the decades after William Penn returned to England the Conestoga Indians continued to meet regularly with the government of Pennsylvania. In June 1717 Lieutenant Governor William Keith and his Council met to discuss "an account of some Disturbance amongst the Indians" on Conestoga Manor. The Conestogas' leader, Civility, had sent a message to Keith with some other Indian leaders, asking him "to come to them without Delay, to consult with them about affairs of Great Importance." Keith agreed to visit Conestoga on July 17 and sent "a belt of Wampum as a Token of friendship & Confirmacon of this message." James Logan and the Council agreed that presents "to the value of Twenty pounds should be provided." What the Conestogas wanted most was reassurance that their bond with Onas was intact. Keith and Logan came to Conestoga as promised in July, met with the "Chiefs & others of the Conestogoe or Mingoe Indians, the Delawares, the Shawnois & Gunawoise [Conoy]," and reiterated the government's commitment to protect them.[1]

When Civility came to Philadelphia in June 1718 his intention was "to Renew the old League of ffriendship." After presenting three bundles of skins, each followed by a speech, the Indians raised a major concern: the impact of liquor on their people. They complained that despite previous agreements "that Rum should not be brought amongst them, it is still carried in great Quantities." A Delaware leader added that Indian youths in the Paxton area "had been lately so generally debaucht with Rum, carried amongst them by strangers, that they now want all manner of Clothing & necessarys to go a hunting." Ulster settlers were busily displacing Indians from the lower Susquehanna Valley at this time, and whiskey was evidently a potent weapon in their campaign. They were master distillers, but Indians had little tolerance for alcohol.[2]

Meetings with the Conestogas and their allies, though important on a local level, were a small part of a larger diplomatic game involving Pennsylvania and the Iroquois confederacy. James Logan devoted much of his energy in the 1720s to creating an alliance with the Iroquois. His goal was not to bring Pennsylvania into the Covenant Chain administered by New York but to create a separate alliance. By building closer ties with Philadelphia the Iroquois hoped to gain leverage in their relations with New York and validate their claim to speak for Pennsylvania's Indians. The provincial government, for its part, saw several advantages in an alliance with the Iroquois. Because of its Quaker pacifist heritage, Pennsylvania had no militia and could not defend itself if Indians attacked. Recognizing Iroquois authority over the tributary nations would help keep hostile Indians in check. This recognition entailed direct purchase of land from the Iroquois rather than the tributary nations who occupied it, which in turn allowed the Penns to gain clear title as a precondition to selling the land to settlers. Both parties to the alliance, in short, had much to gain.[3]

Pennsylvania and the Iroquois consolidated their emerging alliance at a conference hosted by the government of New York in Albany in September 1722. Representatives of the Mohawks, Onondagas, Oneidas, Cayugas, and Senecas attended; a sixth nation, the Tuscaroras, had joined the Iroquois confederacy by this time, but as junior partners they did not have the right to participate in treaties. Although the stated purpose of the conference was to "brighten the links of the Covenant Chain," William Keith also conducted important business privately with the Iroquois in Albany. Two leaders from each of the Five Nations agreed to "freely surrender...all those Lands about Conestogoe which the five Nations have claimed," saying that it was their "desire that the same may be settled with Christians."[4]

That the Iroquois should "freely surrender" land long since purchased by William Penn reveals a fundamental difference between Indian and European understandings of landed property. The Iroquois sold the lower Susquehanna Valley, which included Conestoga Indiantown, to Governor Thomas Dongan of New York in 1683 and Dongan sold the region to William Penn fourteen years later. The Susquehanna Valley Indians ratified Penn's purchase in 1701, and the Iroquois did so again at Albany in 1722. In return for surrendering their claim at Albany the Iroquois requested favorable terms for their traders, along with provisions for their homeward journey. Aware that the Iroquois lacked direct control over the region and that William Penn had acquired firm legal title from New York, William Keith carefully crafted his response to emphasize Pennsylvania's sovereignty while maintaining the impression of Iroquois authority. "You know very well that the Lands about Conestogoe, upon the River Sasquehannah, belong to your old friend & kind Brother William Penn," he told the Five Nations, "nevertheless, I do here, in his name, kindly accept of the offer & surrender, which you have now made to me, because it will put an end to all other claims & Disputes if any should be made hereafter." Yet, because Indians did not believe in absolute or permanent ownership in the English sense, they often sold the same piece of land more than once. On the eve of the American Revolution the Cayugas were still claiming to own Conestoga Indiantown, which they sold to William Penn's grandson, John, in 1768 and again in 1775.[5]

One sign of Pennsylvania's emerging alliance with the Iroquois in the 1720s was the presence of Five Nations representatives at conferences in Philadelphia. The Conestogas tried to counter this presence by invoking their covenant with Onas and turning to the proprietary government for protection. When Civility came to Philadelphia with some of his followers in 1727 "several Chiefs of the five Nations, but most of them of the Nation of the Cayoogas," monitored the proceedings. The Conestogas told the new lieutenant governor, Patrick Gordon, that traders were cheating them on their animal skins and giving them expensive rum instead of powder and shot, and that settlers were encroaching on their land. They asked him to ensure that "there may be no more Settlements made up Sasquehannah higher than Pextan, and that none of the Settlers thereabouts be suffered to sell or keep any Rum there." Invoking their special bond with Onas, they hoped that "the Covenant Chain & the Friendship" between them and Pennsylvania would "be Kept bright & shining to the Sun, & that neither Rain nor Damps nor any Rust may affect it to deprive it of its Lustre." In this way all people living in the province might "ever continue as they have hitherto been, one Body, one Heart & one Blood to all Generations."[6]

In a separate communication Civility asked Logan not to "allow Christians, or white people," to settle west of the river. Logan told Civility, unconvincingly, that restraining aggressive settlers was already government policy. He responded to Civility's request by calling on him to "hinder all Christians, white people, whatsoever, English, Dutch & all other Nations," from settling west of the river, and to "take yͤ. utmost care to prevent yͤ. Marylanders coming thither." Logan apparently hoped that keeping the Conestogas in place on a government-protected enclave would help keep intruders out of the region; Civility may have hoped that this approach was viable. In 1730 squatters from Donegal and Swatara put these hopes to the test, seizing Conestoga Manor by force. Although they were quickly driven off, the future of the Pennsylvania frontier now lay in the hands of hungry Christians in search of idle land.[7]

When Thomas Penn was resident in Pennsylvania the Conestoga Indians dealt directly with him rather than his lieutenant governors. In August 1735 Civility brought a delegation of about thirty Conestogas to Philadelphia, along with representatives of the Shawnee and Conoy Indians. Unsure of their status with Thomas Penn, they wished to renew "the League & Chain of Friendship" they had made with his father. The Conestogas carried with them their copy of the treaty of 1701. To "bind their Words" Civility laid down "three bundles of skins" at the beginning of the conference. He also presented some skins sent to him by a group of Shawnee Indians who were seeking the proprietary's assistance "in composing any Differences that may arise between the Irish People, who are come into those parts, and these Indians, who intend to live & dye where they are now settled." Penn magnanimously reassured the Conestogas that the "great Treaty of Friendship" made in 1701 would last "forever, that is as long as the Sun & Moon shall endure, or Water flow in the Rivers, which is the Language that has always been used on these Occasions." He awarded the Conestogas £30 in gifts, exclusive of "the Charges of their Entertainment in town," and sent them on their way.[8]

Penn's principal interest in Indian policy by this time lay not in the lowly Conestogas but in the Delaware Indians, whose tributary relationship to the Iroquois he turned to Pennsylvania's advantage. The Delawares were still the largest and most powerful Indian nation in Pennsylvania, and the meaning of their tributary status had yet to be put to the test. During his stay in Pennsylvania Penn worked closely with the Iroquois to displace the Delawares from eastern Pennsylvania. The Delawares' fate would determine the future of all Indians in the province.

In August 1732, six days after Penn's arrival in Pennsylvania, representatives of three of the Iroquois nations came to visit him in Philadelphia. Conrad Weiser and the Oneida leader Shikellamy were "appointed as fitt & proper Persons to goe between the Six Nations & this Government, & to be employed in all Transactions with one another." The discussions in Philadelphia, both public and private, continued for more than a week. They concluded with Pennsylvania reiterating its recognition of Iroquois authority over the Shawnees and Delawares. Pennsylvania also promised the Iroquois to "constantly keep a Fire for you here at Philadelphia" and to maintain "an open Road between Philadelphia and the Towns of the Six Nations," marking each promise with a belt of wampum.[9]

It took four years to consummate the new "League and Chain of Friendship & Brotherhood" agreed upon in 1732. In September 1736 about 100 representatives of the Six Nations arrived in Shamokin, "having been expected at

Philadia. these four years past, to confirm the Treaty" made four years earlier. From Shamokin they journeyed to Philadelphia to confer with Thomas
Penn. As Pennsylvania had "received us kindly" in 1732, an Iroquois spokesman announced, "and at that Treaty undertook to provide & keep for us a
Fire in this great City, we are now come to warm our selves there at, & we
hope it will ever continue bright & burning to the End of the World." Laying
down a large belt of wampum, he declared that Onas had "opened & cleared
the Road between this Place & our Nations," which they now desired to see
permanently clear and unobstructed.[10]

The Iroquois and Thomas Penn reached an agreement which would apply
to "all our Nations" in Pennsylvania. In other words, it included the Delawares,
the small nations of the Susquehanna Valley, and all other Indians with whom
the Iroquois were "in League and Friendship." The treaty confirmed that the
Conestogas, having been vanquished in war—by the Iroquois conquest of
the Susquehannocks in 1675—were tributaries of the Six Nations with no territorial or military rights. The Iroquois spokesman declared that "if Civility
at Connestogoe should attempt to make a sale of any Lands to us or any of
our neighbors they must lett us know that he hath no Power to do so, & if
he does any thing of the kind they, the Indians, will utterly disown him."
Penn had no hesitation in recognizing this formal assertion of authority over
the Conestogas. In return for his recognition, the Iroquois once again signed
releases confirming his father's purchase of the Susquehanna Valley from New
York in 1697. And Penn knew that the Conestogas, despite their tributary
status, would continue to regard him as Onas and look to Philadelphia rather
than Onondaga for protection.[11]

Recognizing Iroquois authority over the Delawares held even greater potential advantages for Penn. The real significance of the 1736 conference lay neither in its affirmation of old land purchases nor in its reassertion of Iroquois
authority over the Conestogas. Instead, the conference helped clear a path
toward the dispossession of the Delawares. Hungry for Indian land, John and
Thomas Penn unexpectedly announced that, fifty years earlier, their father had
purchased a vast, but not yet properly measured, region west of the Delaware
River. According to the Penn brothers, their father and the Delawares had
agreed to set the boundary lines for this purchase by conducting a three-day
walk, but they had walked for only a day and a half. The walk must now be
finished to conclude the transaction.

The Penns claimed to have unearthed a deed that proved the purchase had
been agreed on but not completed. The Delawares had no way of knowing

that this document was a copy of an ambiguous and improperly executed deed dating from 1686. Beyond this document no record survived that an agreement to purchase had been made or that a walk had taken place. The Delawares retained a memory of the purchase in oral tradition, but in several different versions. The only other reference to the purchase before the 1730s was in a letter to William Penn, also dated 1686. But Onas/Miquon embodied the power of the written word. And the Penns now used that power to perpetrate the Walking Purchase, the biggest land fraud in Pennsylvania's history.[12]

Even before the Walking Purchase was completed, the Penn brothers began to sell thousands of acres in the area under dispute, known as the Forks of the Delaware, to speculators and favorites. Aware that this land could not realize its full value unless it was cleared of encumbrances, they made plans to complete the supposed purchase of 1686 and expel the Delawares. Thomas Penn and James Logan presented a copy of the deed to Nutimus, the principal Indian leader in the Forks of the Delaware. They demanded that the agreement ostensibly made fifty years earlier be properly enacted. Nutimus replied that his ancestors had indeed sold land to William Penn, but only south of Tohickon Creek, and he insisted that his people had no memory of land being sold north of that point.[13]

Nutimus initially refused to comply with the Penns' demands, but he was in no position to bargain. In August 1737 Logan invited him and other Delaware leaders to his country home to discuss the upcoming Walking Purchase. Logan reiterated Thomas Penn's position: the Delawares had agreed to sell the land under discussion, William Penn had paid them for it, and all that remained was to complete the walk. Presented with a distorted map showing the area north of Tohickon Creek in compressed scale, the Delaware leaders were led to believe that they would be relinquishing land only below the creek, as their forefathers had agreed. On the basis of this map and the deed of 1686, neither of which he could understand, Nutimus was browbeaten into accepting the Walking Purchase. On September 19, 1737, Thomas Penn dispatched not one walker but three, who set out with supply horses and Indian guides. The walk encircled a vast area of 1,100 square miles, or 710,000 acres—almost the size of Rhode Island—stretching from Tohickon Creek to the Kittatinny Mountains and beyond.[14]

At the behest of Thomas Penn the Iroquois took the lead in expelling the Delawares from the land taken from them by the Walking Purchase. The decisive action came at a conference in Philadelphia in July 1742. The

THE WALKING PURCHASE

LAND ACQUIRED BY PENNSYLVANIA
FROM THE DELAWARE INDIANS

NEW
YORK

PENNSYLVANIA

FORKS OF THE
DELAWARE

River

Delaware

NEW JERSEY

Lehigh
River

Tochickon Creek

Schuylkill
River

Delaware River

Trenton

N

0   10   20
Miles

Philadelphia

Delawares were represented by the Shamokin leader Sassoonan and by Nutimus, whose favorite nephew, Pisquetomen, served as interpreter. The Iroquois sent several "Chiefs of the Six Nations," led by a formidable intermediary called Canassatego. The proceedings began with a presentation of goods to the Six Nations in compensation for their releasing their claims on the lower Susquehanna Valley in 1736. Thomas Penn then formally requested that the Six Nations remove their Delaware tributaries from the land acquired in the Walking Purchase. "As you on all Occasions apply to Us to remove all White people that are settled on Lands before they are purchased from You, and we do our Endeavours to turn such People Off," he told the Iroquois leaders, "We now expect from You that you will cause these Indians to remove from the Lands in the fforks of the Delaware, and not give any further Disturbance to the Persons who are now in possession."[15]

Canassatego did as he was asked. Casting the Delawares as "women" without military or territorial rights, he ordered them to leave the region at once and forbade them and their offspring ever to sell land again. The Six Nations, he continued, had perused various papers that Thomas Penn had made available to them. On this basis they had decided to remove these "very unruly People" who are "altogether in the wrong in their Dealings with You. We have concluded to remove them, and Oblige them to go over the River Delaware, and to quit all Claim to any Lands on this side for the future, since they have received Pay for them and it is gone through their Guts long ago."[16]

Then, turning to the Delawares with a belt of wampum in his hand, Canassatego delivered a humiliating rebuke. "Let this Belt of Wampum serve to Chastize You," he declared. "You ought to be taken by the Hair of the Head and shak'd severely till you recover your Senses and become Sober; you don't know what Ground you stand on, nor what you are doing." All Penn wanted, the Iroquois spokesman continued, was "to preserve ffriendship." The Delawares, by contrast, were "maliciously bent to break the Chain of ffriendship with our Brother Onas." Canassatego had seen with his own eyes "a Deed signed by nine of your Ancestors above fifty Years ago for this very Land" (i.e., the deed of 1686). The land therefore belonged to Pennsylvania. Canassatego also wanted to make a deeper point. "But how came you to take upon you to Sell Land at all?" he asked. "We conquer'd You, we made Women of you, you know you are Women, and can no more sell Land than Women."[17]

What did it mean for the Iroquois to label the Delawares women? Womanhood in itself did not necessarily carry pejorative associations because both groups of Indians traced descent through the female line. Senior Indian women assumed honored roles as peacemakers and advisors. Yet it is abundantly clear that the Iroquois intended to humiliate the Delawares by calling them women. Canassatego ordered them to "remove instantly" from the Forks of the Delaware. "We don't give you the liberty to think about it," he declared. "You are Women; take the Advice of a Wise Man and remove immediately." The Iroquois would permit the Delawares to resettle only in Shamokin or the Wyoming Valley, where their activities could be closely monitored. "You may go to either of these Places," Canassatego declared, "and then we shall have you more under our Eye, and shall see how You behave." As Nutimus and Sassoonan absorbed this message, Canassatego approached with a string of wampum. This string, he told them, "serves to forbid You, Your Children and Grand Children, to the latest Posterity, for ever medling in Land Affairs, neither you nor any who shall descend from You, are ever hereafter to presume to sell any Land." Canassatego then seized Nutimus by the hair and dragged him from the room.[18]

The Walking Purchase transformed the landscape of the Forks of the Delaware and doomed the region's native inhabitants. The Penns laid out manors, surveyed the land and sold it to settlers, and founded the town of Easton. They made huge profits, as did several proprietary favorites and speculators. William Allen purchased a substantial amount of land in the region and founded Allentown on the site of an Ulster enclave called Craig's Settlement. Moravian missionaries established settlements at Nazareth and Bethlehem, intending to convert rather than displace the Delawares. Within five years of the Walking Purchase most of the Delaware Indians had been forced out of their homelands, westward to Shamokin, northward to the Wyoming Valley, or westward across the Susquehanna River.

Until Sassoonan's death in 1747 Shamokin remained the most important Delaware settlement in Pennsylvania. Sassoonan had no direct heir, but he had three nephews—Pisquetomen, Shingas, and Tamaqua—and he appointed Pisquetomen his successor in 1741. Both Pennsylvania and the Iroquois, fearing the rise of a powerful Delaware dynasty in the Susquehanna Valley, refused to acknowledge the succession. By the time Sassoonan died six years later his nephews had abandoned Shamokin for the Ohio country, where they were recognized as the Delaware "royal family." Henceforth the center of Delaware power lay west of the Susquehanna River. The insult Thomas Penn and the Iroquois had inflicted on the Delaware Indians remained a burning grievance. The Walking Purchase was the main catalyst for the Delawares eventually going to war against Pennsylvania.[19]

CHAPTER 5

A HUNGER FOR LAND

Land-hungry settlers who could not establish a foothold in Lancaster County began to cross the Susquehanna River into the Cumberland Valley in the 1730s. At the conference in 1742 when Canassatego expelled Nutimus and his people, western Delaware and Shawnee Indians complained that "they were greatly disturbed and injured by the Peoples settling" on their side of the Kittatinny Mountains. In October Lieutenant Governor George Thomas issued a proclamation prohibiting settlement west of the mountains. All settlers that "have presum'd to possess themselves of any Lands there," he declared, "are manifest Intruders; and, as such, liable by the Laws to be removed, and, in Case of refusal, to be committed to Prison and severely Fined." With winter approaching he gave the intruders until May 1, 1743, to vacate. The proclamation had little effect as it could not be enforced west of the river, where squatters continued to settle in increasing numbers.[1]

In August 1749 almost 300 representatives of the Iroquois and other Indian nations came to Pennsylvania "to brighten the Chain of Friendship." The Iroquois renewed their complaints about "Encroachments on their hunting Grounds, and peremptorily insisted on the Removal of the Intruders." The new lieutenant governor, James Hamilton, proposed purchasing land in the Great Cove area of Cumberland County, but the Iroquois "absolutely refused." Instead he purchased some two million acres north of the Kittatinny Mountains, extending eastward from the Susquehanna River to the Delaware River, for the sum of £500.[2]

With this territory open to settlement, Hamilton issued a proclamation "to warn the People against continuing or settling on any unpurchased Land over Sasquehannah on the severest Penalties." As this proclamation again had no effect on squatters west of the river, Hamilton sent Richard Peters and Conrad Weiser to eject them. Weiser was convinced "that if we did not in this Journey entirely remove these People it would not be in the Power of the Government to prevent an Indian War." In May 1750 Peters, Weiser, and Andrew Montour met with some Conestoga and Shamokin Indians at the home of George Croghan to discuss what do about the squatters in Cumberland County. A native of Dublin, Croghan was one of the first English-speaking Indian traders to settle west of the Susquehanna River, establishing a trading post at Aughwick. The Shamokin Indians included two sons of Shikellamy, the Oneida intermediary who had worked closely with Weiser until his death in 1748.[3]

On May 22 local justices of the peace acting under Peters's and Croghan's instructions set out with five of the Shamokin Indians to expel squatters in the Juniata Valley, Sherman's Creek, and Great Cove. They found sixty-one illegally erected dwellings, many of them on land "esteemed by the Indians for some of their best hunting Ground." The squatters were ejected and bound over to appear at the next county court. The eviction party agreed that if the cabins were not destroyed their occupants would return or new trespassers would move in. Weiser pointed out that the Indians "would conceive such a contemptible Opinion of the Government that they would come themselves in the Winter, murder the People and set the Houses on Fire." Shikellamy's sons were especially insistent that the cabins be burned. For Ulster settlers who believed it was "against the laws of God and Nature" to deny them land retained by heathen savages, eviction in the presence of Indian observers must have been especially humiliating.[4]

By evicting squatters in Cumberland County the proprietary government was hoping to maintain harmonious relations with the Iroquois and their tributaries, but it was also acting out of self-interest. Not only did the evictions display the authority of the provincial government to squatters and Indians alike, but they also cleared the way for the Penn family to purchase western land and sell it to legitimate settlers. Beyond the sparsely settled regions along the Susquehanna and Juniata Rivers lay the Ohio country, which as yet had no European inhabitants. This vast region lay within William Penn's charter, and his son was determined that it should come under Pennsylvania's jurisdiction.

Thomas Penn faced stiff competition in his designs on the Ohio country, which stretched westward from the Allegheny Mountains to the Ohio River. Land speculators from Virginia had staked a claim to the territory on the basis of that colony's seventeenth-century charter, which specified no western boundary. They formed the Ohio Company in 1747 and began to send

THE OHIO COUNTRY

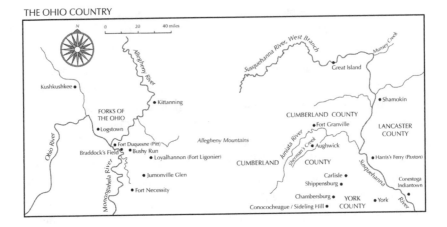

expositions into the territory. Their goals clashed with those of the French, who were erecting a series of forts in the region to consolidate their own imperial claim. The French plan directly challenged British imperial ambitions. The increasingly independent Indians who lived in the Ohio country, meanwhile, claimed that the region belonged to them. And the Iroquois, who regarded these Indians as tributaries, insisted that it was theirs by right of conquest. Out of this tangle of conflicts would emerge the French and Indian War.

The Ohio country Indians were no longer willing to accept Iroquois claims of authority over them. Aware of their diminishing authority, the Six Nations acknowledged a western Iroquois (Mingo) leader named Tanaghrisson as their representative in the region rather than appointing one of their own. Born to a Catawba mother and a Seneca father, Tanaghrisson was taken captive as a child, adopted into the Seneca nation, and raised in New York. In the 1740s he moved to Logstown, an important new Indian settlement on the Ohio River about eighteen miles north of the Forks of the Ohio, where the Allegheny and Monongahela Rivers meet. Located in the remote unpurchased reaches of Pennsylvania's charter, Logstown replaced Shamokin as the most important Delaware and Shawnee town. Tanaghrisson staked out an increasingly independent position as spokesman of both the Mingoes and the western Delawares and Shawnees. In English he was known as the "half-king," a term that probably reflected the relatively low status of the western Indians in Iroquois eyes.[5]

At a ceremony in Logstown in July 1752 Tanaghrisson recognized Shingas, one of Sassoonan's three nephews, as king of the Delawares. Tamaqua stood proxy for his brother Shingas, as the half-king placed a lace hat on his head and presented him with a colorful jacket to recognize his coronation. The ceremony represented a significant diplomatic defeat for the Iroquois, who had opposed Sassoonan's selection of Pisquetomen as his heir. Now Pisquetomen's brother was king. The three Delaware brothers dominated Indian affairs in the Ohio country for the next decade, mounting a serious challenge not only to the Iroquois confederacy but also to Pennsylvania.[6]

Even as the western Delawares were establishing their autonomy from the Iroquois, their fate became entangled in the long-simmering struggle between France and England for imperial mastery over North America. In April 1754 the French seized a small Virginian encampment at the Forks of the Ohio and began to build Fort Duquesne, named after the governor general of New France. In response the government of Virginia authorized a twenty-two-year-old colonel in the colonial militia named George Washington to lead a detachment of Virginia soldiers into the Ohio country. Washington established a base camp at a clearing called Great Meadows, and on the night of May 27, after receiving word that a party of French soldiers was encamped in a nearby ravine, he set out in search of them with about forty men. After an all-night march through the woods Washington's party launched a surprise attack, killing ten Frenchmen and capturing twenty-one. At the end of this brief skirmish Tanaghrisson picked up a hatchet and killed the French commander, Joseph Coulon de Jumonville, who was lying injured on the ground.

Washington retreated to Great Meadows and erected an encampment, which he called Fort Necessity. Tanaghrisson had formed a dim opinion of the Virginia colonel by this time, reportedly saying that he "was a good natured Man, but had no Experience; he took upon him to command the *Indians* as his Slaves, and would have them every Day upon the Scout, and to attack the Enemy by themselves, but would by no Means take Advice from the *Indians*." Tanaghrisson abandoned Washington, eventually making his way back to Paxton town, where he died in October 1754. Jumonville's brother, meanwhile, had defeated Washington at Fort Necessity. As a condition of his surrender Washington signed a document in which, perhaps unwittingly, he accepted responsibility for killing the French commander. French forces and their Indian allies took possession of Fort Necessity on July 4, and the Virginians were forced out of the Ohio Valley.[7]

Frontier settlers, all too aware that Pennsylvania still had no militia, were terrified at the prospect that Indians might attack the province. On July 17, 1754, seventy-five residents of Cumberland County submitted a petition to James Hamilton stating that "the late Defeat of the Virginia Forces" had placed them "in the most imminent Danger by a powerful Army of cruel, merciless, and inhuman Enemies, by whom our Lives, Liberties, Estates, and all that tends to promote our Welfare, are in the utmost Danger of dreadful Destruction." On July 22 fifty-seven residents of Paxton, Derry, and Hanover Townships, including John Harris Jr., sent a petition stating that they were "in great Danger from the French and French Indians." They were willing to fight in their own defense but were without "Arms and Ammunition and unable to purchase them." They pleaded with Hamilton to "make such Provision timeously for Us as may prevent Ourselves and Families being destroyed and ruined by such a Cruel Enemy." From nearby Donegal Township on July 26 ninety-eight inhabitants sent a petition requesting that Hamilton "put Us in a Condition that We may be able to defend Ourselves, and We on our Part will join with all that We can do for the Safety of the Province." For the moment these fears proved groundless; the anticipated attacks on Pennsylvania did not get under way until the following summer.[8]

On July 4, 1754, the day George Washington surrendered to the French at Fort Necessity, commissioners from seven American colonies were meeting in Albany, New York. The Board of Trade, which governed England's overseas possessions from London, convened the Albany Congress with a view to unifying the American colonies in the event of war with France. One hundred fifty Iroquois Indians attended the conference, led by the venerable Mohawk chief Hendrick (Theyanoguin). Born around 1680 Hendrick made a much publicized journey to London with three other Mohawk sachems in 1710 and visited London a second time in 1740. His sentiments were firmly pro-British.

Also present at Albany was Teedyuscung, the self-appointed leader of the Delawares east of the Susquehanna. Born near Trenton around 1700 Teedyuscung lived in New Jersey for the first thirty years of his life. Around 1730 he moved to the Forks of the Delaware, where he reportedly witnessed the conferences resulting in the Walking Purchase. In 1750 he was baptized under the name Gideon at the Moravian mission at Gnadenhütten, but his conversion was short-lived. He broke with the Moravians in spring 1754 and moved to the Wyoming Valley, on the north branch of the Susquehanna River, with sixty-five of his followers. There he proclaimed himself king of the eastern Delawares, uniting scattered bands of Lenape, Nanticoke, Shawnee, and Mahican Indians under his leadership.[9]

Presiding over the Albany Congress was William Johnson. Born to a Catholic gentry family in Ireland, Johnson converted to Anglicanism as a young man. His uncle, Admiral Peter Warren, brought him to New York in

Hendrick (1692–1755). "The Brave old Hendrick (Theyanoguin) the great sachem or chief of the Mohawk Indians." Engraving, London, ca. 1740. Courtesy of John Carter Brown Library at Brown University.

1738 to manage his estates in the Mohawk Valley. In 1746 Governor George Clinton of New York appointed Johnson to supervise the Covenant Chain alliance. Johnson built a limestone house near the Mohawk River, known as Fort Johnson. In 1763 he constructed a grand mansion, Johnson Hall, staffed by servants and slaves, where he lived with his long-time companion, Catherine Weisenberg, and his principal Iroquois mistress, Molly Brant. He took several other Indian mistresses and lovers as well. Fort Johnson and Johnson Hall were the sites of many important conferences with the Iroquois.[10]

James Hamilton, Richard Peters, and twenty-five-year-old John Penn represented the proprietary interest at Albany. A grandson of William Penn, John Penn

Sir William Johnson (1715–1774). Portrait by John Wollaston, ca. 1750–1752. Oil on canvas. Gift of Laura Munsell Tremaine in memory of her father, Joel Munsell. 1922.2. Courtesy of Albany Institute of History & Art.

was there because his uncle Thomas wanted to introduce him to the family business. Conrad Weiser served in his usual role as Pennsylvania's chief interpreter. The Assembly sent two of its most prominent leaders to Albany. Isaac Norris Jr., the fifty-three-year-old speaker of the Assembly, was a member of one of Philadelphia's most prominent Quaker families. His father came to Philadelphia with William Penn and flourished in business and politics. Accompanying Norris was Benjamin Franklin, forty-eight years old at this time and renowned throughout the American colonies and Europe for his scientific work.[11]

The Albany Congress is best known for Franklin's proposal to unite the mainland colonies in a federal union under the Crown. Under Franklin's Plan of Union each colony's legislature would elect representatives to a grand council administered by a president general appointed by the king. The council

Benjamin Franklin (1706–1790). Engraving, 1756. Courtesy of William L. Clements Library, University of Michigan.

would have powers over taxation, defense, and Indian policy. Although the Plan of Union won approval at Albany, none of the colonial legislatures voted in favor, preferring to retain their autonomy under the existing decentralized system of imperial rule. A powerful colonial federation of the type Franklin envisaged was, in any case, far removed from what the Board of Trade had in mind in convening the Albany Congress, and it would not have been approved in London even if the colonies had been in favor.

A much more pressing issue at Albany was the need to renew the Covenant Chain. With the possibility of war between England and France looming large, both the imperial authorities and the various colonial governments needed to ensure that the Six Nations stayed out of the conflict. Hendrick's Mohawks were the only Iroquois nation to adopt an unequivocally pro-British stance.

Some of the Onondagas and Oneidas were reportedly leaning toward the French, and the western Senecas and Cayugas (Mingoes) often had strong French, or at least anti-British, sympathies. But Hendrick prevailed at Albany. The Covenant Chain was renewed, promising official Iroquois neutrality if war broke out.[12]

The delegates then turned their attention to matters of interest to their individual colonies, compared to which Franklin's Plan of Union was an abstraction. Hamilton, Peters, and John Penn had arrived in Albany with instructions to acquire from the Iroquois all unpurchased lands within Thomas Penn's charter—a huge territory on both sides of the Susquehanna River that included the Ohio country. The Indians who lived in this territory sent no delegates to Albany. Even if they had done so, Pennsylvania would not have negotiated with them but with their nominal overlords, the Iroquois. On July 6 the Pennsylvania delegates signed a treaty with the Six Nations, who agreed to sell all previously unceded land in Pennsylvania to Thomas Penn. Iroquois spokesmen later maintained that they had intended the sale to include only those parts of the territory in question where Europeans were already living. Pennsylvania, however, took the deal to include all the land in the region, unsettled as well as settled. In Thomas Penn's mind this territory stretched as far west as the Ohio River. After the conference he gratefully assigned 2,000 acres each to Peters and Weiser for their services in securing purchase of the Ohio country.[13]

Pennsylvania officials seem to have been oblivious to the consequences of this transaction on the Indians living in the Ohio country, who were not consulted. The western Delaware and Shawnee Indians were already predisposed against Pennsylvania and the British because of their expulsion from their eastern homelands. They knew that the British conquered through settlement, whereas the French relied on strategically placed forts and made alliances with Indians. As the Presbyterian schoolteacher and interpreter Charles Thomson noted in 1759, the Albany purchase "ruined our interest with the *Indians*, and threw those of them, especially to the westward of us, entirely into the Hands of the *French*." These western Indians, Thomson observed, knew that they "had nothing to expect but to see themselves in a short Time, at the Rate the *English* settled, violently driven from their Lands, as the *Delawares* had formerly been." Rather than endure this ordeal of displacement yet again, they eventually chose to make war on Pennsylvania.[14]

The Iroquois exempted two sacred sites from the Albany purchase, Shamokin and Wyoming, both located east of the Susquehanna River. "We will never part with the Land at Shamokin and Wyomink," Hendrick declared. "Our bones are scattered there, and on this Land there has always been a great Council Fire." The Iroquois representative John Shick Calamy (Shikellamy's son), had "Orders not to suffer either Onas's People nor the New Englanders to settle any of those Lands." They were exempt from the transfer made in 1754 and would remain so forever. Yet, as the reference to intruders from both New England and Pennsylvania suggested, the region was much coveted by this time.[15]

Flanked by high mountain ridges, the Wyoming Valley extended for about twenty-five miles on either side of the Susquehanna River's north branch. Its name probably came from the Delaware word *maughwauwama* ("extensive meadows" or "large plains between mountains"), shortened to *wauwama* and eventually pronounced "Wyoming." The principal Indian town in the valley, Wyoming, was seventy miles northeast of Shamokin. The valley was sparsely populated, mainly by displaced Delaware and Shawnee Indians, along with a few Nanticokes and Mahicans. Thomas Penn claimed it belonged to him, as it lay within his father's grant. The Iroquois insisted it was theirs by right of conquest over the Susquehannocks. Teedyuscung and his followers, who moved to Wyoming in 1754, claimed the valley by right of occupancy. Settlers and land speculators from Pennsylvania and New England, meanwhile, sensing opportunities for enrichment, were intent on acquiring land in the region for themselves.[16]

Hendrick made it clear at Albany that the Wyoming Valley was not for sale. Yet only five days after the Albany purchase a group of Iroquois Indians signed a deed conveying the Wyoming Valley to John Henry Lydius, an unsavory character who was serving as the agent of a land speculation company from Connecticut. Several of the Indians who had signed the Albany purchase also signed the Lydius deed, as it came to be known. But how could a Connecticut corporation lay claim to a section of northern Pennsylvania? The Susquehannah Company, as it was called, based its argument on the unlimited sea-to-sea rights granted in Connecticut's original charter in 1662, which placed no western limit on the colony's sovereignty. Declaring that its purpose was "To Spread Christianity as also to promote our own Temporal Interest," the Company petitioned the legislature in Hartford for permission to purchase and settle a tract of land in the Wyoming Valley lying, like Connecticut itself, between the forty-first and forty-third lines of latitude.[17]

The Susquehannah Company hired John Henry Lydius to represent its interests at Albany. Both the British and the French suspected Lydius of being a double agent. William Johnson said he "was certain" Lydius was "a Roman Catholick" and doubted he would take the oath of allegiance. Richard Peters and John Penn reported that Lydius was "known to have abjured the Protestant religion in Canada" and was "suspected of carrying on a Secret Correspondence with the Government of Canada." The Lydius deed claimed that seventeen "Chief Sachems & Heads of The five Nations," who were "the Native Proprietors of a large Tract of Land... between the fourty first & fourty Third degrees of North Latitude," conveyed this land to the Susquehannah Company for 2,000 New York pounds. As well as working "to The Benefitt and Increase of our Trade," the deed piously noted, the purchase would introduce to the Wyoming Indians "a more full & Clear Knowledge of the True God and the Christian religion and thereby fix and Establish a more firm Solid & Lasting friendship with His Majesties English Subjects."[18]

From the standpoint of Pennsylvania and the Iroquois Council at Onondaga, the Lydius deed was clearly invalid. The Iroquois held land in common as a tribal trust, and it could not be sold without group approval in open council. Lydius had made his purchase covertly and incrementally, from individual Indians he plied with liquor before extracting their signatures in his Albany home. One of William Johnson's deputies, Daniel Clause, told Richard Peters that Lydius had "the Sum of Fifteen Hundred Dollars" at his disposal for this purpose. Another correspondent noted that more than thirty Oneida Indians came to Albany, ostensibly "to speak with the Commissioners of Indian Affairs," but spent their time instead at Lydius's house, where they were treated "plentifully with victuals and Drink" and received a bribe of $300. The last signatures to the Lydius deed were not affixed until March 4, 1755, almost a year after the Albany Congress.[19]

The Susquehannah Company's intervention could not have come at a worse time for the architects of Pennsylvania's Indian policy. A local conflict in the Wyoming Valley might become embroiled in the larger conflict brewing west of the Susquehanna River. At first Conrad Weiser tried to put an optimistic spin on things, telling Richard Peters in October that although he was "surprized of the Mischief of John Lidius, and the Folly of some of the Indians," he did not "think the Generality of the Chiefs will countenance such a Mischievous action." Nor did he believe that the Indians of the Susquehanna Valley would "suffer the New England Men, nor any Body else to settle on Wayomack Land." As a safeguard against Connecticut incursions, he suggested that Peters summon Hendrick to Philadelphia, set up a conference with the Six Nations, and send some men to Wyoming to build houses for the Indians there. "You will have heard by this time," Weiser added in passing, "that Tanachrishon [i.e., Tanaghrisson], the half King died about a week ago at Paxton, I suppose by his hard drinking." Scarouady (Monacatootha), an Oneida leader who lived in the Ohio country, succeeded Tanaghrisson as half-king.[20]

By the end of October Weiser was growing more anxious. He advised Pennsylvania's new lieutenant governor, Robert Hunter Morris, that the Susquehannah Company must be stopped. "If the Connecticut People shou'd countenance the Deed that Lydius so feloniously got," he told Morris, "and settle upon the Land, there will certainly be Bloodshed, for the Indians always said they would never suffer any white People to settle Wyomink or higher up." Weiser's biggest fear was that the Wyoming Delawares, threatened by New England settlers, would be driven into the arms of the French. If they were "obliged to move way" they could "move only to Ohio," he warned, and there "they would be under the Influence of the French and in their Interest, as the Senecas and Onondagers now are." In November word reached Philadelphia that the Susquehannah Company was planning to send 400 settlers to the Wyoming Valley in the spring.[21]

Hendrick finally arrived in Philadelphia in January 1755. After listening to condemnations of the Lydius deed he declared, "We agree that the Deed should be destroyed. We agree with You that is a false Proceeding." But he insisted that the deed could be invalidated only "by the act of the Council of the Six Nations." Hendrick promised to lend his assistance in securing this outcome. But on September 8, 1755, he was ambushed and killed by French-speaking Mohawks near Lake George in New York. By then it was too late to avert the war that was descending on Pennsylvania and all of North America.[22]

TWO

THEATRE OF BLOODSHED AND RAPINE

CHAPTER 6
BRADDOCK'S DEFEAT

In 1754, responding to the emerging imperial crisis in the Ohio country, the British appointed Edward Braddock as commander in chief in North America. A native of Scotland, Braddock was almost sixty years old at the time of his appointment and had been in the British Army for forty-five years. He arrived in Virginia in March 1755 with two Irish regiments and based them at Wills Creek, Maryland, where the land speculators who formed the Ohio Company had built a storage and supply depot. Braddock enlarged the fort and renamed it in honor of his patron, the Duke of Cumberland, a younger son of George II.[1]

Braddock's assignment was to oversee an elaborate four-pronged strategy to remove the French from North America. He would lead his two regiments, supported by provincial soldiers, across Pennsylvania to capture Fort Duquesne and then proceed northward to Forts Machault, Le Boeuf, and Presqu'Isle. A second British force would attack Fort Niagara, at the western end of Lake Ontario, a prime location for a counteroffensive against Fort Duquesne. A third would attack Fort Beauséjour in Nova Scotia. And a fourth, consisting of regular soldiers supported by provincials and pro-British Iroquois warriors, would attack Fort St. Frédéric (later known as Crown Point) on Lake Champlain. Erected by the French in 1734–1736, this great four-story stone fort controlled northbound movement from New York to Montréal and Québec. The British plan was colossally ambitious but quite unrealistic; they captured only one of the four French forts. Seventeen-fifty-five turned out to be a disastrous year.

At Fort Cumberland General Braddock spent three months assembling the largest army in North American history up to that point. Alongside 1,400 soldiers from the two Irish regiments, his force included 1,000 provincials from Virginia, Maryland, and North Carolina combined—but none from Quaker Pennsylvania, which had no soldiers to offer. Among the provincials

George Washington (1732–1799) in the uniform of a British colonial colonel. Portrait by Charles Willson Peale, 1772. Courtesy of Washington-Custis-Lee Collection, Washington and Lee University, Lexington, Virginia.

in Braddock's army was Colonel George Washington of the Viriginia militia. British military regulations stipulated that all provincial field officers (i.e., majors, lieutenant colonels, and colonels) were inferior in rank to the lowest field officers in the regular army. Rather than endure the dishonor of taking orders from officers of lower rank, Washington chose to serve in Braddock's army as a volunteer aide-de-camp. Knowing that the general carried blank commissions, he hoped to realize his ambition of becoming an officer in the regular British Army.[2]

Although Pennsylvania made no official military contribution to Braddock's expedition, some frontier settlers from that province joined up voluntarily. In December 1754, before Braddock's arrival, Andrew Montour recruited a group of men from Paxton Township to help the Virginia militia fortify the defense camp at Wills Creek. Some of these men stayed on after the work was done and joined Braddock's expedition. Lazarus Stewart, a native of Hanover Township in Lancaster County, raised and commanded a party of volunteers that marched with Braddock. James Smith of Conococheague also partici- pated in the expedition. Captured by Delaware Indians, he was taken prisoner to Fort Duquesne and adopted into the Mohawk nation for five years. When the Indian wars were over he reemerged as the leader of the infamous "Black Boys" of Cumberland County.[3]

In April 1755 General Braddock summoned the governors of Virginia, Maryland, Pennsylvania, and New York to a council of war at Alexandria, Virginia. There he appointed William Shirley, the governor of Massachusetts, to command the Niagara campaign and William Johnson to lead the expe- dition against St. Frédéric. He also appointed Johnson sole British superin- tendent of the Six Nations, a position designed to further the imperial plan, initiated at the Albany Congress, of placing Indian affairs under centralized control. Initially subordinate to the commander in chief, Johnson reported directly to the Crown from 1756 onward. The position provided him with considerable power, prestige, and wealth.[4]

On receiving word of his appointments from Braddock, Johnson sum- moned George Croghan to Wills Creek. A skilled mediator and interpreter, Croghan knew the Ohio country well. His skills were badly needed at Fort Cumberland, for Edward Braddock despised Indians. He scorned the idea of making alliances with the Iroquois or the Delawares, never doubting that traditional British military power, if deployed in sufficient force, would win the day. Braddock had an excellent understanding of the strict discipline, com- plex strategy, and staged battles of European warfare, but no inkling of how irrelevant these qualities would be in the forests and hills of North America. "The great Danger to the General's Army," the pro-Delaware author Charles Thomson noted a few years later, "was, that it might be attacked and routed in its March by the Indians, who are so expert in Wood-Fights, that a very small Number of them are superior to a great Number of our Regulars, and generally defeat them."[5]

When Shingas came to Fort Cumberland at Croghan's suggestion, Braddock remained inflexible. The Delaware leader reportedly offered to support the British in return for a guarantee that his people would retain their land along the Allegheny River. Braddock rejected this proposal out of hand. According to Shingas, when he asked what would happen to land the British took away from the French and their Indian allies, the general answered, "The English

Should Inhabit and Inherit the Land." Asked by Shingas if Indians friendly to the British would be able to live, trade, and hunt in this territory, Braddock flatly retorted, "No Savage Should Inherit the Land." At this affront Shingas declared that his people would refuse to help the British, to which Braddock replied that he had no need of their help.[6]

The first detachments of Braddock's army set out from Fort Cumberland at the end of May 1755. Their destination, Fort Duquesne, had a garrison of only 100 French regulars and 200 Canadian militia, but they were supported by between 600 and 1,000 Indians camped outside the fort. Following the path cut from Wills Creek to Red Stone Fort by George Washington and the Virginia Regiment in 1754, Braddock built a road capable of transporting his troops, artillery, and supply train as the army advanced. Progress was painfully slow—four miles a day on average—as the soldiers had to cut through woods, forests, hills, and mountains. By the time of its completion in July 1755, Braddock's Road extended across the Alleghenies to the Forks of the Ohio.

On June 18, frustrated by the sluggish pace, Braddock made the fatal mistake of splitting his army in two. He and Lieutenant Colonel Thomas Gage advanced with a flying column of about 1,500 men ahead of the baggage and heavy artillery. They crossed the Monongahela River on July 8 within ten miles of Fort Duquesne. The next day they encountered a French-led force of about 900 men, including some 600 Indians, who inflicted one of the worst defeats in British military history. While the French and their Indian allies lost only twenty-three dead and sixteen wounded, the British casualties amounted to two-thirds of the enlisted men and three-quarters of the officers. In all, 977 men were killed, wounded, or missing, including sixty officers. Among those mortally wounded was Edward Braddock. The surviving British soldiers buried his body in the middle of the road, marching over the grave to conceal it from the enemy.[7]

Of the four French forts the British planned to take in 1755, they captured only Fort Beauséjour in Nova Scotia. Important as this conquest was, the real prize in the region, Fortress Louisbourg on Cape Breton Island, remained in French hands. As for Fort Niagara, William Shirley postponed his attack to the spring and returned to Massachusetts. Shirley succeeded Braddock as commander in chief but was recalled to England in 1756 to face treason charges for his failure to proceed against Niagara. He was eventually acquitted, but his disgrace significantly benefited his chief political rival, William Johnson.[8]

Johnson had won the mantle of imperial war hero even before Shirley's removal. On September 8 his force of 3,000 provincials and Indians defeated

Braddock's burial, 1755. LC-USZ62-50571. Courtesy of Library of Congress.

the French at Lac du St. Sacrement. Casualties were about the same on each side, and the British lost their most steadfast Indian ally, Hendrick, in a skirmish before the main battle. But Johnson won control of the south end of the lake and claimed victory on this basis. He renamed St. Sacrement Lake George after the king and built Fort William Henry, naming it for one of the royal grandsons. Johnson then withdrew his force to prepare for an attack on St. Frédéric, but like Shirley he eventually abandoned this plan. Unlike his rival, however, Johnson was not punished for his inaction; instead he received a baronetcy and the sum of £5,000 for his victory at Lake George. He went on to build a spectacular career as the kingpin of Indian diplomacy in British North America.

For settlers on the Pennsylvania frontier Braddock's defeat carried ominous implications. All of Pennsylvania was now open to attack by French and Indian forces. Already on June 22, shortly after the last of Braddock's army had set out for Fort Duquesne, Indians had launched attacks in the vicinity of Wills Creek, killing and scalping three people. Over the next forty-eight hours, John Harris reported from Paxton, twenty more settlers in the vicinity of Fort Cumberland were "found killed, barbarously murder'd and missing." Harris suspected that Indians from the Paxton area were involved, and he was terrified by the prospect of attacks closer to home. "Upon the first Alarm of Murder being committed among us," he warned, "the general part or Majority of our Settlers will run off and leave their Habitations and Effects, Grain, &ᶜᵃ; You may certainly depend on it, For in the Situation our People are they cannot make any Defence."⁹

Edward Shippen found Harris's position alarmist. From Lancaster he wrote to his cousin William Allen that of "all the Persons I have talked with John Harris at Pexton is the greatest Coward, and discourages the Folks most, buzzing them in the Ears of their great Danger. But I hope to put a Stop to his silly Proceedings." Rather than evacuate the region as Harris wanted, Shippen urged the "Back Settlers . . . to be resolute and to stand their Ground, and to put themselves into the best Posture of Defence they possibly can." He advised that two or three families should group together in houses "where Water is handy" and make loop holes in the walls for small arms. Single men, he continued, should join volunteer companies to patrol the countryside and reap the grain while others kept guard. The threat to western Lancaster County was imminent, Shippen warned Allen, but the settlers would fight rather than flee at first sight of the enemy.¹⁰

The extent of the threat, however, depended on the western Indians rather than the settlers. As tributaries of the Iroquois, the Delawares and Shawnees were not supposed to transact in land or wage war. Yet if Britain and France went to war these Indians knew they would have no choice but to take sides, as both powers coveted the land on which they lived. In the spring of 1754, a year before Braddock's arrival in America, they had sent a wampum belt to the Iroquois Council at Onondaga, seeking assistance in the event of a French attack. The white portion of the belt, as interpreted by Conrad Weiser, conveyed the following message: "Uncles the United Nations, We expect to be killed by the French your Father; We desire, therefore, that You will take off our Petticoat that we may fight for ourselves, our Wives and Children; in the Condition We are in You know we can do nothing." The Iroquois were not prepared to grant this request. But the Ohio country Delawares were ready to reclaim their manhood for themselves. Neither pro-French nor pro-British, they were prepared to make an alliance with either side in order to survive. But siding with the French would involve a decisive break with their putative Iroquois overlords, whose official neutrality amounted on balance to a pro-British stance.¹¹

In September 1754 Tamaqua pressed the Delawares' case with the Iroquois once again. At a conference at Aughwick he addressed his Iroquois "uncles" through the half-king, Tanaghrisson. "I still remember the time when You first conquered Us and made Women of Us...and told Us you took Us under your Protection," Tamaqua declared, "and that We must not meddle with Wars, but stay in the House and mind Council Affairs." The Delawares had been prepared to follow this instruction during peacetime, but now, he warned, "a high Wind is rising." Braddock's defeat in July 1755 changed everything. With the Iroquois still refusing to accede to their demands, the Ohio country Indians decided to attack the Pennsylvania frontier. They set out to revenge the humiliations inflicted on them by Pennsylvania and the Iroquois, of which the Walking Purchase was the most painful and enduring. In doing so they defiantly cast off their supposed status as women. Seven decades after William Penn inaugurated his holy experiment, war had finally come to the once Peaceable Kingdom of Pennsylvania.[12]

The Ulster settlement of Penn's Creek lay about four miles west of the Susquehanna River and four miles south of Shamokin. Delaware and Shawnee warriors attacked the settlement on October 16, 1755, killing at least thirteen residents, scalping several of the victims, and capturing twenty-eight more. A petition to Lieutenant Governor Robert Morris reported the details, including a description of one man who "lay on his back barbarously burnt and two Tomahawks sticking in his forehead." Inspired by Braddock's defeat, the western Delawares and Shawnees launched repeated attacks on both sides of the Susquehanna River in October and November.[13]

The attack on Penn's Creek had a chilling effect in the Susquehanna Valley. The vulnerability of frontier settlements, Benjamin Franklin noted, was "a natural Consequence of the loose manner of Settling in these Colonies, picking here and there a good Piece of Land." The settlers lived "at such a distance from each other, as that a few Indians may destroy a Number of Familys one after the other, without their being even alarm'd or able to afford one another any Assistance." Led by Shingas the western Indians used tactics designed to instill maximum terror. Parties of as many as fifty warriors sometimes attacked forts and more densely populated settlements, but the typical raiding party consisted of fewer than twenty Indians. Specializing in surprise attacks on individual homesteads or small farming communities, especially at harvest time, these parties slaughtered men as they worked in the fields, killed or captured women and children, burned crops and buildings, and mutilated the dead. The object of the attacks was to intimidate the settlers, drive them out, and turn them against the provincial government. In so doing the Indians hoped to recover lost land, or at least retain the land they occupied, as the basis of an equitable peace.[14]

Writing to Robert Morris on October 20, John Harris requested that the Assembly agree on some method to defend the province. Otherwise, if just one "company of Indians come & Murder but a few Families hereabouts, which is daily expected," Harris warned, "the situation we are in would oblige numbers to abandon their places, and our Cattle and Provisions, which we have plenty of, must then fall a prey to the Enemy." Abandoning farms was a desperate measure; the crops would be left unharvested and the refugees would have no source of food or income. As Edward Shippen had predicted in July, many settlers tried at first to defend themselves and stay on the land. The petitioners from Penn's Creek reported that almost all the "back Inhabitants" had fled, but that they and "a few more" were "willing to stay and endeavour to defend the Land." They might be unable to do so, however, "for want of Guns and Ammunition." Without immediate assistance they too "must fly and leave the Country to the mercy of the Enemy." Frontier settlers would long resent the provincial government's failure to provide assistance when they needed it most.[15]

A week after the Penn's Creek massacre, John Harris Jr. headed upriver from Paxton with a party of forty men to bury the dead. Along the way he stopped at Shamokin "to learn the best Intelligences." On his return Harris reported to Robert Morris, "The Indians on the West Branch of Sasquehannah certainly killed our Inhabitants on Mr. Penn's Creek." They had also sent "a hatchet and two English Scalps" up the north branch of the Susquehanna to the Wyoming Indians, Harris reported, "to desire them to strike with them if they are men." Andrew Montour told Harris that there was already "a body of French with 1,500 Indians coming against us, . . . & are now not many days' march from this Province and Virginia, which is appointed to be attacked at the same time." A French officer had reportedly been spotted with "a party of Shawonese, Delawares, &ᶜᵃ·, within six miles of Shamokin two days ago, & no doubt intends to take possession of it."[16]

John Harris had good reason to be afraid. Although his latest reports betrayed some of the alarmism Shippen disliked, his trip back from Penn's Creek to Paxton had been fraught with peril. On October 25 Harris's party was attacked in the woods by a party of twenty or thirty Indians. Harris reported to Robert Morris that about fifteen of his men "took to Trees and attacked the Villains, killed four of them on the spot, and lost but three men." As they crossed the Susquehanna River one of the men riding behind Harris "was shot from off an horse." Harris's own horse "was wounded, & falling in the River I was obliged to Quit him and swim part of the way." Another four or five of his men were drowned crossing the river. Harris believed he had been betrayed by the Indians around Paxton town. Deeply distrustful, he asked Morris "to cause them to be removed to some place, as I don't like their Company."[17]

Conrad Weiser told a version of this story less favorable to the Paxton men. When Harris and his party arrived at George Gabriel's inn, about five miles south of Shamokin, they learned that the bodies at Penn's Creek had already been buried. They went to Shamokin instead, where they were "seemingly well received, but found a great number of strange Indians, tho' Delawares, all painted Black." The next day Harris's men "got up early in order to go back, but they did not see any of the strangers; They were gone before them." Andrew Montour, who "was there painted as the rest, advised our people not to go the same Road they came, but to keep this side [i.e., east of the] Sasquehannah and go the old Road." Ignoring Montour's advice they crossed the Susquehanna River "in order to go down on the West Side of that River as far as Mahanoy." As they were fording John Penn's Creek they were ambushed by Indians. In addition to the dead, twenty-six men went missing. Harris had omitted most of these details in his report to Robert Morris, but it was little wonder that he was so fearful and suspicious.[18]

By the end of October Harris was making preparations for the anticipated French and Indian attacks on the lower Susquehanna Valley. Given its economic and strategic significance, Paxton was a prime target. "We expect the Enemy upon us every day," Harris wrote to Shippen on October 29, "and the Inhabitants are abandoning their Plantations, being greatly discouraged at the approach of such a number of Cruel Savages, and no sign of Assistance." An army of 1,500 French-led Indians was said to be advancing steadily, "their Scouts Scalping our Families on our Frontiers daily." Montour had told Harris, "There was forty Indians out many days, and intended to burn my House & destroy myself and Family." Harris had therefore "cut holes" in his house; he was determined to hold out to "the last extremity if I can get some men to stand by me, few of which I yet can at present, every one being in fear of their own Families being cut off every hour (such is our situation)." The greater part of the Susquehanna Indians, Harris told Shippen, "is actually in the French interest." To tell friend from foe, he suggested, "We ought to insist on the Indians declaring either for or against us."[19]

Learning from Harris's reports that a French and Indian army was about to cross the Susquehanna, Conrad Weiser prepared to lend assistance to the people of Paxton. He assembled 200 mostly German settlers from the Tulpehocken area in Lancaster County and "gave orders to them to go home and fetch their

Arms, whether Guns, Swords, pitchforks, axes, or whatsoever might be of use against the Enemy," along with "three days provision in their Knapsacks." Weiser divided the settlers into companies of thirty men, with each company choosing its officers. They marched west toward the Susquehanna, now 300 strong, but when they arrived in Paxton there was no sign of the anticipated invasion. Deciding that "we did not come up to serve as Guards to Paxton people, but to fight the Enemy if they were come so far as we first heard," Weiser's men returned home to "take care of our Townships."[20]

Despite the false alarm in Paxton, Weiser emphasized to Morris that Pennsylvania was "in great Danger." Although "most of the Inhabitants would do their Duty," he advised the lieutenant governor, "without some Military Regulations we shall never be able to defend the Province." Weiser informed Chief Justice William Allen, "All our Indians are gone off with the French, or rather joined them because they could not stand their Ground against the French and their Indians." Even worse, he told Allen, "the French are about Fortifying themselves this side of the Allegeny Hills," and perhaps even in the Shamokin area, where the inhabitants had abandoned their farms, leaving their corn and cattle behind.[21]

Attacks by the western Delaware and Shawnees reached their full intensity in November. On the first of the month Shingas led about ninety Delaware, Shawnee, and Mingo warriors in an attack on Great Cove, an Ulster settlement on the west bank of the Susquehanna River in lower Cumberland County. Indians also attacked the nearby settlement of Little Cove. The sheriff of Cumberland County estimated "that 27 Plantations were burnt and a great quantity of Cattle killed" and that "of ninety-three Families which were settled in the two Coves & the Conolloway's [a neighboring settlement] 47 were either killed or taken and the rest deserted."[22]

In mid-November Indian raids penetrated across the river into Lancaster County and as far east as Berks County. Delaware and Shawnee warriors attacked Swatara and Tulpehocken in Lancaster County. One resident of Tulpehocken, where nine settlers were killed, reported to Conrad Weiser, "We are in great Danger for to Lose our Lives or Estates. Pray, therefore, for help, or else whole Tulpehoccon will be ruined by the Indians in a short time, and all Buildings will be burned down & the people scalped." Beleaguered settlers in Berks County were incensed at the Assembly for failing to provide adequate defense. "This night," one settler reported, "we expect an attack, truly alarming is our situation. The people exclaim against the Quakers, & some are scarce restrained from burning the Houses of those few who are in This Town."[23]

On November 9 the Rev. John Elder wrote to the provincial secretary, Richard Peters, with the latest news from Paxton town. Within the previous few weeks, he told Peters, "upwards of 40 of His Majesty's Subjects" had been "massacred on the Frontiers of this and Cumberland Cʸ, besides a great number carried into Captivity." Yet the legislature and the executive continued to engage in "nothing but unreasonable Debates... instead of uniting in some probable Scheme for the Protection of the Province and the preservation of its Inhabitants." Unless "vigorous methods" were "speedily used to prevent it," Elder warned, "we in these back Settlements will unavoidably fall a sacrifice & this part of the Province will be lost." For the present those "vigorous methods" were based on the brutal, extralegal actions of Ulster settlers. At the end of December Weiser reported that some "Paxton people took an enemy Indian" and, having interrogated him, "they shott him in the midst of them, scalped him and threw his Body into the River."[24]

The finality of war in the once peaceable kingdom of Pennsylvania hit home in December 1755, when Teedyuscung and the Wyoming Delawares launched devastating raids in Pennsylvania's Northampton County. "Tho' our Uncles have made Women of Us," Teedyuscung had declared to the provincial Council in April 1755, "yet in time to come We may have children, who when born may look up and see the Sun and Sky clear and the Road open between Us and You." Teedyuscung sensed an opportunity to establish autonomy from the various parties seeking control over the Wyoming Valley: the Six Nations; their patron, Sir William Johnson; the Penn family; settlers and squatters; and land speculators from Connecticut. In December he decided to join the western Delawares and wage war against Pennsylvania, which was now under attack on two fronts, northern as well as western. By March 1756 Indian raids had killed an estimated 700 settlers in Pennsylvania, Virginia, and North Carolina. Thousands more settlers had abandoned their farms. Still lacking an official militia, Pennsylvania was about to enter the deepest crisis in its history.[25]

CHAPTER 7
PENNSYLVANIA GOES TO WAR

Before the French and Indian War Pennsylvania had made only one attempt to form a provincial militia. In 1747, during King George's War, Benjamin Franklin organized an "Association" to defend Pennsylvania in the event of an attack by French-allied Indians. This volunteer force did not enjoy formal recognition from the government, it provided no pay, and the men elected their own officers. "Associators" in Lancaster County followed Franklin's example, creating two voluntary military companies east and west of the Susquehanna River. Fears of an attack on Pennsylvania proved groundless, and the voluntary associations quickly disbanded.[1]

When western Indians commenced their raids in 1755 frontier settlers banded together in informal military groups known as "Rangers" or "Volunteers." The members of these forces, like many frontier settlers, wore Indian-style leggings, moccasins, animal pelts, and blanket coats. They mastered Indian methods of "irregular" forest warfare, including the use of ambushes and raiding parties. Presbyterian ministers were active in organizing local military efforts. Among them was the Rev. John Steel of Conococheague in Cumberland County, who put together a company of Rangers after Braddock's defeat and was elected their captain. He erected a stockade around his church, which became known as "Fort Steel." A neighboring Presbyterian minister, Andrew Bay, also organized a volunteer force.[2]

The Anglican minister Thomas Barton organized a local volunteer militia in the Carlisle region, but his chief service to the proprietary interest was as a propagandist. He published a sermon on the theme "unanimity and public spirit" in 1755, with an introduction by his fellow minister William Smith, arguing that the emerging French and Indian alliance in the west threatened the survival of Protestantism. The French papists and their heathen allies, if victorious, would trample on Pennsylvania's religious liberties. In this time of grave need, Barton concluded, political self-interest should be secondary to the public good. In other words, the Quaker assemblymen should do whatever the proprietary demanded on military defense. Barton's mentor, William Smith, published several tracts attacking the Assembly's defense policy and was briefly imprisoned for contempt.[3]

The Assembly had the authority to create a militia and construct forts and to raise money to fund these efforts. But passing military legislation presented formidable difficulties in Pennsylvania. Despite Anglican and Presbyterian accusations to the contrary, Quaker pacifism was not the principal obstacle. Only a small minority of Quakers insisted on absolute nonviolence by this time. Most members of the Assembly belonged to the Society of Friends, but they approved of defensive wars. As far back as 1711, Isaac Norris Sr., the father of the speaker of the Assembly, had pushed through a vote of £200 "for the Queen's use," a euphemism that assuaged Quaker scruples by making no mention of war. A large majority of the assemblymen in the 1750s favored the creation of a militia to defend Pennsylvania, but they disagreed with the lieutenant governor on questions of command and discipline. Robert Morris wanted to exert direct control over the militia by serving as its commanding officer, appointing the officers, and enforcing strict military rules. The assemblymen, who had no intention of vesting this degree of control in the executive branch, favored a much looser model of military discipline.[4]

These disagreements could eventually be resolved by the normal process of political give and take, but there was a more intractable problem: How was the militia, regardless of its structure, to be funded? When the Assembly decided to levy a general tax on property for this purpose, a dispute arose over whether the Penn family's estates would be included. This dispute would endure for the next ten years, poisoning relations between the executive and legislative branches of the provincial government. Thomas Penn's lieutenant governors had standing instructions not to sign bills that taxed the proprietary estates. Penn enforced these instructions by requiring them to sign penal bonds whereby they would forfeit sizable funds if they disobeyed orders. Throughout the late 1750s, whenever the Assembly passed a supply bill that included a tax on the proprietary estates the lieutenant governor responded by exercising his veto. From the perspective of frontier settlers, the resulting gridlock in government looked like callous indifference.[5]

The battle over Pennsylvania's first militia law began in the spring of 1755, when General Braddock was assembling his army, and ended in November with the province reeling under Indian attack. Urged on by Robert Morris, the Assembly passed a bill at the end of July raising £50,000 "for the King's use," to be funded by a tax on all property, real and personal, including proprietary lands. Reminding the Assembly of his instructions from Thomas Penn, Morris returned the bill on August 5 with an amendment exempting the proprietary estates from taxation. The Assembly rejected the amendment, and there the matter rested until November.[6]

Not until the Ohio country Delawares and Shawnees began to attack Pennsylvania did the government turn its attention to frontier defense once again. On November 3 Morris called the Assembly into special session to respond to the latest Indian raids. The Assembly presented a new "Bill for striking Sixty thousand Pounds in Bills of credit, and for granting the same to the King's use," with the funds to be raised by a general property tax that once again included the Penns' estates. By way of compromise, the bill stipulated that the question of taxing proprietary lands ought to be referred to the Privy Council (the king's advisory body) for adjudication. From Morris's point of view this was no compromise; because the bill taxed the proprietary estates he had no choice but to veto it. He upbraided the assemblymen for being more interested in "regaining the Affections of the Indians now employed in laying waste the Country and butchering the Inhabitants, and of inquiring what injustice they have received," than in drafting a bill he could sign.[7]

It would have been better, Morris told the Assembly, to pass two separate bills. Pointing out that the Privy Council approved or rejected entire bills rather than sections of bills, he suggested that most of the £60,000 could have been raised by a bill that excluded the proprietary estates, which he would have signed immediately. A separate bill, taxing the proprietary estates alone, which he would have vetoed, could then have been referred to the Privy Council. From the assemblymen's perspective, however, this approach amounted to a capitulation, not a compromise. It conceded the issue in dispute, which concerned not just money but also the balance of power in the provincial government.[8]

A series of events in mid- and late November broke the logjam. After Indian raiding parties struck Lancaster and Berks Counties in mid-November Robert Morris demanded a proper militia law and "an immediate Supply of money." The Assembly continued to insist that the proprietary estates could not be exempted. Then, on November 24, Delaware warriors attacked the Moravian mission of Gnadenhütten, killing eleven missionaries and burning the settlement to the ground. That same day word arrived in Philadelphia that as many as 2,000 inhabitants of Chester County were preparing to march on the city "to compel the Governor and Assembly to agree to pass Laws to defend the Country and oppose the Enemy." Conrad Weiser reported that "another considerable number" of men (estimates varied from 300 to 700) were on their way from Berks County. These reports turned out to be overblown, but several hundred mostly German farmers, led by a tavern keeper from the Lancaster turnpike named John Hambright, did make their way into the city.[9]

At this critical moment, whether by serendipity or design, Morris revealed that he had received a letter from Thomas Penn authorizing a gift of £5,000 in lieu of taxes on the proprietary estates. The Assembly accepted the gift as the equivalent of a proprietary tax, and the impasse over the supply bill was resolved. Morris approved a bill appropriating £60,000, of which £55,000 would come from a property tax that exempted the proprietary estates and the remainder from Thomas Penn's gift. "This timely and generous Instance of the Proprietaries care & anxiety for the Inhabitants," Morris declared, "cannot fail of making the most lasting impressions upon the minds of every well wisher to this country." Penn's gesture, however, was not what it seemed. Although he presented the £5,000 "as a free Gift from us to the publick," he stipulated that the money was "to be paid out of our Arrears of Quit-Rents." In other words, it was to be funded from his bad debts, which the Assembly was charged with collecting. The assemblymen seem not to have realized this when they accepted the gift in lieu of taxation.[10]

Pennsylvania could at last proceed to organize its first official militia. Yet for all the controversy that attended its making, the force created in November 1755 was a ramshackle and loosely disciplined outfit. It consisted of 1,400 men arranged into twenty-five companies under the command of three principal officers. The men west of the Susquehanna River were to be commanded by John Armstrong of Cumberland County and those east of the river by Conrad Weiser and James Burd of Lancaster County. Service was voluntary, and the men could not be forced to serve for a duration of more than three weeks, nor to travel beyond three days from the parts of the province inhabited by Europeans. Officers were elected by the rank and file. This was the army that was supposed to defend the Pennsylvania frontier against the French and their formidable Indian allies. From a military perspective, William Allen was justified in dismissing the whole affair as "a Solemn Farce." But the creation of an official militia marked a decisive break in the history of Quaker Pennsylvania. And it provoked a bitter dispute within the Society of Friends about the legacy of William Penn and his holy experiment.[11]

The principle of nonviolence stood at the heart of the original Quaker vision of human dignity and equality. The founder of the Society of Friends, George Fox, laid down the precepts of Quaker pacifism during the English Civil War. "I...doe deny the carrying or drawing of any carnall sword against any, or against thee Oliver Crumwell or any men," Fox wrote to the lord protector of England in 1654. At the end of one of his terms in prison Fox explained his position further: "All that pretend to fight for Christ, are deceived; for his kingdom is not of this world, therefore his servants do not fight. Fighters are not of Christ's kingdom, but are without Christ's kingdom; his kingdom starts in peace and righteousness, but fighters are in the lust." People who took up the sword in the name of the gospel, Fox insisted, were deceived, "for the Gospel is the power of God, which was before the devil, or fall of man was; and the gospel of peace was before fighting was." Those who "would be wrestlers with flesh and blood, throw away Christ's doctrine." Only by turning the other cheek and loving their enemies could people remain within this doctrine. But Fox's absolute proscription on violence did not withstand the test of time in eighteenth-century Pennsylvania, where Quakers had to deal with the practicalities of government.[12]

A minority of Pennsylvania Friends remained true to the original Quaker teachings as late as the 1750s. Of these strict pacifists, the Pemberton brothers, Israel Jr., James, and John, were the most influential. Known as the "King of the Quakers," Israel Pemberton Jr. served two terms in the Pennsylvania Assembly, but his real influence lay outside the formal institutions of politics. As clerk of the Philadelphia Yearly Meeting from 1750 to 1765 he held the pre-eminent office in American Quakerism. He was on close terms with Quaker leaders in London as well as Philadelphia, knew all of Pennsylvania's religious and political figures, and had extensive contacts among the Delaware Indians. His brother James led the strict pacifist faction in the Assembly before resigning his seat in protest at the Assembly's militarism in 1756. John, the youngest brother, took a strict pacifist stance as well. The Pembertons were joined in their endeavors by several leading Pennsylvania Friends and by the itinerant Quaker missionary John Woolman.[13]

In blaming the Quakers in general for their plight, frontier settlers reduced the Assembly to Quakerism and Quakerism to pacifism. From this perspective the Assembly was at best ineffective and at worst indifferent to frontier suffering. The so-called Quaker party continued to dominate the Assembly in the 1750s, but, although most of its members were Quakers, very few of them were strict pacifists. Only four assemblymen, for example, voted against the militia bill in November 1755. And some members of the Quaker party—notably Benjamin Franklin—did not even belong to the Society of Friends. These subtleties were lost on the frontiersmen, who denounced Quakers as an undifferentiated whole and found in Israel Pemberton Jr. the embodiment of everything they hated about Philadelphia's political elite.[14]

The leaders of the Quaker party, meanwhile, had little patience for the lofty idealism of Israel Pemberton and John Woolman. Isaac Norris Jr., the speaker of the Assembly, was a pragmatist, like most successful politicians. Strict pacifists saw the endorsement of defensive warfare as a betrayal of Quaker principles, but Norris saw it as a necessity. He knew that Quakers would lose political credibility if they refused to sanction the use of force in the current crisis. Yet the strict pacifists, though few in number, were vocal and highly committed. They would do everything they could to prevent Pennsylvania's taking the momentous step of declaring war against the Delaware and Shawnee Indians.[15]

On April 12, 1756, the pacifist Quakers presented a "Humble Address" to Robert Morris invoking the memory of William Penn in a last plea for peace. Pennsylvania, they reminded Morris, had a unique heritage and an ongoing historical mission. "The Settlement of this Province was founded on Principles of Truth, Equity, and Mercy," they wrote, "and the Blessing of Divine Providence attended the early Care of the first Founders to impress these Principles on the Minds of the Native Inhabitants." On this basis the Indians, "when their Numbers were great and their Strength vastly Superior," had received William Penn and the founding generation "with Gladness, relieved their Wants with open Hearts, granted them peaceable Possession of the Land, and for a long Course of Time gave constant and frequent Proofs of a cordial Friendship." The spirit of war ran counter to everything that Pennsylvania stood for. Rather than rushing into declaring war Morris ought to investigate the source of the Delawares' grievances and seek to make peace with them.[16]

The "Humble Address" had no effect on Morris, who had already decided on war. On April 13 he informed the Council that "a great Body of the Inhabitants of the Back Counties" were planning to march from Lancaster to Philadelphia to pressure the government into declaring war. The following day, before the marchers could assemble, Morris issued a declaration of war against "the *Delaware* Tribe of *Indians*, and others in Confederacy with them." The declaration stated that the Delawares and their allies had "for some Time past, without the least Provocation, and contrary to the most solemn Treaties, fallen upon this Province, and in a most cruel, savage and perfidious Manner killed and butchered great Numbers of the Inhabitants." They had "carried others into barbarous Captivity, burning and destroying their Habitations, and laying waste the Country," despite "the friendly Remonstrances made to them by this Government." The Delawares and their allies were therefore deemed "Enemies, Rebels and Traitors to His Most Sacred Majesty."[17]

Morris's proclamation did more than declare war. To the horror of pacifist Quakers, it also offered scalp bounties. Every male Indian above the age of twelve captured and taken prisoner would fetch a reward of 150 "*Spanish Dollars or Pieces of Eight*" (silver coins, often cut into four or eight pieces, which were legal tender in the American colonies due to a chronic shortage of currency). For the scalp of any such male the bounty would be 130 Spanish dollars. For women and children the rates were slightly lower. Soldiers in the pay of the province would receive half the going rates. All Indians were thereby declared legitimate targets. The bounties encouraged attacks on the most vulnerable and defenseless and blurred the fading distinction between "friendly" and "enemy" Indians. By April 1756, as the "Humble Address" put it, Pennsylvania had degenerated into a "Theatre of Bloodshed and Rapine."[18]

CHAPTER 8
NEGOTIATIONS

In May 1756 Pennsylvania's lieutenant governor, Robert Morris, sent two messengers to the Wyoming Valley to see if Teedyuscung was interested in making a separate peace. The lieutenant governor and the Indian leader had a mutual interest in reaching a compromise: Morris's incentive was to stop the attacks on Pennsylvania's northern front, Teedyuscung's to retain a permanent homeland in the Wyoming Valley. At the end of May the messengers returned to Philadelphia with word that the Delaware king "was willing to renew the Treaties of Friendship which *William Penn* had made with his Forefathers." The Delaware leader "begged that what was past might be foregotten" and declared that he had "laid down the Hatchet, and would never make Use of it any more against the *English.*" Morris suggested that he and Teedyuscung meet so "that they might have an Opportunity of making these mutual Declarations at a publick Convention." In the meantime Pennsylvania would observe a thirty-day ceasefire against the Wyoming Indians.[1]

Even as these overtures were being made the western Delawares and Shawnees continued their attacks on Lancaster County. Near Harris's Ferry in early July "a Lad at Plough was chased by two Indians, who would certainly have taken him, had not two Men appeared, who fired their Guns, and sounded a Horn, upon which the Indians ran off." From Bethel Township it was reported that "one Martin Coppeller, and his Wife, were killed and scalped by three Indians; and that they also knocked down and scalped a Girl at the same time." In Bethlehem "friendly Indians" reported that "some Hundreds of our Enemy Indians, of different Nations, in and about the Allegheny Mountains, are gone to hold a Council, and form themselves into a Body, in order to come down and harass this and the neighbouring Provinces." A number of disaffected local Indians were said to have joined them.[2]

In seeking reconciliation with Pennsylvania the "King of the Delawares" had the support of Israel Pemberton Jr., the "King of the Quakers." Pemberton believed that his small but disciplined cadre of strict pacifists could become an independent political force by inserting themselves as mediators between the provincial government and the Delawares. Just after the declaration of war he hosted a dinner at his Chestnut Street home in Philadelphia attended by Scarouady, prominent Quaker pacifists, Conrad Weiser, Andrew Montour, and William Johnson's deputy, Daniel Clause. Several more meetings followed, and in July about 120 Quakers subscribed £2,000 to create an organization that became known as the Friendly Association for Regaining and Preserving Peace with the Indians by Pacific Measures.[3]

The conference with Teedyuscung took place in the town of Easton in late July 1756. Located on the Delaware River, Easton was in the heart of the territory taken from the Delawares by the Walking Purchase. Robert Morris and Richard Peters headed the Pennsylvania delegation, with Weiser as their chief interpreter. The Seneca leader Captain Newcastle represented the Six Nations. Also present, on their own initiative, were forty Quakers led by Israel Pemberton Jr., ready to support Teedyuscung and bearing abundant gifts for the Indians. Teedyuscung did most of the talking, identifying the loss of ancestral lands rather than French intrigue as the principal reason the Delawares had gone to war. He had reportedly witnessed Canassatego dragging his uncle Nutimus by the hair in 1742 when the Iroquois banished his people from the Forks of the Delaware after the Walking Purchase.[4]

The imperial government looked unfavorably on the proceedings at Easton. Pemberton had earlier asked Scarouady and Clause to present the Friendly Association's ideas for a peace initiative to the Six Nations and Sir William Johnson. Johnson and his Iroquois allies, predictably, saw the Quakers' intervention as unwarranted third-party meddling in diplomatic affairs. Already annoyed by Pennsylvania's unilateral declaration of war, Johnson believed that individual colonies should not conduct negotiations with Indians. The Iroquois, meanwhile, insisted that tributary nations such as the Delawares lacked the authority to negotiate, let alone to make war.[5]

Although little of practical importance was achieved at Easton, Teedyuscung used the conference to publicly cast off his people's role as female subordinates of the Six Nations. On July 29 he presented a wampum belt he had received from the Iroquois with which, he claimed, they "have lately Renewed their Covenant Chains with us." In the center of the belt was a square, signifying Indian land; at either end was the figure of a man, one English and the other French. The implicit message was that the Delawares should unite with the Iroquois in preventing both European powers from seizing their land. But Teedyuscung wanted independence from the Iroquois, not just from the English and the French. Cleverly interpreting the Iroquois belt as a liberation from tributary status rather than an assertion of Iroquois authority, he declared, "We were Accounted women, and Employed only in women's business, but now they have made men of us, and as such we now come to this Treaty, having this Authority as a man to make Peace." On the basis of this supposed agreement, Teedyuscung went so far as to claim that he was speaking on behalf of ten nations at Easton—the six Iroquois nations, his own Lenapes, and his Unami, Munsee, and Mahican allies—a formulation the Iroquois must have found absurd as well as offensive.[6]

Conrad Weiser subsequently asked the Iroquois delegate Newcastle about the wampum belt Teedyuscung unveiled at Easton. Newcastle's interpretation of the belt's message was much less favorable to the Delawares than Teedyuscung's. "You will remember that you are our women," Newcastle's account of the Iroquois message began, "our forefathers made you so, and put a petticoat on you, and charged you to be true to us & lie with no other man." Lately the Delawares had abandoned their obligation to the Iroquois and to Pennsylvania: "You have Suffered the string that tied your petticoat to be cut loose by the French, and you lay with them, & so became a common Bawd, in which you did very wrong and deserve Chastisement." Nonetheless, as the Iroquois continued to esteem the Delawares, they were prepared to recognize some of their pretensions to autonomy. By going to war the Delawares had "thrown off the Cover of your modesty and become Stark naked, which is a shame for a woman." In light of this fact the Iroquois were prepared to begin the process of restoring the Delawares' manhood—or, as they put it, to "give you a little Prick and put it into your Private Parts, and so let it grow there till you shall be a compleat man." But they admonished their tributaries "to act as a woman . . . be first instructed by us, and do as we bid you and you will become a noted man."[7]

In the Iroquois scheme of things, the Delawares were no longer women, but they were not yet fully men. Their revived masculine status did not come with permission to make war or to buy or sell land. Although Teedyuscung had declared the Delawares liberated from womanhood at the Easton conference in July, Newcastle reported to the provincial Council in October the story of how a Mohawk chief named Canyase had subsequently met with the Delaware king and tried to set him straight. "I told him that the Delawares were women," Canyase said to Newcastle, "and always treated as such by the Six Nations." Canyase's Mohawk nation had taken the Delawares under their protection, and it was up to the Mohawks to decide their status. "We, the Mohocks, are Men; we are made so from above," Canyase told Teedyuscung, "but the Delawares are Women and under our Protection, and of too low a kind to be Men." Like the rest of the Six Nations leadership, Canyase was prepared to "join and help to cut off your Pettycoats, and so far make a Man of you." But that was as far as the Delawares' masculinity would go. "I do not put the Tomahawk in your hand," Canyase pointedly reminded Teedyuscung. "I know what is for your good and therefore, I will not allow you to carry a Tomahawk." Despite his bombast at Easton in 1756, Teedyuscung was still a long way from achieving the autonomy he desired. And peace between Pennsylvania and the Delawares, especially west of the Susquehanna, was nowhere in sight.[8]

On July 30, the day before the Easton conference ended, Ohio country Indians led by Shingas attacked Fort Granville on the Juniata River in Cumberland County, killing or capturing all of the garrison and the settlers who had taken refuge there. This attack cut off supplies to British posts further west and, as settlers fled the region, pushed the western limit of European settlement back to the town of Carlisle. Pennsylvania's local struggle, moreover, was now bound up in the larger conflict known as the Seven Years' War. Word reached the American colonies that England had declared war on France on May 18 and France had responded in kind on June 9. Even as the peace negotiations at Easton were proceeding, Pennsylvania was commencing construction of Fort Augusta at the Forks of the Susquehanna, near the recently abandoned town of Shamokin, once the center of Indian culture in the lower Susquehanna Valley. And, between sessions with Teedyuscung, Morris was planning a surprise attack on the western Delaware stronghold of Kittanning. The war in Pennsylvania was only just beginning.[9]

By the summer of 1756, with western Indians intensifying their attacks on the frontier, the lower Susquehanna Valley was in turmoil. In August a resident of Derry Township named James Galbreath wrote to Edward Shippen about conditions in Lancaster County's upper end. "There is nothing but Bade nuse Every day the Last week," he reported, "...if there is not a stope put to these savages; we shall be all broke in these parts." More and more residents were fleeing daily, "Leaving almost there all behind them...so that the Enemy will have nothing to do but tak what we have worked for." Galbreath informed

Robert Morris that "the name or sight of an Indian maks allmost all mankind in these parts to trimble, there Barbarity is so Cruel." Thomas Barton sent similar reports from Cumberland County, informing Richard Peters, "Such a Panick has seized the Hearts of People in general, since the Reduction of Fort Granville, that this County is almost relinquished." He told of a horrific funeral at which a party of Indians descended upon the mourners, "open'd the Coffin, took out the Corps and scalp'd her."[10]

Forty-seven desperate residents of Cumberland County, nearly all of them of Ulster origin, sent a petition to Robert Morris on August 21, 1756, seeking military assistance. They feared the Indians would learn "of the Weakness of this Frontier, and how incapable we are of defending ourselves against their Incursions," which would encourage them "to redouble their Attacks, and in all probability enforce the Remaining Inhabitants of this County to evacuate it." The petitioners therefore requested that Lord Loudoun, the new commander in chief of British forces in North America, be asked to provide some of his troops to defend them. With this assistance they hoped "to continue a Frontier if possible" (i.e., remain as the western vanguard of settlement) and allow the remaining inhabitants to harvest "a part of the immense Quantity of Grain which now lies exposed to the Enemy & subject to be destroy'd or taken away by them." Petitioners from neighboring York County pointed out that abandoning the harvest would not simply deprive settlers of food and property, but would provide the enemy with abundant provisions and thereby enable them "to carry their Hostilities even to the Metropolis." They too urged that Loudoun be informed of their "truly deplorable Condition" so that he might take some measures to help them.[11]

Pennsylvania became even more vulnerable with the fall of Fort Oswego to the French. Located on the southeast shore of Lake Ontario, this complex of three forts was essential to British offensive capabilities in the northwest. On August 20 Lord Loudoun informed Robert Morris that Oswego, "with all its Stores and Ammunition and the train placed there, is lost, the Garrison made Prisoners, and our Naval power on the lake destroyed." The fall of Oswego posed a grave threat to Pennsylvania, Loudoun warned, and "as you may now expect the weight of the French Indian power on your back, I must caution you to put your Frontiers immediately in the best posture of defence you are able." Far from being able to send the troops that the frontier petitioners requested, Loudoun demanded that Pennsylvania send recruits to him. Compounding the terror on the frontier, settlers soon learned that Indians had slain more than thirty residents of Oswego's hospital and killed or captured many others in the woods after the fort was taken. Settlers in Cumberland County frantically petitioned the provincial government for help throughout September.[12]

In this month of confusion and panic Pennsylvania scored one partial but important victory, at the Delaware town of Kittanning. The attack was the first foray by Pennsylvania forces into the Ohio country. Located on the Allegheny River about forty miles from Fort Duquesne, Kittanning was home to the warriors Shingas, Tamaqua, and Captain Jacobs. John Cox, a young man who was taken prisoner by the Delawares, described the ordeal of the fifty English prisoners he encountered in the town. He noticed several scalps affixed to a pole when he arrived. The Indians "made an Example of one Paul Broadly," he recalled, whom they "beat for half an hour with Clubbs and Tomhawks, and afterwards fastning him to a Post cropt his Ears close to his head and chopt his Fingers." All the prisoners were called together "to be Witnesses to this Scene of their inhuman Barbarity." Yet, despite this show of terror, Cox reported, the Indians and their prisoners "during the whole Summer have been in a starving Condition, having very little Venison & Corn, and reduced to the necessity of living upon Dog Flesh and the few Roots and Berrys they could collect in the Woods." Several of the prisoners had died "for want of Food." Their Indian captors "talked several times of making Peace with the English, and many of them observed that it was better to do so than Starve." Kittanning was vulnerable.[13]

The man chosen to lead the expedition was Colonel John Armstrong. A native of Ulster, Armstrong was appointed deputy surveyor of Cumberland County in 1750, a position that allowed him to amass considerable landed wealth for himself. When Pennsylvania created its militia he was given command west of the Susquehanna River. Armstrong assembled a force of 360 men, including the Presbyterian minister John Steel, and marched west to Kittanning in September 1756. They attacked on September 8, when most of the warriors were absent, killing between thirty and fifty Indians, including Captain Jacobs. After redeeming eleven captives, they destroyed the town. Seventeen of Armstrong's men were killed, thirteen were wounded, and nineteen were reported missing. These were heavy casualties, but in an otherwise dismal year the destruction of Kittanning was widely celebrated. The city of Philadelphia struck a medal in Armstrong's honor. Thomas Penn rewarded him with a sword and belt. Yet the destruction of Kittanning intensified rather than curtailed Indian raids on Pennsylvania. In October Delaware and Shawnee warriors began to cross the Susquehanna once again, striking

Lancaster and Berks Counties. The settlers were "moving away, leaving their Barnes full of Grain behind them," Weiser warned, "and there is a lamentable cry among them."[14]

On November 4, 1756, the *Pennsylvania Gazette* reported that "King Teedyuscung, with a Number of Indians, and several white Prisoners" was on his way to Easton for another conference. Four Iroquois representatives accompanied Teedyuscung, but Captain Newcastle was not among them; he had contracted smallpox and lay dying in Philadelphia. Richard Peters and Conrad Weiser were in attendance, and the Assembly had sent Benjamin Franklin and three other commissioners. Also present, after much vacillation and complaint, was the new lieutenant governor of Pennsylvania, William Denny.[15]

The source of Denny's hesitation was a written instruction from Lord Loudoun forbidding him to make treaties with Indians. The king, said Loudoun, had "entirely taken out of the Hands of the Governments and Governors all right to Treat with, Confer, or make War or Peace, with the Five Nations" and instead entrusted it "wholly and solely" in Sir William Johnson. Faced with this reminder of imperial power, Denny initially decided not to go to Easton. Weiser and other influential voices on the Council, however, persuaded him to attend the conference on technical grounds, arguing that the arrangements had been agreed on before Loudoun's letter arrived.[16]

When the conference opened Teedyuscung articulated the grievances that lay behind his decision to take up the hatchet against Pennsylvania. At the first Easton conference in July he had stated that these grievances concerned land; now he identified the core issue as the Walking Purchase of 1737. To the despair of Pennsylvania's seasoned Indian negotiators, Denny bungled his way through the conference, insisting that the Delawares publicly state their grievances. On November 12 he questioned Teedyuscung directly about how the "League of Friendship" between them came to be broken. "Have we, the Governor or People of Pennsylvania, done you any kind of injury?" he asked. The Delaware king "thanked the governor" for the opportunity to answer this question—as well he might—"and desired time to consider till to-morrow morning."[17]

The following day Denny asked Teedyuscung again to state "freely and fully without any reserve" any "Grievances received by the Indians from this and other Governments." Coached by his patron, Israel Pemberton Jr., Teedyuscung had prepared a specific and highly effective reply. Declaring that he did not have "far to go for an answer," he stated, "This Ground that is under me is mine, and has been taken from me by Fraud and Forgery." Teedyuscung did not have quite the claim to the land that he was asserting; both he and his uncle originally came from New Jersey. But by raising the Walking Purchase and Nutimus's humiliation at the hands of Canassatego, he focused his complaints on a highly emotive episode in Delaware history. When Denny pushed him to explain his position, Teedyuscung stated succinctly, "When one man has formerly Liberty to purchase Lands, and he took a Deed from the *Indians* for it, and then dies, if, after his Death, his Children forge a Deed like the true One, with the same *Indians* Names to it, and thereby take Lands from the *Indians* which they never sold: This is Fraud."[18]

Teedyuscung identified "the young Proprietaries," Thomas and Richard Penn, as the perpetrators of the Walking Purchase fraud. They "came and got it run by a straight Course by the Compass," he declared, "and by that Means took in double the Quantity intended to be sold." At this, the provincial secretary, Richard Peters, threw down his pen in anger and announced that he would no longer take the minutes of the conference. Having conspired with Thomas Penn to perpetrate the fraud, Peters had a strong interest in excluding Teedyuscung's charges from the provincial records. Like Weiser, Peters had advised Denny against giving Teedyuscung an opportunity to state his case at Easton. Denny, however, not only allowed Teedyuscung to answer his questions, but he also ruled that a set of notes taken independently by Charles Thomson, who was openly sympathetic to the Delawares, be adopted as the official record. Denny rounded out the day by inviting Benjamin Franklin and several Quaker leaders, staunch antagonists of the proprietary interest, to dine with him and Peters. Denny's performance at Easton worked very much in Teedyuscung's favor. Yet there is no evidence that the lieutenant governor had any clear agenda; he has been described variously as "quarrelsome," "weak-minded," and a "bumbling dunderhead."[19]

As the Easton conference was under way, the Pennsylvania Assembly was busy considering measures that would create a more effective fighting force. Shortly after the declaration of war in April, the Assembly had passed an act placing all provincial forces under the same discipline as British regulars who served with them in joint operations. This law, designed to strengthen the power of officers, did not achieve its goals. On November 3, therefore, the Assembly passed legislation creating a new Pennsylvania Regiment, which William Denny immediately approved. As in 1755, the legislation authorized a force of 1,400 paid provincial volunteers organized in twenty-five companies.

Enlistment terms remained short, but in a significant departure from the existing militia system officers were to be commissioned by the lieutenant governor rather than elected by their men. Conrad Weiser of Lancaster County was appointed to command the 1st Battalion, John Armstrong of Cumberland County the 2nd, and James Burd, a son-in-law of Edward Shippen of Lancaster, the 3rd.[20]

But how was this new force to be paid for? Denny's instructions from Thomas Penn included the standard prohibition on bills taxing the proprietary estates. His instructions also reiterated a directive Penn had issued in 1751, that the deputy governors should not approve excise or paper money bills without retaining veto power over expenditure of the funds raised. As the excise was one of the Assembly's few mechanisms for raising revenue, the assemblymen were not prepared to concede this point. In September 1756 the Assembly had passed a supply bill appropriating £60,000 for military spending, to be funded by a twenty-year extension of the excise on liquor. Denny vetoed this bill because it did not grant him veto power over expenditure of the funds (and because Penn had instructed him to veto bills extending the excise for more than ten years). To appropriate the necessary funds for the Pennsylvania Regiment the legislators therefore reverted to the mechanism that had caused so much controversy the year before: a general property tax, including the proprietary estates.[21]

In January 1757 the Assembly passed a supply bill to this effect, which Denny vetoed. Seeing no other way to fund the Pennsylvania Regiment, the assemblymen capitulated, passing an amended supply bill that exempted the Penns' estates. To their surprise and irritation Denny vetoed this bill as well, on the grounds that it violated other relatively minor instructions from Thomas Penn. The Assembly then elected Benjamin Franklin as its agent, and he spent the next five years in London representing its grievances to the Penn family and the British government. Not until late March 1757, when word reached Philadelphia that as many as 800 French soldiers and their Indian allies were preparing to attack the garrison at Fort Augusta, did Denny finally sign the supply bill. Although the new force was far from adequate for Pennsylvania's needs, it was a significant improvement on the existing militia. What frontier settlers would most remember, however, was that an elementary defensive measure had once again taken months of squabbling to produce.[22]

CHAPTER 9
WESTWARD JOURNEYS

At the end of March 1757 as many as 160 Indians gathered at Paxton to meet Sir William Johnson's deputy, George Croghan. Each of the six Iroquois nations was represented. Among the Indians were thirty Conestoga men, women, and children—probably the entire remnant of their once proud nation. They were led by Sheehays, who, according to Benjamin Franklin, had "assisted" at the treaty his father Connoodaghtoh signed with William Penn in 1701. John Harris Jr. and the Rev. John Elder, the two most prominent residents of Paxton town, attended the meetings. So too did Colonel John Armstrong, the hero of Kittanning. On this occasion Elder and Armstrong must have encountered Sheehays and the Conestogas face to face.[1]

During the French and Indian War peaceful Indian enclaves such as Conestoga Indiantown came under great suspicion. In January 1756 Robert Morris had summoned the Conestogas to Lancaster to "give them Assurances of a future Support and a small Present as a Testimony of the Regards of the Government for them." He declared that he was willing to "ratify and confirm the several Treaties of Peace, Amity, and Friendship subsisting between us," but warned the Conestogas not to "harbour any strange Indians." Sheehays reassured him that "if any strange Indians come amongst us, we shall give you the earliest Notice." Declaring that he was "lame and infirm," Sheehays asked for protection for his people once he was gone. "You see, Brother," he told Morris, "that the Connestogoe Indians, formerly a large Tribe, are reduced to these few, and that there is never an old man among them but myself, and I must die soon." Despite his fears Sheehays remained headman of the Conestogas for another seven years, until December 1763.[2]

Nothing much could be accomplished at Paxton until Teedyuscung arrived. He had reportedly gone looking for support among the western Senecas and promised to come soon with a retinue of 200 followers. But Teedyuscung was grandstanding; he never arrived in Paxton. At Croghan's suggestion the assembled Indian delegates retired to Lancaster town, where William Denny arrived on May 9 to preside over a conference in the courthouse. Once again Teedyuscung did not show up. Israel Pemberton Jr. and other members of the Friendly Association were there, however, despite orders from Lord Loudoun and Sir William Johnson not to meddle in Indian affairs. Their presence was an affront not only to the imperial authorities, but also to embattled frontier settlers. During the conference a group of settlers came to Lancaster bearing the scalped and mutilated bodies of three men and a woman who had recently been killed at Swatara, just below Paxton. They dumped the four bodies outside the courthouse and demanded that Denny come outside to see them, which he prudently declined to do.[3]

With little business to transact in Teedyuscung's continued absence, a Mohawk spokesman named Little Abraham explained to the Pennsylvania government that his people had tried to rein in the rebellious Delaware and Shawnee Indians, who "wou'd acknowledge no Superiority that any other Nation had over them." Openly defying the Mohawks and Sir William Johnson, these Indians had declared, "We are men, and are determined not to be ruled any longer by you as Women." As a sign of their newfound manhood they were "determined to cut off all the English, except those that may make their escape from us in Ships." And they made an extraordinarily defiant threat to their putative Mohawk overlords. "So say no more to us on that Head," they declared, "lest we cut off your private Parts and make Women of you as you have done of us." This threat was mostly bluster, yet it was clear from Little Abraham's account that the Iroquois had lost control over the Ohio country Indians.[4]

The Iroquois retained more control over the Wyoming Delawares, but in the summer of 1757 Teedyuscung was dreaming of autonomy from the Six Nations as well as from Pennsylvania. He agreed to attend a conference in Easton, the third in that town, in mid-July. The Delaware king arrived with about 160 of his people and more than 100 Indians described as western "Senecas and others of the Six Nations." Six unidentified Iroquois leaders accompanied the party to monitor the proceedings. A large number of Quaker pacifists, led by Israel Pemberton Jr., came to advise Teedyuscung. The Quakers claimed they were there simply to observe the proceedings, which nobody could prevent them from doing. Thomas Penn, however, insisted that they had no right to be in Easton, and he forwarded to Philadelphia a letter from the Earl of Halifax, a high-ranking imperial official, condemning the Quakers.[5]

William Denny presented a summary of this letter to the Council on July 7. Halifax denounced the Quakers' intervention in treaty negotiations as "the most extraordinary Procedure he had ever seen, In Persons, who were on the same Footing, only, with all others of the King's private Subjects, to presume to Treat with Foreign Princes." That "One Part of the King's Subjects" should set themselves up "as Mediators between a Province, in which they live, and any Independent People," according to Halifax, "is the highest Invasion of His Majesty's Prerogative Royal, and of the worst Consequence, as It must tend to divide the King's Subjects into different Parties and Interests." Penn therefore instructed Denny "not to suffer those People, or any other particular Body or Society, in Pennsylvania, to concern themselves in any Treaty with the Indians." Nor were the Quakers to be permitted to distribute presents at conferences, either solely or in conjunction with the provincial government.[6]

Halifax's words had no effect. Pemberton and his followers once again orchestrated the proceedings at Easton. In consultation with Pemberton, Teedyuscung made his first move before the public business of the conference got under way on July 21. Having witnessed Richard Peters throw down his pen rather than record distasteful information the previous November, the Delaware king requested permission to appoint his own scribe, who would take notes along with the provincial secretary. Denny initially responded that, by arrangement with Sir William Johnson, the only person permitted to take notes would be a secretary appointed by George Croghan. When Teedyuscung threatened to leave Easton at once if his request was not satisfied, Denny relented, assigning the task to Charles Thomson, who had assumed that role informally after Peters's tantrum in November. A native of Ulster who came to America in 1740, Thomson was outspokenly critical of the proprietary government's policy toward Indians. He later published a history of the shady land dealings behind Teedyuscung's grievances.[7]

Buoyed by the presence of Thomson and Pemberton, Teedyuscung pursued his goal of securing a safe and permanent home for his people. He laid out this agenda early in the conference, once again emphasizing the Walking Purchase as a means to achieve his end. "As we intend to settle at *Wyomen*," Teedyuscung declared, "we want to have certain Boundaries fixed between you and us, and a certain tract of Land fixed, which it shall not be lawful for us or our Children ever to sell, nor for you or any of your Children ever to buy." He asked Denny to honor this request by sending workmen to build housing in Wyoming town. Denny responded that because Pennsylvania did not own

Charles Thomson (1729–1824). Autographed portrait engraving. Record ID 20040830001. Courtesy of Collections of the University of Pennsylvania Archive.

Wyoming, which had been exempted from the Albany Purchase in 1754, he had no authority in the matter. The land belonged to the Iroquois, but Denny said he would intercede with them on Teedyuscung's behalf.[8]

Teedyuscung's chances of achieving his goals were undermined by a tragic flaw: his alcoholism was now on full display. The Delaware king drew more attention at Easton for his drunken bombast than for his negotiating skills. For the rest of his life he had a reputation as a drunken buffoon, an image carefully cultivated by his enemies but rooted in fact. He had considerable political skill and evident charisma; without alcohol he might have become the great and dignified leader he claimed to be. Those who wished to exploit his weakness supplied him with a steady flow of liquor. According to Thomson, the Delaware king was "kept almost continually drunk" for the first five days of the conference. It was scarcely surprising that when he came to give his first speech, parts of it were "dark and confused."[9]

When sober Teedyuscung could perform very effectively. Asked by Croghan if he still believed in the charges of fraud he had leveled at Easton in November 1756, Teedyuscung said that he did. He insisted on seeing the deeds by which Pennsylvania held the land acquired in the Walking Purchase so that "a full Satisfaction shall be made to the true Owners." Denny sent Croghan and Weiser to Teedyuscung with some of the relevant documents, but as Thomson noted, they were by no means "sufficient to throw full Light into the Matters in Dispute." Beyond this partial concession Denny bypassed the issue by insisting that ultimate authority rested with Sir William Johnson.[10]

Teedyuscung was prepared to offer peace to Pennsylvania, but he wanted to do so independently of the Six Nations, Johnson, and the western Delawares. On August 3 he presented two belts of wampum tied together in a knot to "brighten the chain of friendship" between his people and the provincial government. He also gave Denny a "Pipe and good Tobacco of Friendship," which he claimed his "Uncles" the Iroquois had given him to signify that they would no longer regard him as a woman. Denny reciprocated with a large white belt with the figures of three men on it, representing George II taking hold of an Iroquois king with one hand and Teedyuscung with the other. This form of British control cannot have been what Teedyuscung had in mind when he dreamed of independence from the Iroquois.[11]

Throughout the conference Teedyuscung tried to assert his independence by emphasizing his reinvigorated masculinity. "I was stiled by my Uncles, the Six Nations, a Woman, in former Years," he declared, "and had no Hatchet in my Hand, but a Pestle or Hominy Pounder." But now that he had become a man the Six Nations had given him a tomahawk too. As a mark of his fealty to Pennsylvania and the British, he declared that he would "take that Tomahawk and turn the edge of it against your Enemies, the French." Yet, though Teedyuscung spoke the language of reconciliation with Pennsylvania, his grievances concerning the Walking Purchase remained unaddressed. And despite his oscillation between defiant bluster and protestations of loyalty, he was still a pawn in a larger game controlled by the Iroquois and Sir William Johnson.[12]

The "King of the Quakers," meanwhile, faced accusations of disloyalty for openly assisting Teedyuscung at Easton. Criticism of Pemberton and his Friendly Association intensified after the conference, as Indian raids on Pennsylvania continued. In September 1757 the members of the Friendly Association sent an address to Denny expressing surprise at recent accusations against them and insisting that they had always acted with the government's approbation. Pennsylvania, they reminded Denny, "was settled on terms very different from most of the other colonies." In return for clearing land "from all titles, claims, or demands of the *Indian* natives, or any persons whatsoever," the proprietaries charged a quitrent, which they used to fund further purchases from the Indians. This system was designed to ensure "the original intention and agreement of honestly purchasing the land of the people, who had a native right in it." The Delawares had complained "of diverse kinds of frauds" and demanded "an impartial enquiry," and the Friendly Association supported them in their efforts. In doing so, they insisted, they were loyal both to the Crown and to the legacy of William Penn.[13]

Although the pacifist Quakers endured considerable criticism, especially with the resumption of Indian attacks east of the Susquehanna directly after the Easton conference, they succeeded in advancing Teedyuscung's cause. In the spring of 1758 the provincial government sent workers to the Wyoming Valley to build cabins, with the Friendly Association funding the effort. About sixty carpenters, masons, and laborers set out from Philadelphia in May and worked with scarce provisions until the end of the month, when one of the masons "was kill'd and Scalped by Six of the Enemy Indians." Despite this attack they stayed in Wyoming for one more week, and by the time they left they had built ten houses, laid fences, and dug some ground for planting. Teedyuscung had secured a home—but only on the sufferance of Sir William Johnson and the Iroquois, who allowed him to stay in Wyoming as a buffer against speculators and squatters.[14]

Teedyuscung was steadily being pushed to the margins. His hopes of establishing himself as a mediator between Pennsylvania and the Ohio country Indians were increasingly unrealistic, as neither the western Delawares nor the Pennsylvania government was prepared to grant him this degree of authority. The Delaware king agreed to attend a fourth conference at Easton later in the year, but William Denny was now ready to deal directly with the Indians of the Ohio country. Philadelphia's attention had turned westward to the true center of Delaware power.

In the spring of 1758 the British unveiled an elaborate plan to defeat the French in all theaters and expel them from North America. In the north the new commander in chief, James Abercromby, was to attack Fort Carillon (later renamed Ticonderoga), on the portage between Lake George and Lake Champlain, clearing the way for an assault on Québec and Montréal. In the northeast Jeffery Amherst was assigned to capture Fortress Louisbourg on Cape Breton

THE WAR IN THE WEST, 1754-1763

Island, the strongest defensive structure in North America, which guarded the mouth of the St. Lawrence River and the rich Newfoundland fisheries. Amherst, who joined the British Army as a teenager, was exceptionally well organized and ambitious. His reputation and Abercromby's would stand or fall on what they accomplished in 1758.

In the western theater John Forbes was assigned to complete the task Edward Braddock had so disastrously failed to accomplish three years earlier. His orders were to launch an expedition against Fort Duquesne, expel the French, and thereby secure the Ohio country. From April to June Forbes assembled an army consisting of about 1,700 regular British troops and 5,500 provincial soldiers, including the Pennsylvania Regiment (by now

2,500 strong) under the command of Colonel John Armstrong. Virginia sent two regiments of 1,000 men each, one commanded by Colonel George Washington.[15]

Like Edward Braddock in 1755, General Forbes built a road as he progressed westward, but he chose a different route. Braddock's road, originating at Fort Cumberland (Wills Creek) in Maryland, had cut a trail favorable to Virginia land speculators. Forbes, by contrast, built his road straight across Pennsylvania from Carlisle, over the Allegheny Mountains, to the Monongahela River and Fort Duquesne. The forward elements of Forbes's army, led by Colonel Henry Bouquet, began to move out in mid-June. They reached Raystown on June 24, where they began constructing a base camp that Forbes later renamed in honor of the Duke of Bedford, the lord lieutenant of Ireland.

John Forbes (1710–1759). Courtesy of Library and Archives Division, Historical Society of Western Pennsylvania, Pittsburgh.

Forbes had learned many lessons from the disaster that befell Braddock. The most important was that he needed Indian allies. Israel Pemberton Jr., acting on his own initiative, urged Forbes to make peace overtures toward the Ohio country Delawares. Forbes realized that, by furthering Pemberton's peace initiative, he might deprive the French garrison at Fort Duquesne of its Indian support. He conferred with William Denny, Richard Peters, and Conrad Weiser about this idea in June 1758. The result was a joint invitation from Forbes and Denny asking Teedyuscung to attend a conference in Philadelphia as a stepping-stone to peace negotiations with the western Delawares. Forbes dispatched Charles Thomson and the Moravian missionary Christian Frederick Post to the Wyoming Valley, where they met Teedyuscung on June 12. Post had spent seventeen years living among the Mahican Indians, married two Indian women, and served as a messenger and interpreter for the Pennsylvania government throughout the 1750s. He visited Teedyuscung for a second time at the end of June, and on this occasion the powerful western Delaware leaders Keekyuscung and Pisquetomen were present. After the talks in Philadelphia Denny dispatched Post with Pisquetomen on a peace mission to the Ohio country.[16]

Post and Pisquetomen reached Fort Augusta on July 25, where they learned "the disagreeable News that our Army was, as they said, entirely cut off at *Ticonderoga*." On July 5 a British force of about 6,300 regulars and 9,300 provincials under General James Abercromby—the largest army assembled in North America up to that point—had advanced up Lake George against Fort Carillon. Abercromby's second in command, Lord George Howe, was killed in a skirmish with the French on July 6. Two days later Abercromby launched a massive, futile, and ruinously self-destructive frontal attack, which the French commander Montcalm easily repelled. Apparently lacking any plan, Abercromby sent wave after wave of soldiers forward to be slaughtered, without artillery support. The casualties were massive: 464 British regulars and 87 provincials dead, 1,117 regulars and 239 provincials wounded. The numbers were even worse than at Braddock's defeat. But the British had more than one target in 1758. The great fortress at Louisbourg finally fell to Jeffrey Amherst and James Wolfe at the end of July. Everything now depended on Fort Duquesne.[17]

On July 29, 1758, as Amherst and Wolfe were taking Louisbourg, Christian Frederick Post and Pisquetomen crossed the Susquehanna River at Great Island and headed west toward the Ohio country. "My companions were now very fearful," Post recalled, "and this Night went a great Way out of the Road to sleep without Fire, but could not sleep for the Musquetoes and Vermin." Along the way they came upon three of the "Little Hoops on which *Indians* stretch and dress the raw Scalps" of their conquests, and on one of them "there remained some long white Hair." They saw several poles, painted red, where prisoners were tied at night. By August 10 the expedition had reached the outskirts of Kushkushkee, a Delaware settlement about twenty miles from Fort Duquesne. As Post described it, Kushkushkee was "divided into four Towns, each at a Distance from the others, and the whole consists of about 90 Houses and 200 able Warriors." He asked Pisquetomen to enter the settlement with four strings of wampum bearing the message that he carried "Words of great Consequence from the Governor and People of *Pennsylvania* and from the King of *England*." When Post followed Pisquetomen into Kushkushkee he announced that he brought "joyful News" not only from the government and people of Pennsylvania but also from "your Children the *Friends*." The Delaware leader Tamaqua provided the guests with accommodation in "a large House."[18]

Tamaqua quickly dispelled any illusions that the western Delawares recognized Teedyuscung's pretensions to authority. On being informed "that *Teedyuscung* had said he had turned the Hatchet against the *French* by Advice of the *Allegany Indians*," Tamaqua flatly declared that "they had never sent him such Advice." The western Delawares urged Post to "lay aside Teedyuscung and the Peace made by him; for that they had nothing to do with it." They regarded the eastern Delaware leader as an upstart of minor lineage. Though they may have welcomed his attacks on Pennsylvania, they alone had the authority to negotiate on behalf of the Delaware nation.[19]

The negotiations at Kushkushkee continued for several weeks. On August 26, speaking "in the Name of the Government and People of *Pensilvania*," Post addressed a large audience that included some French officers. He presented a belt of wampum with eleven rows to "take every Thing out of the Way that the bad Spirit has brought between us, and all the Jealousy and Fearfulness we had of one another, and whatever else the bad Spirit might have poisoned your Heart and Mind with." Presenting a second belt, he asked his "Brethren at *Allegheny*, every one that hears me, if you will join with us in that brotherly Love and Friendship, which our Grandfathers had." He assured them that "all past Offences shall be forgotten." With a third belt, Post reminded his listeners that Pennsylvania had already "made Peace with part of your Nation Twelve Months past" (Teedyuscung's Wyoming Delawares) and opened "the Road from *Allegheny* to our Council-Fire, where your Grandfathers kept good Councils with us." For "unless a Road be kept open, People at Variance can never come together to make up their Differences." Presenting a "large Peace Belt," Post took the western Delawares "by the Hand" and led them "at a Distance from the *French*." "Come away on this Side of the Mountain," he urged, "where we may oftner converse together, and where your own Flesh and Blood lives." He concluded by requesting that the Ohio country Indians release their captives as a condition of any peace treaty.[20]

Shingas, the most feared of the Ohio Delaware warriors, was understandably skeptical about Post's assertions of "brotherly Love and Friendship" and the claim that "all past Offences shall be forgotten." He asked Post if he "did not think, that if he came to the *English* they would hang him, as they had offered a great Reward for his Head." Post assured him that "twas all forgotten and wiped clean away; that the *English* would receive him very kindly," to which one of Shingas's companions replied, "Don't believe him, he tells nothing but idle lying Stories." Shingas promised that "he would do all in his Power to bring about an establish'd Peace" but "wished he could be certain of the *English* being in earnest." Shingas and his brothers were worried about more than their personal safety; their principal concern was the long-term impact of a British presence in the Ohio country. They made it clear to Post that they had "great Reason to believe, you intend to drive us away and settle the Country, or else why do you come to fight in the Land that God has given us." This land belonged to the Delawares, they reminded Post, not to the British or the French. "Tis plain that you white People are the Cause of this War," Shingas and his companions declared, "why don't you and the *French* fight in the old Country, and on the Sea? Why do you come to fight on our Land? This makes every Body believe you want to take the Land from us, by force, and settle it."[21]

Given the difference between French and British policy toward Indians, the Delawares would need some persuading to switch allegiances. As Charles Thomson noted, "The *English*, in order to get their Lands, drive them as far from them as possible, nor seem to care what becomes of them, provided they can get them removed out of the Way of their present Settlements." The French, by contrast, "who enjoy the Friendship of the *Indians*, use all the Means in their Power to draw as many into their Alliance as possible." By this means the French befriended Indians, whereas the British excelled in turning them into their "most bitter Enemies." This interpretation had some merit, yet the western Indians had sided with the French out of necessity rather than affection. Shingas and his brothers made it clear to Post that the French during wartime were no better than the British. It seemed as though "the white

People think we have no Brains in our Heads," they told him. Rumors were circulating that the two European powers had started the war deliberately to "waste the *Indians*" and "divide the land" between them. They were "big" and the Indians "small," but that did not mean the Indians were powerless. "When you hunt for a Rattle-Snake," Shingas and his brothers warned, "you cannot find it, and perhaps it will bite you before you see it."[22]

Post worked hard to persuade the Delawares and Shawnees that the British were preferable to the French in all respects. One of his arguments concerned religion. The French were "papists" and, he claimed, they were assisted by others of that faith: runaway Irish servants who disseminated rumors about how the British were fomenting war solely to seize the Indians' land. As Post put it, the French "buy *Irish* Papist Servants and promise them great Rewards to run away to you and strengthen you against the *English* by making them appear as black as Devils."[23]

On September 3, 1758, the western Delawares delivered their response to Post's initiative. A spokesman declared that he welcomed Pennsylvania's interest in renewing "that Peace and Friendship we had formerly," and he promised to send the "great Peace-Belt" presented by Pennsylvania on August 26 "to all the Nations of my Colour, they will all join to it and we all will hold it fast." Presenting a belt of wampum, he asked that Pennsylvania "let the King of *England* know what our Mind is as soon as possibly you can." A leader named Delaware George expressed his regret for having befriended the French and assured Post that now his "Heart sticks close to the *English* interest." But Shingas and his brothers remained skeptical. Unsure of French as well as British motives, they told Post on the eve of his departure that they could not conclude a treaty at this time. Instead they sent a message with Post to William Denny seeking reassurance on British military intentions.[24]

Shingas and his brothers had good reason to be skeptical. If British intentions were pure, why was General Forbes still marching on Fort Duquesne? "If you had brought the News of Peace before your Army had begun to march," they told Post, "it would have caused a great deal more good." Traders and runaway servants were saying that the British and French "intended to join and cut all the *Indians* off." On September 6 the western Delawares formally bade farewell to Post. Later that day the forward elements of General Forbes's expedition, led by Colonel Henry Bouquet, reached Loyalhannon Creek. Numbering about 1,500 men, the advance guard included the 2nd Battalion of the Pennsylvania Regiment under Colonel James Burd, along with four companies of Highlanders and some Royal Americans.[25]

Pisquetomen and Post had a difficult time on their homeward journey, negotiating their way through woods and swamps in heavy rain. Traveling down "a vast steep Hill" on September 11 they almost lost their horses, which they "expected every Moment...would fall Heels over Head." They reached the Susquehanna River on September 15, hunted for food on Great Island, and arrived at Fort Augusta two days later. Thankful for his delivery from "the Country of dreadful Jealousy and Mistrust," Post felt confident his peace mission would have its desired effect. Just before he arrived at Fort Augusta, however, the British forces advancing on Fort Duquesne suffered a disaster that brought back the worst memories of Braddock's defeat.[26]

The advance guard of Forbes's army intended to reconnoiter the area around Fort Duquesne and, if the opportunity arose, launch a surprise attack. A small expedition advanced to within a few hundred yards of the fort, only to be ambushed by about 1,000 pro-French Indians on September 14. The British suffered more than 200 dead or wounded. Only the ability of the vanquished troops to fall back on Loyalhannon prevented a repeat of 1755. French and Indian forces attacked Loyalhannon on October 12, but the garrison, commanded by Burd, repulsed the attack. At the time of this attack hundreds of delegates had assembled for the fourth Easton conference, which turned out to be the most important in Pennsylvania since 1701. This conference would foreclose the last of Teedyuscung's ambitions, seal the fate of the French garrison at Fort Duquesne, and transform the course of the French and Indian War.

CHAPTER 10
CONQUEST

The great Easton conference opened on October 8, 1758, with more than 500 representatives from thirteen Indian nations, including each of the Six Nations, in attendance. George Croghan represented Sir William Johnson, and Conrad Weiser and Henry Montour were the principal interpreters for Pennsylvania. Teedyuscung was there with his Wyoming Delawares, supported by Israel Pemberton Jr. and other members of the Friendly Association. More significantly, the western Delawares were represented by Pisquetomen and an Indian named Thomas Hickman, who had joined the return party from Kushkushkee after the negotiations there.

Teedyuscung, though still supported by Pemberton and the Friendly Association, faced formidable obstacles at Easton. Not the least of these was his alcoholism, which gave advantage to those who wished to deceive or discredit him. Another was the determination of the Iroquois, who held Teedyuscung accountable for taking up the hatchet without their permission, to formally reassert their control over him. The Ohio country Indians and the government of Pennsylvania, meanwhile, refused to recognize Teedyuscung's claim to be the Delawares' principal spokesman. On October 13 he arrived at the proceedings drunk, demanding that Lieutenant Governor William Denny show him "a Letter that the *Alleghanians* had sent by *Pisquetumen*" in response to Christian Frederick Post's overtures. Richard Peters replied that this request could be considered, if at all, only when the Delaware king was sober. In an effort to preserve his credibility Teedyuscung reasserted his charges of fraud in the Walking Purchase and demanded compensation. But in a speech on October 20 he poignantly admitted his impotence in the face of the Iroquois. "I sit here as a Bird on a Bow," Teedyuscung declared. "I look about and do not know where to go; let me therefore come down upon the Ground, and make that my own by a good Deed, and I shall then have a Home for Ever."[1]

The key to peace, as everyone at Easton knew, lay with the western Delawares. On October 24 they reached an agreement with Pennsylvania, subject to formal approval by the council at Kushkushkee. Before the conference began Sir William Johnson had prevailed upon Thomas Penn to give up a large part of the enormous territory he had purchased from the Iroquois at Albany in 1754. Weiser and Peters executed a deed at Easton by which Pennsylvania renounced all land "Westward of the Allegheny or Applaccin Hills"—in other words, the Ohio country, where the western Delawares and Shawnees lived. European settlement would be prohibited west of the Alleghenies. The Easton treaty of 1758 thereby established a precedent for a series of ever more westerly boundary lines that would be set in the 1760s and 1770s.[2]

The deal struck at Easton was the best the Ohio country Indians could hope for. Pennsylvania did not deed the land beyond the Alleghenies to these Indians, any more than it had purchased it from them in 1754. Instead, the Ohio country was returned to the Iroquois, who claimed to own it by right of conquest. The new boundary line on European settlement did, however, allow the Ohio country Indians to dissolve their marriage of convenience with the French. If British settlement was to be prohibited, they would no longer need the French as a counterweight. And although the Easton treaty recognized Iroquois overlordship, the Ohio country was too far from Iroquoia to allow for direct control. The deal offered at Easton in 1758 therefore had its attractions. Everything would depend on what the British did when they expelled the French. The Delaware leaders had no illusions on this point, yet with Forbes's army approaching they had little choice but to break with the French and accept the British terms. The biggest winner in the negotiations was the man with the most military power: General Forbes. He knew that if the Indians accepted the treaty the French garrison at Fort Duquesne was doomed.[3]

For the Iroquois, like the Delawares, the treaty was at best double-edged. They regained nominal control over the Ohio country and the western Delawares and Shawnees. Yet their understanding of what it meant to buy and sell land continued to differ markedly from that of Thomas Penn. The Iroquois believed that the Albany purchase of 1754 had covered only land that was already populated by Europeans. Penn, however, insisted that the purchase covered unsettled as well as settled land. The Albany agreement included considerable territory east of the Alleghenies, which Penn retained when he returned the Ohio country to the Iroquois in 1758. Because much of this territory remained unsettled, the Easton treaty confirmed Penn's ownership of a vast amount of eastern land that the Iroquois claimed they had not intended to sell in 1754. "Yet now by the Deed as drawn," an anonymous observer of the Easton conference wrote, "ten Times, nay I may say twenty Times as much Land is conveyed as was then settled." The Indians "to whom the Lands have been given for hunting Grounds," he predicted, would "disapprove this Grant as they did before, and maintain their Right by Force of Arms." The Easton deed, moreover, was executed in the midst of "a public Entertainment" for the Indians, unfortunate timing "considering the *Indians* Fondness for Liquor." The duplicity in Pennsylvania's policies reflected the brutal realities of power by this time: Forbes was marching west, he would crush the local Indians if necessary, and the momentum of history was such that Thomas Penn could reclaim the Ohio country whenever he chose to do so. The Easton cession was, in the end, a nicely crafted diplomatic fiction.[4]

What would happen if the western Delawares and Shawnees abandoned the French and the British conquered Fort Duquesne? Who but the most optimistic and powerless Indian could hope that the new boundary line would hold? Could the diplomatic transfer of the Ohio country to the Iroquois prevent European settlers from encroaching on the land? Shingas and his brothers had received no reassurance on these questions from Post in September. Nor did they receive reassurance at Easton in November. Even if European intruders stayed out of the region, securing permission from the Iroquois to remain on land they regarded as rightfully theirs was scarcely what the western Indians had been fighting for since 1755. They would take some persuading that the Easton treaty was worth accepting. Accordingly, as soon as the conference ended, Post and Pisquetomen embarked on their second peace mission to the Ohio country.[5]

The delegation set out from Philadelphia on October 25. Two days later, in Conrad Weiser's hometown of Reading, Post met Teedyuscung's son, Captain Bull. Also in attendance was the Oneida intermediary John Schick Calamy, overseer of the Susquehanna Valley Indians for the Six Nations. Post read a message from William Denny asking his companions to alter their route so that they could meet General Forbes along the way. They agreed to this plan and set out for Paxton, which they reached on the evening of October 28. After crossing the river they passed by the Ulster settlement of "*Chambers Fort*" (Chambersburg), where "some of the *Irish people*, knowing some of the *Indians*, in a rash manner exclaimed against them" and had to be driven away. Schick Calamy was familiar with people of this sort; he had left Paxton in 1756, abandoning "his Guns, Cloaths, and all that he had" because "the Irish People did not use him well and threatned to kill him."[6]

The incident at Chambersburg must have aggravated Indians' fears that the conquest of Fort Duquesne would merely pave the way for European incursions onto Indian land. Pisquetomen asked Post whether Forbes would "claim the land as his own, when he should drive the *French* away?, or whether the *English* thought to settle the country?" "Look, brother," he asked Post, "what makes you come with such a large body of men, and make such large roads into our country; we could drive away the *French* ourselves, without your coming into our country." On November 8 Post and his party made their rendezvous with Forbes at Loyalhannon. The main British force had by now joined the advance guard at Loyalhannon, which Forbes renamed Fort Ligonier after the British supreme military commander. The general asked all Indians who "had any love for the *English* nation, to withdraw from the *French*." If they did not, he warned, he would have no choice but to treat them as enemies. The expedition pressed on to Kushkushkee the following day. That evening they "heard the great guns fire from *fort Duquesne*," and whenever he looked toward the fort, Post recalled, he "felt a dismal impression, the very place seemed shocking and dark."[7]

The talks at Kushkushkee began on October 20. Sixteen Delaware leaders met in council that afternoon. In the evening messengers arrived from the French commander at Fort Duquesne, reiterating the claim that the British were coming to destroy the Indians as well as the French and urging all young Indian men to drive out the invaders. But when the wampum string accompanying this letter was placed in front of the first Delaware "captain," he declared that he would not go to help the French. "He then threw the string to the other fire place, where the other captains were; but they kicked it from one to another, as if it was a snake." An Indian named Captain Peter picked up the string with a stick and flung it "from one end of the room to the other," saying that it should be given to a French officer who had "boasted much of his fighting" and for whom the Delawares had often ventured their own lives. The officer, Post recalled, was "mortified to the uttermost; he looked as pale as death."[8]

As Post was negotiating with the Delaware warriors in Kushkushkee, the final British advance on Fort Duquesne was under way. On November 18 a force of 2,500 men, including George Washington and his Virginia Regiment, left Fort Ligonier and headed toward the Ohio River. On November 22, with General Forbes only fifteen miles away, "the *French* . . . uncovered their houses, and laid the roofs around the fort to set it on fire, and made ready to go off, and would demolish the fort." Two days later they blew up Fort Duquesne. General Forbes took possession on November 25 and renamed the structure Fort Pitt, in honor of the British prime minister. Confirming the worst fears

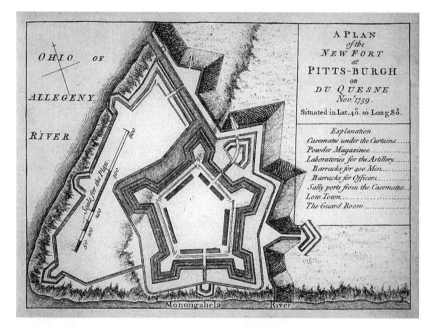

Fort Pitt, 1763. In John Roque, *A set of plans and forts in America, reduced from actual surveys* (London: M. A. Rocque, 1763). Courtesy of William L. Clements Library, University of Michigan.

of the Ohio country Indians, the British soon built a fort ten times the size of Fort Duquesne, capable of housing 1,000 men. Fort Pitt became a stark new symbol of the British imperial presence in the Ohio country.[9]

On November 25, the day General Forbes took possession of Fort Duquesne, Shingas and Tamaqua arrived in Kushkushkee. Any decision on the Easton agreement would rest primarily with them and their brother, Pisquetomen. Presenting four strings of wampum, Post delivered a message on behalf of William Denny. "I perceive your bodies are all stained with blood," he read, "and observe tears and sorrows in your eyes: With this string I clean your body from blood, and I wipe and anoint your eyes with the healing oil, so that you may see your brethren clearly." Offering a second string, he took a soft feather "and with that good oil, our grandfathers used" opened and cleared the ears of his listeners so that they could hear and understand his words. With the last two strings he cleared the dust from their throats and "the passage from the heart to the throat," and took all bitterness from their hearts, so that they might speak freely with the British.[10]

Post then presented Denny's answer to the message the western Indians had sent to Philadelphia after the first peace expedition in September. Pennsylvania had "never let slip the chain of friendship," Denny wrote, "and it has never dropt out of our hands. By this belt we desire that you will dig up your end of the chain of friendship, that you suffered, by the subtlety of the *French*, to be buried." Denny reassured the Indians that he would speak in their favor to the king to ensure that past wrongs be forgiven. He then presented two large wampum belts tied together. The first belt represented the British and the Ohio country Indians taking hands. By this belt, Denny declared, "I make a road for you, and invite you to come to *Philadelphia*, to your first old council fire, which was kindled when we first saw one another." The second belt had "the figure of a man, at each end, and streaks of black, representing the road from the *Ohio* to *Philadelphia*." These two belts, Denny said, "signify our union and friendship for each other; with them we jointly take the *tomahawks* out of your hands, and bury them under ground." Post also presented a message from General Forbes urging the Ohio country Indians to let the French "fight their own battles, as they were the first cause of the war, and the occasion of the long difference, which hath subsisted between you and your brethren, the *English*."[11]

After Post's presentation the Cayuga chief Petiniontonka urged the Ohio country Indians, on behalf of the Iroquois, to make peace with the British. "We desire you would lay hold of the covenant, we have made with our brethren, the *English*, and be strong," he said. "We likewise take the *tomahawk* out of your hands, that you received from the white people; use it no longer." Petiniontonka advised the Delaware leaders to "fling the *tomahawk* away; it is the white people's; let them use it among themselves; it is theirs, and they are of one colour; let them fight with one another, and you be still and quiet at *Kushkushking*." Post asked that this same message be conveyed to "our grandchildren, the *Shawanese*." The Cayuga spokesman presented a belt of wampum with eight diamond figures "signifying the five united nations, and the three younger nations, which join them" (the Tuscaroras, Delawares, and Shawnees). For outward ceremonial purposes at least, Tamaqua was willing to go along with this ritual. Resuming the status of "niece" to the Iroquois, he meekly declared, "I have not made myself a king. My uncles have made me like a queen, that I always should mind what is good and right."[12]

Following these exchanges the Delaware leaders retired into private council, beyond Post's reach. Their response to his presentation, delivered on November 27, was not what he had hoped for. They wished "the *English* only would go back, after having drove away the *French*, and not settle there." Post responded disingenuously that the British only wanted to set up trading posts. The following day Tamaqua announced his approval of Pennsylvania's peace overture, but "in a most soft, loving and friendly manner" requested that Forbes and his army would "go back over the mountain, and to stay there; for if you do that, I will use it for an argument, to argue with other nations of *Indians*." After a return journey through bitter cold and heavy snow, Post crossed the Susquehanna and arrived in Lancaster on December 10 to report that the western Indians had accepted peace.[13]

Following the Easton treaty and the great British victories of 1758, the North American phase of the Seven Years' War drew quickly to a close. In 1759 the French abandoned Forts Venango and Presqu'Isle and the British captured Fort Niagara, Fort Carillon (Ticonderoga), St. Frédéric (Crown Point), and Québec. On September 8, 1760, Jeffery Amherst captured Montréal. With it fell New France and all dreams of a French empire in North America. Yet no sooner had the Peace of Paris been signed in 1763 than the largest Indian war in colonial American history erupted. And in the midst of this conflict, known as Pontiac's War, the Paxton Boys wrought a terrible revenge on the Conestoga Indians.

THREE

ZEALOTS

CHAPTER 11

INDIAN UPRISING

In June 1762 Sir William Johnson came to Easton to preside over the fifth and last of the Indian conferences in that town. He was determined to settle forever the dispute over the Walking Purchase and to consign Teedyuscung to a position of permanent subordination under the Iroquois. He also wanted to silence Israel Pemberton Jr. No Iroquois representatives attended, but Johnson promoted their interests, and thereby his own. In Thomas Penn he had a new and previously unlikely ally. Penn had long undercut Johnson's authority by seeking an independent alliance with the Iroquois and dealing unilaterally with the Delawares. But the two men shared a strong dislike of Teedyuscung and Pemberton and had a common antagonist in the Susquehannah Company of Connecticut. The outbreak of the French and Indian War had forced the Company to postpone its plan to colonize the Wyoming Valley, but in May 1762 the directors voted to send 100 men to the valley, where they established a settlement called Mill Creek, near Wyoming town. The Company's claim threatened Penn's political sovereignty and financial interests as well as Johnson's carefully crafted system of Indian diplomacy.[1]

Exploiting the Connecticut threat to their mutual advantage, Johnson and Penn achieved all of their goals at Easton. They humiliated Teedyuscung, reprimanded Pemberton, boosted Iroquois authority, and fended off the challenge of the Susquehannah Company, at least for the present. Much to their satisfaction, Teedyuscung issued a formal complaint about the Company's intrusions in the Wyoming Valley. Johnson replied that the solution lay with the Iroquois, who owned the land on which Teedyuscung lived, thereby confirming the Six Nations' authority over the Delawares. As for Pemberton, Johnson demanded to know on whose authority the Quaker leader saw fit to interfere in matters of state. For six years Johnson had tolerated the Quakers' interference; now he threatened to terminate the conference if they persisted in disobeying his orders, which, as he reminded them, came on royal authority. With Pemberton silenced, Johnson guided the proceedings toward the conclusion he desired. On June 28 he prevailed on Teedyuscung to withdraw his long-standing charges of fraud against Pennsylvania. James Hamilton declared that Thomas Penn would provide an unspecified sum to the Delawares in return for Teedyuscung's retraction. Meeting with Hamilton in Philadelphia in April, Teedyuscung had suggested that £400 might suffice.[2]

The final question to be decided at Easton was what to do with Teedyuscung and his people. Would they be allowed to stay permanently in Wyoming, as the Delaware king wished? Johnson and the Iroquois agreed to keep him there as a buffer against the Susquehannah Company. Although Teedyuscung had at last received the financial compensation he had been demanding, along with permission to stay in Wyoming, his power was utterly broken. Iroquois authority over the eastern Delawares was fully restored. When Indian leaders gathered in Lancaster in August to ratify peace between Pennsylvania and the Ohio country Delawares, Teedyuscung begged the Iroquois for a deed giving him and his heirs ownership of Wyoming, vainly threatening to leave if his request was denied. This time the Iroquois ordered rather than permitted him to stay in Wyoming.[3]

When Teedyuscung returned to Wyoming at the end of September he found more than 100 Connecticut colonists there, equipped with tools for building and farming. Adding to his humiliation, one of the colonists reportedly stole his horse. A large party of Delaware and Iroquois warriors drove out the intruders. Teedyuscung drank away the winter in the cabin the provincial government had built for him. Then, on April 19, 1763, unknown assassins, almost certainly associated with the Susquehannah Company, set fire to his cabin as he slept, killing the Delaware king and his wife. The killers burned the town of Wyoming, and within two weeks a dozen Connecticut families had taken possession of the site. More than 150 New Englanders soon settled there. The remaining Wyoming Indians relocated to the west branch of the Susquehanna River, their dream of a permanent home gone forever.[4]

By this time the Wyoming dispute was under consideration at the highest levels of government. At the Easton conference in 1762 Sir William Johnson had claimed that authority to resolve the dispute lay solely with the Six Nations, an argument designed to augment Iroquois authority over the Delawares. After the conference Johnson shifted position, asking the Board of Trade to resolve the dispute. The Board ruled on April 27, 1763, that responsibility lay with Pennsylvania and Connecticut rather than the king. Each colony was to appoint a commissioner to negotiate terms, but the Connecticut settlers were required to leave the region as a precondition to a resolution. The Susquehannah Company responded by suspending further settlement in the Wyoming Valley but refused to withdraw the settlers who were already there. This proved to be a fatal misjudgment. In July 1763 the Susquehanna Valley came under sustained Indian attack for the first time in five years. By the time Pennsylvania appointed its commissioner in October, Delaware warriors had destroyed the Connecticut settlement at Mill Creek.[5]

No sooner had Jeffery Amherst emerged as the conqueror of North America than he unwittingly began to plant the seeds of the largest Indian rebellion in colonial American history. Never sympathetic to Indians, he decided in the fall of 1761 to terminate the practice of distributing gifts among them. This short-sighted policy proved disastrous. Gift giving was essential to Indian diplomacy; no conference was complete without an exchange of presents, the value of which was carefully weighed by both sides. But Amherst believed that distributing gifts, including alcohol, merely encouraged Indians' natural tendency toward idleness. Removing the scourge of alcohol from diplomacy and trade had clear advantages for Indians, but discontinuing gift giving not only insulted the Indians, it exposed them to economic hardship and in some cases starvation.

The ban on gifts included powder and ammunition. As a military man Amherst had good reasons for depriving Indians of arms, yet guns were essential for hunting as well as war, and their absence caused great deprivation among the Indians. The resulting "powder famine," more than any other short-term cause, accounted for the eruption of Pontiac's War, which began in the Great Lakes region in the spring of 1763 and quickly spread to the Ohio country. By denying supplies to the Indians, Amherst had provoked just the outcome he was trying to avoid. From Lancaster on June 6 Edward Shippen reported George Croghan's belief "that it is highly probable there will be a General Indian War." Croghan had foreseen this "many months ago," Shippen wrote, "& thinks it might have been prevented if the Great Man now at New York [Amherst] had paid any regard to General Johnson."[6]

The immediate origins of the war can be traced to April 27, 1763, when Pontiac presided over a council of more than 400 Indians near Fort Detroit to discuss the possibility of a revolt against the British. Pontiac is thought to have been born near Detroit around 1720 to an Ottawa father and an Ojibway mother. He sided with the French in the 1750s and may have fought against General Braddock at the Monongahela River in 1755. Inspired by the teachings of the Delaware prophet Neolin, who preached resistance to English culture as the only means of Indian survival, Pontiac and his followers laid siege to Fort Detroit from May 9 to October 15. During this period Seneca, Chippewa, Miami, Potawotomi, Wyandot, Munsee, and Huron Indians, as well as the Ohio country Delawares and Shawnees, rose up against British rule. Although the rebellion bears his name, Pontiac was not so much the military leader as the central inspirational figure. By the end of July the rebels had captured eight British forts. Pitt, Detroit, and Niagara were soon the only western forts remaining in British hands.[7]

To have any chance of success the uprising needed French support. Reviewing the origins of Pontiac's War, Benjamin Franklin noted rumors that it resulted from the circulation of "a large Belt" by a French commander promising supplies and assistance to Indians who renewed their war against the English. This belt was "carried round thro' the Nations." When Pontiac's War began, many Indians—and apparently some French soldiers as well—did not know that the Seven Years' War had ended two months earlier. Franklin predicted that the rebellion would crumble when it was confirmed that "a Peace is concluded between England & France." A letter from Detroit in November, two weeks after Pontiac's siege was lifted, stated that a French officer had "brought a Belt and Letter to the Savages, with an Account of the Peace between England and France, which neither the Savages nor French here believed till now." When it became widely known that French support would not materialize, the rebellion began to dissipate, as Franklin had predicted. In the summer of 1763, however, the prospects for an Indian rebellion looked favorable. Within weeks of Pontiac's laying siege to Detroit the Pennsylvania frontier came under attack by Delaware and Shawnee warriors. The mastermind of these attacks, just as in the late 1750s, was Shingas.[8]

In June 1763, following Pontiac's move on Fort Detroit, Indian warriors made rapid advances across the west. A report from Fort Pitt on June 16 stated that Shawnees, Delawares, and Mingoes "have frequently appeared in small Parties, and have taken one Scalp, shot and stole our Horses and some Cowes, and came and fired on the Fort." In mid-June Seneca warriors captured Forts Venango, Le Boeuf, and Presqu'Isle. On June 21 Delaware and Shawnee warriors attacked Fort Ligonier and Fort Bedford in Cumberland County. Three parties of volunteers, one of them led by Colonel John Armstrong, set out to bury the dead in Cumberland County. Passing houses in flames and burned fences and fields, they noticed that "the Hogs had fallen upon and mangled several of the dead Bodies." According to a report from Carlisle, the Indians intended "to carry the War to as great an Extent as they can," destroying the harvest and killing "all that fall into their Hands." Settlers were once again abandoning their farms, and those who returned to save their crops did so "at the Risk of their Lives."[9]

From Lancaster the Rev. Thomas Barton contemplated the latest developments with great anxiety. "The Barbarians have renew'd their Hostilities against us," he wrote, "And our Country bleeds again under *Savage Knife*. The dreadful News of Murdering, burning & scalping is daily convey'd to us, and confirm'd with shocking Additions." Every "Stable, Barn, or Hovel" in Carlisle and Shippensburg, he told Richard Peters, was "crowded with miserable Refugees." More than 50,000 acres "of as fine Wheat & other Grain as any in the World [was] left to rot, or fall a Prey to a cruel Enemy." What the people wanted most, said Barton, was the restoration of scalp bounties for the Indians they killed and captured. This measure would not only demonstrate the government's commitment to the settlers' cause, but it would boost the enlistment of young men, who "would be prompted by Revenge, Duty, Ambition, & the Prospect of the Reward, to carry Fire & Sword into the Heart of the Indian Country."[10]

Pennsylvania not only lacked scalp bounties at this time; it once again had no militia. The Pennsylvania Regiment had been dissolved after the termination of hostilities in the province in 1758. The summer of 1763 therefore brought back terrible memories of the French and Indian War, when frontier settlers had borne the brunt of Indian attacks as the Assembly and lieutenant governor squabbled over money. The frontier was under attack again, but how would the government in Philadelphia respond? On July 4, 1763, James Hamilton sent a message pressuring the Assembly for support. From "a Dread of being cruelly butchered," he wrote, "the miserable People, throughout almost the whole Frontiers of the Province," had deserted their settlements and sought refuge further east. They had repeatedly beseeched Hamilton to help them "to make a Stand, and repel the Enemy, in Case they should be attacked." They needed military assistance to bring in the harvest. Hamilton urged the assemblymen to pass legislation enabling him "to raise a Body of Men" for these purposes and "for the Protection of the Country at this dangerous and critical Juncture."[11]

The Assembly responded by passing a resolution taking "into immediate pay of this Province" up to 700 "Back Inhabitants and others" for a three-month period. Lancaster, Berks, and Northampton Counties would provide 100 men each, and the remaining 400 would come from Cumberland County. Intended for defensive purposes only, the new frontier force fell far short of the settlers' needs, but from their perspective it was a significant step in the right direction. The two most prominent Presbyterians in the lower Susquehanna Valley, the Rev. John Elder of Paxton and Colonel John Armstrong of Carlisle, were appointed to command the new recruits in Lancaster County and Cumberland County. With the onset of Indian raids in June 1763 local settlers

Paxton Presbyterian Church. Photograph. Courtesy of Ron Wix.

had already banded together in volunteer groups, known as the "Cumberland Boys" west of the river and the "Paxtang Rangers" or "Paxton Boys" in western Lancaster County. Elder and Armstrong organized these and other men into the new militia units authorized by the Assembly in July.[12]

John Elder was fifty-seven years old by this time. The new secretary of the provincial Council, Joseph Shippen, a son of Edward Shippen of Lancaster, had recommended Elder's appointment and explained to the pastor what to expect in commanding his men. It was "very necessary," he told Elder, "that some Gentleman of sense Prudence & Influence on the Spot should encourage & superintend the raising of them & direct the Services of them." As Elder was "well respected by every Body on your Frontier," he would be "of the greatest Use in this Matter." Shippen reassured him, "It is not expected that You will ever accompany the Soldiers to any Part." Instead, he would give his men "the necessary Orders where to proceed & what to do for the Protection of the Inhabitants, from time to time, as Circumstances may change." Elder was to divide his 100 men into two companies. Asher Clayton, who had served as an officer in the Pennsylvania Regiment, would captain one of these companies, and Elder would appoint the captain of the other.[13]

Tensions ran high in Paxton at this time as rumors spread that Indians would soon cross the Susquehanna River. The trader and interpreter Thomas McKee warned James Burd that attacks east of the river were imminent. He added that he was having "a good deal of Difficulty, By the Inhabitants of this place," who were threatening to scalp the Indians, telling them "that they have fifty Dollars reward from the Governor, for Every one theyle take." The previous night, McKee reported, four Paxton residents were "going to Smite Down" three Indians, and but for the efforts of a young man named Patterson, "they would have Shott them." McKee thought that "it would be far weller, to have killed them, than Exasperate them in the manner they have done, And leaving them to Revenge these Barbarities, perhaps on Some Innocent family." The aggrieved Indians, he feared, would "Represent there usuage to their Nation, and Exasperate them against us." Everyone in Paxton "must be in great Terror, night and day," Edward Shippen told his son Joseph, "and the Poor ffamilys that are come thither from Juniata & other Places, in great want of the Necessarys of Life." For the present, Shippen could think of only one practical solution: "A good reward offered for Scalps would be the most effectual way of quelling the Indians."[14]

It was at this low point in British fortunes that the most notorious incident in Pontiac's War took place. It became infamous only in retrospect; at the time it was scarcely noticed. In July 1763 Colonel Henry Bouquet was leading an expedition across Pennsylvania to relieve Fort Pitt, which was under siege by western Indians. Jeffery Amherst wrote to Bouquet from New York City on July 7, insisting that no Indian prisoners were to be taken during the expedition. In a postscript he inquired of Bouquet, "Could it not be contrived to send the small pox among the disaffected tribes of Indians? We must on this occasion use every stratagem in our power to reduce them." Bouquet responded, "I will try to inoculate the Indians by means of Blankets that may fall in their hands, taking care however not to get the disease myself." Lamenting the loss of British life involved in fighting Indians directly, Bouquet added, "As it is a pity to oppose good men against them, I wish we could make use of the Spaniard's Method, and hunt them with English Dogs Supported by Rangers, and some Light Horse, who would I think effectively extirpate or remove that Vermine." Amherst replied approvingly from New York on July 16. "You will Do well to try to Inoculate the Indians by means of Blankets," he told Bouquet, "as well as to try Every other method that can serve to Extirpate this Execrable Race." Amherst also approved Bouquet's plan for "Hunting them Down by Dogs," but lamented the lack of suitable breeds in North America.[15]

Jeffery Amherst (1717–1797). Engraving based on Joshua Reynolds's portrait-in-armor of the victor of Montréal. Courtesy of William L. Clements Library, University of Michigan.

Bouquet and Amherst appear to have been unaware that germ warfare had been put into effect in Pennsylvania only a few weeks earlier. On June 24 Captain Simeon Ecuyer, the commander of Fort Pitt, presented two visiting Delaware leaders with blankets and handkerchiefs that had been infected with smallpox at the fort's hospital. An epidemic swept across the Fort Pitt region in June and July. Although smallpox was already in the area before this incident and the epidemic cannot be traced definitively to Ecuyer's experiments, British intentions are clear. The most poignant note is one of silence: after the smallpox epidemic Shingas and Pisquetomen disappear from the historical record.[16]

CHAPTER 12

RANGERS

Alarming rumors continued to circulate through the Susquehanna Valley in the summer of 1763. "Three Indians came down the River late last night with intelligence," according to an unsigned letter from Paxton town on July 21. "They bring an Account of two Nations, the Senecas and Cayoways [Cayugas] declaring War against the English, and joining the Indians to Westward." These western Senecas and Cayugas (Mingoes) had not actually declared war, but they were sufficiently anti-British to make the rumor plausible. Once the Indians had taken Fort Pitt, the letter continued, they intended to march in a force 900-strong to the west branch of the Susquehanna "and afterwards to march with that Body down the Country."[1]

Settlers who had abandoned their farms were once again seeking refuge in the towns of Cumberland and Lancaster Counties. The *Pennsylvania Gazette* reported that more than "a Thousand Families" in Cumberland County were "driven from their Houses and Habitations, and all the Comforts and Conveniences of Life." By July 25, according to the *Gazette*, there were 1,384 refugees in Shippensburg: 301 men, 345 women, and 738 children. Large numbers of them were living in "Barns, Stables, Cellars, and under old leaky Sheds, the Dwelling-houses being all crowded." Many of these families had suffered "the same Losses and Distresses" and were deprived of their "worldly Substance, and some their dearest Friends and Relatives" during the French and Indian War. Christian compassion dictated that the people of eastern Pennsylvania should help them, but so too did practical self-interest. As the *Gazette* pointed out, if Cumberland County were lost, then Lancaster or even Philadelphia would become "the frontier of this Province."[2]

In Paxton town, meanwhile, John Elder was addressing himself energetically to the task of raising his two companies. On August 4 he reported to James Hamilton that both would be complete within a few days. "There are now upwards of 30 Men in each exclusive of Officers," he told Hamilton, "who are now and have been employ'd Since their Enlistment, in Such Service as is thought most Safe & encouraging to the Frontier Inhabitants." The settlers "here and every where else in the back Counties," he added, were "quite sunk & dispirited, so that it's to be feared that on any attack of the Enemy, a considerable part of the Country will be evacuated, as all seem inclinable to seek Safety rather in flight, than in Opposing the Savage Foe."[3]

As Elder was writing this report in early August, Colonel Henry Bouquet was fast approaching Fort Pitt with a force of 460 British regulars and a detachment of volunteer Rangers. Their goal was to break the siege in place since late May. The expedition ran into serious trouble near the Forks of the Ohio, where previous British expeditions had suffered crushing defeats in 1755 and 1758. On August 5 some 400 Indians, mostly Delawares and Shawnees, ambushed Bouquet's men at a place called Edge Hill, twenty-six miles from Fort Pitt. As a participant in the ensuing battle recalled, this location was "very advantageously chose by a Savage Enemy, surrounded on every side by Rising grounds, except one, and that a Morass; but by the Intrepidity and Coolness of our Men, they were soon put to flight." Having repulsed the attack, Bouquet's soldiers "formed a Circle around our Convoy and Wounded, upon which the Savages collected themselves, and continued hooping and popping at us all the Evening." The next morning, "having mustered all their Force," the Indians "began the War Hoop, [and] attack'd us in Front." But Bouquet feigned a retreat, drew the enemy "to an eager pursuit," and struck back "on their right & left Flanks."[4]

After a bloody two-day engagement the British claimed victory. They lost fifty dead, including two officers, and sixty were wounded—one-quarter of the regular force. The Indians also suffered heavy casualties, though the extent is unknown. According to the soldier who left the eyewitness account, "The Indians never had so severe a drubbing since they knew the use of Powder. Twenty of their great Warriors were found dead, besides the Numbers wounded and dragged away by their fellows." Among those slain were Keekyuscung, the western Delaware leader who had visited Philadelphia with Pisquetomen in 1758, and his son Wolf. Faced with these casualties, the Indians lifted their siege of Fort Pitt and dispersed. Bouquet relieved the garrison on August 10, and reapers went out at once to save the grain. The unplanned Battle of Bushy Run, named for a nearby creek, duly assumed its place in history as a glorious victory.[5]

Although the loss of Fort Pitt would have been catastrophic for frontier settlers, its relief by no means ended the threat to their security. In Paxton John Elder continued his organizing efforts. He divided each of his two companies into six divisions, "station'd about 6 miles from one another." These groups of men, he explained to James Hamilton, were to range a given distance "from their respective Stations" each day. If a division was attacked by the enemy, it would be reinforced by the two nearest divisions. If settlers were attacked, three divisions would "hurry directly to their assistance." Elder was aware of how formidable a task he faced in seeking to defend the frontier. He told Hamilton that he would not have been inclined to divide his men into so many parties but had to "cover certain Gaps in the Mountain that afford the Enemy an easy Passage into ye Settlem^{ts}. & through which they always in the late war made their incursions on the Inhabitants." Defending the isolated settlements "scattered along the River almost up to Augusta, & among the mountains in remote places," he concluded, was "quite impracticable."[6]

The temporary force authorized by the Assembly in July was intended for strictly defensive purposes. Elder knew, however, that his men could never become an effective defense force. What the Paxton pastor really wanted, contrary to the legislature's instructions, was to turn them into an offensive force that would launch punitive expeditions against Indians. If the government refused this request, he was prepared to act unilaterally.

On both sides of the Susquehanna River the frontier force authorized in July 1763 quickly exceeded its mandate. The Rangers who volunteered to serve in this force were settlers whose agenda overlapped with that of the provincial government only up to a point. They wanted security and land and would use whatever means were needed to achieve their goals. On August 20 Edward Shippen reported to his son Joseph that "a Company of Voluntiers consisting of 110 men" had set out from Harris's Ferry "in order to attack our Indian Enemys wherever they would find them." Without clearing the expedition with Hamilton in advance, these volunteers—referred to as Paxtang Rangers, Paxton Boys, and Cumberland Boys—intended to attack the Delawares on Great Island, in the west branch of the Susquehanna River. Shippen was impressed by their commander, Captain William Patterson, whom Thomas McKee had praised the previous month for preventing the murder of three Indians in Paxton. He described Patterson as "a very formidable fine young fellow & very brave into the Bargain," with "the same natural martial Spirit" and physical appearance as Colonel Henry Bouquet.[7]

On the morning of August 21 the expedition arrived at a place called Munsey Hill. After following Indian tracks leading to "a long fire place" alongside Munsey Hill Creek, Patterson "concluded there had lain the night before, between forty and fifty Indian Warriors." At this moment the Rangers suddenly came under attack by "a large Party of the Great Island Warriors." They inflicted "considerable loss" on the Indians, Shippen told his son, but had four of their own men killed and six wounded. The "Paxton and Shippensburg brave Boys," as Shippen called them, "defeated and repulsed about 50 naked, black painted serpents." The ambush intensified suspicions that "friendly" Indians in the Susquehanna Valley were collaborating with the enemy, passing on intelligence, and providing safe havens for raiding parties. Despite the heavy casualties they had incurred, the Paxton Boys claimed victory at Munsey Hill. After the ambush Captain Patterson and some of his men stumbled on three Moravian Indians returning from Bethlehem after selling their pelts, shot them in the back, and scalped them. Exulting in having taken the offensive for the first time, the Paxton Boys looked forward to their next battle. "The Young fellows are in high Spirits," Shippen concluded, "and resolve as Soon as possible to take another Trip."[8]

In early September Indian raids penetrated beyond Lancaster County into Berks County, within sixty miles of Philadelphia. Raiding parties killed or captured sixteen settlers in the vicinity of Reading. Incensed by these attacks, Elder wrote to Hamilton proposing further expeditions up the Susquehanna River by his men. "If your Hon^r. approves of the Expedition up Susquehanna lately carried on by a Number of Young Adventurers from this & Cumberland County, & Shall Judge it necessary to encourage Such Expeditions for the future," he wrote, "Our two Companies, Officers & Soldiers wou'd gladly be employ'd." As for the possibility that the volunteer force might not be renewed when its three-month term expired in October, Elder warned Hamilton, "The consequences will be fatal, the frontier Settlem^{ts}. will immediately be laid waste, & the poor Inhabitants expos'd to the ravages of a Savage Foe." Hamilton had already sent a message to the Assembly urging renewal of the frontier force, warning that the recent respite in Indian attacks on "our Frontiers" was not due "to Remorse for the cruelties they have already exercised, or to any desire of reconciling themselves to us, of which no Overture has hitherto been made." Once they regrouped, he believed, the Indians would "renew their Hostilities against our Frontiers with redoubled Force."[9]

To the fury of the frontier settlers, negotiations between the Assembly and the legislature once again bogged down in disputes of the kind that had hobbled defense efforts during the French and Indian War. On September 27, 1763, the Assembly passed a supply bill raising £25,000 in legal tender to fund a force of 800 men for another three months. Hamilton vetoed the bill, arguing that it violated a ruling issued by the Privy Council in 1760 that quitrents must be paid either in sterling or in local paper money adjusted for depreciation. Thomas Penn had been demanding payments in this form since the 1730s. The Assembly, however, ignored the Privy Council's reading and continued to issue local paper money as legal tender, which could therefore be used at face value to pay quitrents. The dispute dragged on into early October, even as Delaware and Shawnee warriors continued to ravage Pennsylvania. When the unamended supply bill died after Hamilton's third veto the Assembly accepted defeat and raised £24,000 from its own meager sources. These funds kept the volunteer force in place until February 1. Embittered frontier settlers were left to wonder why the provincial government—and, from their perspective, the Quaker Assembly in particular—seemed to care so little about their plight and so much about money and power.[10]

Eager to avenge the ambush at Munsey Hill, Colonel John Armstrong decided to launch a second raid against the Great Island Indians at the end of September, without seeking Hamilton's authorization. As in August, this extra-legal expedition included volunteers from both sides of the river. If Armstrong hoped to repeat his victory at Kittanning in 1756 he was soon disappointed. On October 6 the expedition arrived at Great Island, only to find that the settlement had been abandoned "about twelve or fifteen Days before." A volunteer recalled that the Indians had moved upriver "and carried with them their Cattle and Horses." Armstrong's men set about destroying "the Corn, Beans, Pompions [pumpkins], &c., which was effectually done, by cutting down, battering, and casting into the River." Armstrong, meanwhile, sent a reconnaissance party to "a small Town, called Myonahequa, about 30 miles up the River," where he believed the Indians might have gone.[11]

The following day Armstrong and about 150 of his men set out upriver for Myonahequa. Arriving within a mile of the town by early evening, "they observed several Indians running among the Houses, and, from the Appearance of the Buildings, apprehended that they were fortified, or at least resolved to make a Stand, and accordingly surrounded the Town, and rushed in." Once again, however, "the Indians had made their Escape, leaving their Victuals warm on Pieces of Bark, used by them for Tables." Armstrong found "a quantity of Corn, that had been carried up from the Island; Eels and Pompions; a Number of Swine, three Black Cattle, and Seven Horses; with a Variety of Implements, taken most probably from our Frontier." Further pursuit, Armstrong decided, "would be in vain, as it would be impracticable to overtake them, thus alarmed of our Design."[12]

As Armstrong was setting out for Great Island, Elder wrote to Hamilton proposing another expedition by his Paxton Boys up the Susquehanna River "to Scout a little way into the Enemy's Country." The "Inhabitants of Paxtang the Frontier township in Lancaster County," as an official report later put it, "formed themselves into an Association under pretence of making incursions into the Indian Country to destroy their towns." Elder had a specific target in mind. His intention was to destroy the corn harvested "by the New England men at Wioming," to prevent it from falling into the hands of Indians who might attack the Mill Creek settlement. His men would proceed from there to the town of Wyalusing, another fifty miles up the north branch of the Susquehanna River. Elder and the Paxton Boys were convinced that the supposedly peaceful Moravian Indians of Wyalusing were cooperating with the enemy and even engaging in attacks on settlers. The Rangers, Elder informed Hamilton, "design with y^r. Hon^{rs}. Approbation, to Strike these in order to Root out a Nest of Banditti lodged there consisting of Delawares, Nanticokes & others, our bitter Enemies, & who its thought committed the Barbarities lately in Berks County." Elder was referring here to the raids near the town of Reading in early September, followed a few weeks later by attacks on Northampton and Lehigh Counties led by Teedyuscung's son Captain Bull, which killed thirty-one settlers.[13]

In light of the October attacks, the Paxton Boys decided to embark on their expedition without waiting for Hamilton's authorization or Armstrong's return from Great Island. Led by Asher Clayton, Matthew Smith, and Lazarus Stewart, they set out from Harris's Ferry on October 11. At Fort Augusta they were joined by another twenty-four men, and the combined force left for the Wyoming Valley on October 15. That same day Captain Bull and his raiding party attacked the Mill Creek settlement, killing ten Connecticut settlers and taking another twelve prisoner. By "the way the Savages came in Wyomen," Elder later confirmed to Hamilton, "it appears that they were the same party that committed the Ravages in Northampton County." When the Paxton Boys arrived at the scene on October 17 they discovered the Wyoming massacre.[14]

Writing from Paxton on October 23, a participant in the expedition described what he had seen. "Our Party, under Captain Clayton, is returned from Wyoming," he reported, "where they met with no Indians but found the New Englanders, who had been killed and scalped a Day or two before they got there." They buried "nine men and a woman, who had been most cruelly butchered, the woman was roasted, and had two Hinges in her Hands, supposed to be put in red hot, and several of the men had Awls thrust into their Eyes, and Spears, arrows, Pitchforks, &c sticking in their Bodies." Mutilation of this sort was designed to inflict maximum terror on all settlers who were considering intruding on Indian land. The Paxton men burned the remaining houses and destroyed "a Quantity of Indian Corn." Rather than proceeding to Wyalusing they headed back downriver to Harris's Ferry. Thus ended the first attempt by the Susquehannah Company to plant a permanent colony in northern Pennsylvania.[15]

CHAPTER 13
CONESTOGA INDIANTOWN

Despite the efforts of the Paxton Boys and the Cumberland Boys, the Pennsylvania frontier was more exposed than ever by October 1763. Sir Jeffery Amherst wrote to James Hamilton emphasizing the threat to British imperial interests. The Delaware Indians, according to Sir William Johnson's sources, were still intent on taking Forts Pitt and Augusta, which they regarded "as the greatest Eyesores to the Indians in those parts." Having taken these forts, they would "proceed towards Philadelphia," while the Ottawas, Hurons, and other Indians "would demolish Detroit and Niagara." Given the magnitude of this threat, Amherst expressed his "Surprize at the infatuation of the People in your Province, who tamely look on while their Brethren are butchered by the Savages."[1]

Hamilton shared Amherst's rebuke with the assemblymen, hoping to provoke them into action. They replied that they were at a loss to understand Amherst's criticism. The general, it seemed, was "unacquainted with the vigorous Measures which this Government has pursued, much beyond any of the rest of the Colonies, for the Protection and Defence of their long extended Frontier." The 700 men raised in July had "intercepted and repulsed" several parties of Indians, protecting frontier settlers "from the intended Massacres." John Armstrong had just led the second expedition against Great Island, "which has heretofore served as a Station, from whence the Savages usually issue for the Annoyance of our Settlements." Yet Amherst saw fit to chastise the government of Pennsylvania. Neatly turning the tables on Hamilton, the assemblymen decried this "hard Censure" but wondered "for what Part of the Government it was intended." If the rebuke was "intended for your Honour," they assured him, with grating insincerity, "we have Reason to believe you have done every Thing, as Commander in Chief of the Forces, that could be expected."[2]

Seeking more direct control over Pennsylvania affairs, Thomas Penn appointed his nephew John to replace James Hamilton as lieutenant governor.

John Penn had spent a couple of dissolute years in Philadelphia in the mid-1750s but had little political or administrative experience. He arrived in the city with his brother Richard on October 30, 1763, to considerable fanfare. The members of the Council, along with the mayor, sheriff, and other Philadelphia officials, marched to City Hall, where Penn's commission was read in public. The bells of Christ Church rang out and guns were fired from the battery. Philadelphia's merchants delivered a welcoming address, and a reception followed at the State House. "I have hardly had a moment to myself since I came on Shore," Penn wrote to his uncle on November 15, "my whole time has been almost employ'd in receiving visits & addresses & attending feasts & entertainments which as they were made on purpose for me I could not by any means avoid tho' it was the hardest duty I ever went thro' in my life."[3]

Letters and petitions came in from around the province, some to welcome Penn and others to make him aware of the tribulations of frontier life.

John Penn (1729–1795). Society portrait. Courtesy of Historical Society of Pennsylvania.

From Carlisle on November 12 John Armstrong emphasized the need for frontier defense over effusive words. "Congratulatory addresses, Laudible as they are, may justly become burthensome thro' their number or other attending circumstances, as well as carry in them an air of insincerity," Armstrong wrote, "especially at present when your introduction to the Government happens at a time of general disquiet amongst the Inhabitants thro' the cruel depredations of a Savage Enemy not easily Suppress'd." Armstrong brusquely informed Penn on November 14, "We are almost out of Ammunition, especially Lead, the Patroling partys being now serv'd only with Buck & Swan Shot." As he wrote these words he was unaware that Indians had attacked the nearby settlement of Great Cove the previous day, with "five persons Kill'd & Six missing—whether taken prisoners or Kill'd is not known."[4]

The Conestoga Indians also welcomed John Penn, who they saw as the latest incarnation of their protector, Onas. On November 30, seeking to renew their bond with Onas, they composed an address bearing the marks of Sheehays and two others. As the Conestogas were "settled at this place by an Agreement of Peace and Amity established between your Grandfathers & ours," they told Penn, they looked forward to the same "favour and protection" in the future. Although they had once again proved their loyalty by living "in Peace and Quietness with our Brethren & Neighbours round us during the last & present Indian Wars," they were no longer able to support their families by hunting. The Conestogas therefore urged Penn to consider their "distressed Situation, & grant our Women and Children some Cloathing to cover them this Winter." In the past the provincial government had faithfully furnished them with provisions and appointed an agent to protect them. But there was no agent now, and neighboring settlers had "encroach'd upon the Tract of Land reserved here for our use." The Conestogas therefore asked Penn to appoint Captain Thomas McKee, an Indian trader "who lives near us and understands our Language, to take care, and see Justice done us." His appointment, they hoped, would renew the bond between them and the Penn family.[5]

Early in December the Philadelphia weeklies carried news that further enflamed tensions on the frontier. On October 7 George III had issued a proclamation setting a new boundary line on western settlement. As it took six to eight weeks to cross the Atlantic in those days, the royal proclamation was not printed in Philadelphia until December 8. A blueprint for the postwar imperial order, it divided the land acquired from France under the Peace of Paris into four "governments"—Québec, East Florida, West Florida, and Grenada—and extended the privileges of British subjects to all Europeans lawfully living in these areas. Building on the boundary line principle established at Easton in 1758, the proclamation prohibited settlement on western lands "beyond the Heads or Sources of any of the Rivers which fall into the Atlantic Ocean from the West and North West." It thereby reserved the vast western territory beyond the Appalachian Mountains, including the Ohio country, for Indians rather than European settlers. Though widely ignored in practice, the proclamation exacerbated relations between the American colonists and the imperial government. Its immediate impact in Pennsylvania was to heighten the sense among frontier settlers that all forms of government were conspiring against them.[6]

Although the Paxton Boys claimed that their expeditions targeted only enemy Indians, the local communities referred to as "friendly" Indians were the most vulnerable. The Conestogas, who had lived in precarious harmony with Pennsylvania for three generations, came under close scrutiny during Pontiac's War. So too did the several hundred mainly Delaware Indians who lived in the Moravian missions of Bethlehem, Nain, and Wichetunk. Unlike the Conestogas, they were Christian converts. After the failed expeditions against Great Island and Wyalusing in the autumn of 1763, the Paxton Boys began to insist that the Moravian Indians were in league with the enemy and that the distinction between "friendly" and "enemy" Indians was invalid. All Indians were enemies and must be treated accordingly.

Despite their extreme position, the Paxton Boys were not alone in viewing Indians this way. In October 1763 the Assembly's commissioners submitted a report stating that the Indians at Nain and Wichetunk were in danger from hostile settlers in part because they were secretly trading with enemy Indians and supplying them with arms and ammunition. The commissioners, moreover, believed "that there is much Reason to suspect the said *Moravian Indians* have also been principally concerned in the late Murders committed near *Bethlehem*, in the County of *Northampton*." But, though the commissioners agreed with the Paxton Boys that the Moravian Indians were in league with the enemy, they did not favor punitive raids.[7]

On the contrary, the commissioners recommended that the Indians be removed to Philadelphia, "where their Behaviour may be more closely observed." On the basis of their report, the Assembly resolved to evacuate from the frontier all Moravian Indians who were willing to leave, whether "from their Attachment to the Government, or Regard for their own Safety." A party of 127 Indians from the missions at Nain, Wichetunk, Nazareth, and Bethlehem set out for Philadelphia on November 8. Their removal, John Penn informed his uncle, was designed "to quiet the minds of the Inhabitants of Northampton County who were determined either to quit their settlement or take an opportunity of murdering them all, being suspicious of their having been concerned in several murders in that County." The Indians were housed in the Province Island pesthouse, a quarantine station about six miles south of Philadelphia.[8]

On November 30 a second party of twenty-two Moravian Indians arrived in Philadelphia from Wyalusing, the town the Paxton Boys had hoped to destroy in October. Their leader, Papounan, had initially told James Hamilton that he saw no reason for disagreement between Pennsylvania and his people, who concerned themselves "with nothing but the worship of God." Hamilton reassured Papounan, "We do not look on you and your Indians as our Enemies, but rather our Friends." But he warned him that others would not make this distinction. The attacks led by Captain Bull in Northampton County in October, he told Papounan, "enraged & provoked my People greatly; and in revenge some of them have gone into the Indian country to take their Satisfaction." Hamilton was referring to the Paxton Boys' expedition against Wyalusing, which they had abandoned after discovering the Mill Creek massacre.[9]

Forty-five miles downriver from Paxton, the Conestoga Indians were also under suspicion. Conestoga Indiantown, once a crossroads of diplomacy and trade, was by now in permanent decline. The Conestogas had several times considered abandoning the town. Back in 1758, for example, Sheehays and his younger kinsman Will Sock had come to Philadelphia to see William Denny. The Conestogas needed food and supplies. They could no longer hunt for fear of being mistaken for enemies. They asked for "Matchcoats [blankets worn as outer garments] and Moccasins and other necessaries." One faction wanted to leave Conestoga Indiantown. The hunting, they believed, would be better further north, beyond Shamokin. Will Sock, who had a reputation as a firebrand, spoke for those who favored leaving. He was known to have visited Seneca Indians, some of whom leaned toward the French. John Hughes, who had supervised the construction of cabins for the Wyoming Delawares in 1758, reported that Teedyuscung seized a French flag "from Will Sock and his Companions." Sock was also rumored to have killed an old man near Fort Augusta and an Indian named Chagrea.[10]

As the dominant member of the younger generation of Conestogas, Will Sock evidently had a lot of influence. But Sheehays had more. Sheehays wanted to renew the covenant with Onas. A fire "was kindled at Conestogoe," he declared, "that had burnt a long while." Sheehays had been born there, lived there all his life, and intended to "stay and lay his Bones at Conestogo." The Conestoga headman prevailed; with their business in Philadelphia concluded, Sheehays and his people went home to stay. Two years later, at a conference in Lancaster, Sheehays reiterated his people's commitment to remain in Conestoga Indiantown. "You may, perhaps, think I will go away," he declared, "but I tell you I will always stay at Conestogo, and these that are with me will stay too." But Sheehays had grown weary and longed for the days of William Penn, who "loved, indeed, all the Indians, but there was a singular love between him and the people who came with him and the Conestogo Indians." Speaking for his "young men, and all the Women and Children," he asked the government to continue to protect the Conestogas, who had "ever held fast our friendship with William Penn's people."[11]

With the resumption of war in Pennsylvania in 1763, the Conestogas needed government protection more than ever. The bands of Rangers patrolling the countryside suspected them of spying or harboring enemy Indians. Will Sock came under particular suspicion. The Paxton Boys accused him of giving information to enemy Indians and of planning or participating in attacks on local settlers. The only Conestoga Indian accused of specific offenses, he was a marked man.[12]

Will Sock was not in Conestoga Indiantown on the morning of December 14, 1763. But Sheehays was, along with his son Esscanesh, a brother of Sock's named Waashen (known as George), and three other Indians. The remaining fourteen Conestogas were away from the town, most of them selling brooms and baskets. The Paxton Boys, armed with guns and tomahawks, rode downriver through the night and attacked at dawn. They slaughtered the six Indians they found at home.[13]

Rhoda Barber, who grew up in the nearby Quaker settlement of Wright's Ferry, wrote an account of the massacre in her old age, based on "the facts which I have heard related over and over since my childhood." In December 1763, she recalled, "a company from Paxton township under the name of the Paxton Boys agreed to come by night and destroy the poor Indians at their town." One very cold morning that month, Barber continued, "a German neighbour came to my father's house requesting him to go with him in pursuit of some who had been at his house the preceding night whom he termed robbers." These men had "behav'd in a very disorderly manner such as melting the pewter on the stove and other things of the same kind." Barber's father, "supposing it had been some persons in a frolick advis'd him to take no notice of it." But the German had scarcely left Barber's home "when five or six [men] came in, they had guns which the[y] left outside, they were very cold, their coats cover'd in snow and sleet." Barber did not think that her father "was personally acquainted with them, though we knew from what part of the county they came."[14]

As the men took morning refreshments, they demanded to know "why the indians were suffer'd to live peaceably here." Mr. Barber told them that "they were quite inoffensive." The men then asked him "what would be the consequences were they destroy'd," and he replied, "They would be as liable to punishment as if they had destroyed so many whites." In the meantime, Rhoda Barber's two brothers, age ten and twelve, "had been out looking at the strangers horses (as such boys are wont to do) which were hitched in a waggon shed which stood near the door." After the strangers left, her brothers said the horses "had tomahawks tyed to their saddles and they were bloody." The strangers also had a gun belonging to an Indian friend of the boys named Chrislie. Soon after they left, a message arrived "telling of the dreadful deed" at Conestoga Indiantown. An inquest was held, and the coroner contributed some money to bury the victims. Barber's father "and some others went down to see them buried, shocking indeed was the sight, the dead bodies lay among the rubbish of their burnt cabins like half consum'd logs." The fourteen surviving Conestoga Indians were removed to Lancaster town for their safety. Edward Shippen suggested that they be conveyed from there to Philadelphia, but they remained in Lancaster, where they were lodged in the workhouse "as the Place of greatest Safety."[15]

On the evening of the massacre Edward Shippen wrote to John Penn reporting "that a Company of People from the Frontiers had killed and scalped most of the Indians at Conestogoe Town early this Morning." By sad coincidence, this letter was read before the Council on the same day as the Conestogas' welcome address to John Penn. John Hay, the sheriff of Lancaster County, sent Penn a list of the dead Indians and their "Effects and Papers." A number of documents were found in the burned-out remains of the town, including two belts of wampum, two communications with James Logan, and two letters from Lieutenant Governor William Keith to the Conestoga leader Civility. The documents also included "A Writing, on Parchment, purporting An Article of Agreement between William Penn, Proprietary, &ca, of Pennsylvania, and the King of the Indians inhabiting in or about the River Susquehanna, and other Indian Nations." This document, dated April 23, 1701, was the Conestogas' copy of their foundational treaty with their protector Onas, one of their most prized possessions.[16]

Who killed the Conestoga Indians? The perpetrators were members of the Paxtang Rangers that John Elder had raised in Paxton and Hanover Townships during the summer. As early as September 1763 the term "Paxtang Rangers" was being used interchangeably with "Paxton Boys," the name by which the killers are known to history. Although they were part of the volunteer force created by the government, they had their own agenda; they were in one sense agents of the state, but they also threatened its interests and legitimacy. Having failed in their expedition against the Delaware Indians of Wyalusing in October 1763, they unleashed their accumulated rage on the Conestoga Indians, whose long-standing protection by the provincial government they detested. Claiming that the "friendly" Conestoga Indians were conspiring against Pennsylvania during wartime, the Paxton Boys set out to annihilate them.

The authorities in Lancaster had little difficulty finding witnesses to affirm the individual or collective guilt of the Conestogas. The affidavits sworn to this effect, however, consisted for the most part of hearsay and circumstantial evidence. One witness stated that an Indian woman named Cannayah Sally told him that Conestogas had killed Jegrea (Chagrea) because he would not go to war with them against the British. Another said that during her captivity at Kittanning, "the French Officers were furnish'd weekly, or once in two Weeks, with the *Pennsylvania* Gazette" by "strange *Indian* Messengers" (i.e., Conestogas), who, she was told, "were willing to take up the *Hatchet* against the ENGLISH, whenever the *French* would request them to do it."[17]

Will Sock was the main focus of suspicion. A local gunsmith stated that Sock and another Conestoga Indian had several times "threatened to *scalp* him, for refusing to mend their Tomahawks, and swore they would *scalp* him." A "Lady of Character" from Lancaster town swore that Sock had come to her home and threatened her life, claiming that "*this Place* (meaning *Lancaster*) *is mine and I will have it yet.*" Captain John Hambright, "an eminent Brewer of the Borough of *Lancaster*," who led the march on Philadelphia in favor of a militia bill in 1755, provided evidence about Sock's supposed participation in the murder near Fort Augusta in 1757. As an officer in the Pennsylvania Regiment at that time, Hambright had happened to encounter Sock and a companion the day after the murder, and when he called out to them they halted and "ran off with their greatest Speed." Sock had been a frequent visitor to Fort Augusta before the murder; afterward he did not return for four months, and when he reappeared "he behaved in a different Manner than usual, not coming into the Fort, nor being so familiar as formerly."[18]

This was thin evidence on which to build a case against Will Sock, let alone the Conestogas generally. The eighteenth-century historian Robert Proud, unconvinced by any rationale he heard for the massacre, stated the matter plainly. "A number of, not improperly named, *armed demi-savages*, inhabitants of Lancaster county, principally from the townships of *Paxtang* and *Donegal*, and their neighbourhood," he wrote, "committed the most horrible *massacre*, that ever was heard of in this, or perhaps, any other province, with impunity!" They did so, Proud continued, "under the notion of extirpating the Heathen from the earth, as Joshua did of old, that these saints might possess the land alone, they murdered the remains of a whole tribe of peaceable, inoffensive, helpless *Indians*, who were *British subjects*, young and old, men, women and children."[19]

The Rev. John Elder had some explaining to do. On December 16 Edward Shippen wrote to Elder from Lancaster, demanding to know how the Conestoga massacre could have taken place. Elder wrote to John Penn that day exempting himself from responsibility, though he admitted that he had received information the day before the attack "that a number of persons were assembling on purpose to go & cut off the Indians at Connestogoe." After consulting with a local magistrate, Elder claimed to have "hurried off an Express, with a written message to that party, entreating them to desist from such an undertaking." Elder insisted that he knew "not of one person of Judem^t or prudence that has been anywise concerned in it." The massacre, he said, was perpetrated "by some hotheaded, ill advised persons, & especially by such, I imagine, as suffer'd much in their relations by the Ravages committed in the late Indian War." Elder had warned them that private persons had "no right to take the lives of any under the protection of the Governmnent" and that their proposed action was "barbarous & unchristian in its nature." If they "proceeded in that affair," they must prepare "to meet with a Severe prosecution, & become liable even to capital punishment." Or so, at least, Elder remembered the details of what he had told the Paxton Boys. More interesting than the advice he supposedly offered them is how much he evidently knew about their movements in advance.[20]

When John Penn received word of what had happened on Conestoga Manor his response was strangely muted and ineffective. He went through the motions of instructing the magistrates of Lancaster, York, and Cumberland Counties to take appropriate measures to bring the perpetrators to justice. He sent a message to the Assembly seeking its cooperation in moving the remaining Conestogas to Philadelphia, as they had complained that they did not feel safe in Lancaster. He also requested that "the few friendly Indians" left at

Wyalusing by Papounan be brought down to Province Island. The Assembly approved the removal of both groups and promised to defray the expenses. Penn's only other measure was a proclamation issued on December 22, denouncing those who had "in cool blood barbarously killed" six Indians who had "lived peaceably and inoffensively among us during all our late Troubles, and for many Years before, & were justly considered as under the protection of this Government and its Laws." The proclamation was posted in public places and printed in the *Pennsylvania Gazette* and *Journal*, yet it offered no reward. Anyone with a rudimentary knowledge of life on the frontier at this time ought to have known that the Paxton Boys would have regarded the massacre of December 14 an unfinished job.[21]

CHAPTER 14

LANCASTER WORKHOUSE

On December 27 the Paxton Boys rode into Lancaster town in broad day-light. "A number of Persons to the amount (by their appearance), of fifty or Sixty, armed with Rifles, Tomahawks, &ca., suddenly, about Two o'Clock, rushed into the Town," Sheriff John Hay wrote to John Penn that evening, "& immediately repaired to the Work House where the Indians were con-fined." Brushing aside the sheriff and coroner, they "killed all Indians there, being the fourteen . . . to have survived the former Affair at their Town." The victims consisted of three married couples and their eight children. The adults were Will Sock and Kaniangas ("Molly"), Kyunueagoah ("Captain John") and Koweenasee ("Betty"), and Sasquieshattah ("John Smith") and "Peggy" (Sheehay's daughter). The children included "Chrisly" (Tongquas), the boy Rhoda Barber remembered as Chrislie, a playmate of her brothers. Eyewitnesses emphasized the brutality of the attack, including scalpings and systematic dismemberment.[1]

How could the Lancaster massacre have been permitted to happen? The city magistrates knew that the first massacre was unfinished, which is why they moved the survivors to Lancaster. A detachment of Highlanders was stationed in the town at this time. Why were they not guarding the workhouse on December 27? The Quaker assemblyman Samuel Foulke wrote in his journal that the Lancaster massacre was "to the Eternal Shame & reproach of ye Magistrates of that Town, who tamely Suffer'd the Cruel Massacre when they might Easily have prevented it by Calling on ye Commander of the regular troops then under Arms within Call." According to some accounts, Captain Robinson and his Highlanders stood by and let the massacre take place. Others claimed that the soldiers were in a dif-ferent part of town when the massacre occurred. Yet Lancaster, though large by colonial American standards, was not a very big town. Some reports suggested

"Massacre of the Indians at Lancaster by the Paxton Boys in 1763." In James Wimer, *Events in Indian History* (Lancaster, Penna.: G. Hills, 1841). Courtesy of Library Company of Philadelphia.

that the soldiers wanted to guard the workhouse, but the magistrates denied their request. Foulke went so far as to charge that the Lancaster authorities had several days' warning of the intended attack.[2]

Edward Shippen, the proprietary official most directly accountable in this affair, wrote a long self-justifying letter to his son Joseph on January 5, 1764, acknowledging but not responding to the accusations concerning his conduct. According to a "Report Spread by Somebody in Philadelphia," Shippen told his son, the magistrates of Lancaster had "certain Information" a day or two before the massacre that the killers were coming to "destroy the Indians in the Workhouse." Shippen conceded that he had indeed received advance warning. A few days before the attack the Lancaster "Prison Keeper" had come to his house with news that "a parcel of the Rioters who had killed ye Conestogoe Indians at the Mannor, were collected together at a Tavern on the Donegal Road about four or five miles off." They would be joined "by a larger Number before midnight & then they were to come in a Body & break open the Workhouse, and kill all the Indians." The Lancaster magistrates resolved to send out two constables "as Spies to a Couple of Taverns about the distances abovementioned, and to bring us word as soon as possible."[3]

If the rumors proved true, the magistrates were to "immediately alarmn the Borough, and do the best we could to prevent the Indians being killed." The inhabitants of Lancaster town, being "indisciplined & miserably armed," Shippen wrote to his son, "could have made but a poor stand against 80 or 100 Desperadoes well armed at least." The battle would have taken place in darkness and in "excessive cold" as the streets were "full of Snow & ice." Shippen also claimed, implausibly, that calling for military assistance was not an option because he "had not heard of any Commanding Officer with his Highlanders Soldiers being in the Borough." At around one o'clock in the morning "the Constables returned, almost perished with the Cold," and reported that "there were no Rioters" in the taverns they had checked, "nor had any of them been thereabouts Since they came from the Conestogoe Town." There the matter rested, and Shippen and his fellow magistrates "were in hopes we should have no more disturbance from those People."[4]

Only a few days later, to Shippen's complete surprise, the Paxton Boys "rushed into the Town at Noonday on horseback with their Muskets, Tomahawks, & Scalping knives, broke open the workhouse and killed the Indians." Shippen claimed to have been unaware of the attack as it was happening. "I never heard any word of it till it was just over," he told his son, "and the Rioters were returning from the bloody Place where the Indians were." The killers, it was said, "were not more than eleven or twelve minutes perpetrating their Tragical Scene." Even "if the Magistrates & Burgesses had thought of calling upon Captain Robinson for assistance," Shippen concluded, "it could have been of no service" for his men were "mostly billetted up and down the town (as was understood) and quite off their guard." With nothing more to say in his defense, Shippen assured his son "This is a faithful Account of the affair, and is the best excuse I can make for the Magistrates and therefore conclude."[5]

Looking back a generation later, the historian Robert Proud was not impressed by this "faithful Account." With characteristic bluntness, he concluded that the last fourteen Conestogas "were through the connivance, if not the encouragement, of the *Christian-professing* Magistrates, and other principal persons of that town, all inhumanly butchered, in cold blood, even enfants at the breast, by the same party of armed ruffians [as on December 14], at midday." The Lancaster massacre, he wrote, occurred "without opposition, or the least molestation!—to the lasting infamy of the inhabitants of that place, who had power sufficient to prevent it!"[6]

Who were the Paxton Boys, who had now struck twice with terrible effect against the Conestoga Indians? The men most likely to know the answer to this question were John Armstrong and John Elder, the two most influential Presbyterians in the region extending westward from Hanover and Paxton Townships, across the Susquehanna River to Carlisle, where the Paxton Boys originated. Elder, however, had already told John Penn that he knew none of the men involved, even though he must have known most of them. Armstrong likewise pleaded ignorance. Writing to Penn from Carlisle on December 28, he insisted "that not one person of the County of Cumberland so far as I can learn, has either been consulted or concerned in that inhuman and scandalous piece of Butchery." Such exploits, the hero of Kittanning suggested, were beneath the martial prowess of his men. "I should be very sorry," he told Penn, "that ever the people of this County should attempt avenging their injuries on the heads of a few inoffensive superannuated Savages, whome nature had already devoted to the dust."[7]

John Penn responded to this letter with understandable exasperation. Armstrong's Cumberland Boys, after all, had launched a joint expedition with the Paxton Boys against the Great Island Delawares in September. Even if Armstrong was not directly involved in the Conestoga massacres, Penn was convinced that he must know the perpetrators' identities. "As it is supposed, not without great Reason, that the Chief part of the Rioters live on the frontiers of Cumberland & Lancaster Counties," he informed Armstrong, "it cannot be doubted but, if you are diligent & strict in your Enquiries, you will soon make a Discovery of them." The Paxton Boys, he pointed out, could not have assembled and marched "thro' the Country without being seen & known by a great Number of people." Penn instructed Armstrong to use all means at his disposal, "both as a civil & Military Officer, to discover & apprehend the Ringleaders of those Riots & their Accomplices, that they have to be brought to Justice." He told him also "to be extremely active in discouraging & suppress[g] all such Lawless Insurrections among the People, & to give me the earliest Notice of their future Motions & evil Designs."[8]

Although Penn could not establish a direct link between Armstrong and the December massacres, he had no such difficulty in the case of John Elder. Matthew Smith and Lazarus Stewart, identified in most accounts as the leaders of the Lancaster massacre, were commanders of Elder's Paxtang Rangers. Along with Asher Clayton, Smith and Stewart had led the expedition against Wyalusing in October that discovered the remains of the Connecticut settlement at Mill Creek. Thwarted in their attempt to punish the Moravian Indians at Wyalusing, they attacked the Conestoga Indians instead. The fifty men who attacked the Conestoga Indians were drawn from Elder's two companies of Paxtang Rangers. The Rangers exceeded their mandate by launching punitive expeditions against Indians, but they operated under the authority of the provincial government. In ordering the Wyalusing expedition in October, Elder had defied government authority; the Conestoga massacres now made his command untenable.[9]

On December 29 Penn wrote to Elder summarily removing him from office. Clayton had been dismissed after the unauthorized expedition against Wyalusing, but as the most experienced man available he was now reinstated with command of all provincial forces east of the Susquehanna River. Armstrong, despite Penn's skepticism and frustration, retained command of forces west of the river. Penn ordered Elder to deliver to Clayton "all the Provincial Arms, Accoutrements, Ammunition & other Military Stores remaining in your possession, with an exact Account of those you have distributed among the two Companies." He also instructed Elder, in his civil capacity, "to discourage and Suppress all Insurrections that may appear among any of the people, over whom you have an Influence" and to "take all the Pains in your power to learn the Names of the Ringleaders & Perpetrators of those Barbarities."[10]

On January 2, 1764, Penn issued a second proclamation against the Paxton Boys, enhancing the rather feeble effort of December 22. Since he had issued his first proclamation, Penn noted, "a large party of armed Men again assembled and met together in a riotous & tumultuous manner...and butchered and put to death fourteen of the said Conestogoe Indians, Men, Women, and Children," in the Lancaster workhouse. In so doing they had attacked the authority of the government and the rule of law, for these Indians "had been taken under the immediate Care and Protection of Magistrates of the said County, and lodged for their better Security in the said Workhouse, till they should be more effectually provided for by Order of the Government." Both "common Justice" and "the Laws of the Land, (upon the preservation of which not only the Liberty and Security of every Individual, but the being of the Government itself depend)," Penn concluded, "require that the above Offenders should be brought to condign Punishment."[11]

The new proclamation offered a reward of £200 for the arrest of any three ringleaders. Accomplices, "not concerned in the immediate shedding the Blood of the said Indians," who turned in three of the ringleaders were also eligible for the reward and would receive "all the weight and influence of the Government for obtaining his Majesty's Pardon for his Offence." Despite these incentives, the second proclamation was no more effective than the first. As Benjamin Franklin noted in his *Narrative of the Late Massacres in Lancaster County*, "These Proclamations have as yet produced no Discovery; the Murderers having given out such Threatenings against those that disapprove their Proceedings, that the whole County seems to be in Terror, and no one durst speak what he knows." Letters from the Paxton region "in which any Dislike is expressed of the Rioters," he reported, were being sent unsigned.[12]

Aware that his measures against the Paxton Boys were ineffective, Penn wrote to General Thomas Gage seeking military assistance. He apprised the commander in chief of the recent massacres in Conestoga Manor and Lancaster and warned that, despite his best measures, "these lawless rioters, flush'd & embolden'd by their Success, and encouraged by their numbers, may possibly carry their insults upon the Government & its Laws still further, & raise such Tumults and Insurrections as it may not be in my power to suppress without the aid of a Military Force." Provincial volunteers were not to be trusted, Penn told Gage, even if they could be spared; they "could not be brought to act vigorously against their Friends, Neighbours, and relations." The force John Elder had raised in the summer of 1763, after all, was the nucleus of the Paxton Boys.[13]

Penn therefore requested the assistance of British troops "to support the Civil Authority in the Execution of the Laws in case of need, and to give a check to these daring attacks upon Government." As three companies of British regulars were quartered in Carlisle for the winter, he wondered if their commanding officer might be instructed to assist him in "the present Emergency." Gage replied positively to Penn's request. Although he could not spare the troops from Carlisle, he ordered the commanding officer there to obey Penn's instructions if the crisis worsened. Gage was expecting three companies of Royal Americans to arrive in New York City within a few days and promised Penn he would send them directly to Philadelphia, "there to wait your further Orders."[14]

Penn also took steps to address the repercussions of the Conestoga massacres in the wider world of Indian diplomacy. The Iroquois, who claimed the Conestogas as their tributaries, would need an explanation. As Edward Shippen put it to his son-in-law, James Burd, the massacres not only delivered a "high Insult" to government, but they might have "fatal Consequences…with the six

Nations, from whom the Conestogoe Indians are descended." Council member William Logan predicted "great Confusion if not a Civil War" in Pennsylvania, and "a perpetual Indian War on the Province." Penn therefore wrote to Sir William Johnson about the Paxton affair and asked him "to represent it to the Six Nations in its true light, that they may not impute any Breech of Faith to this Government." He begged Johnson to "take the properest method of acquainting them with the Truth of this Transaction, & of removing any disadvantageous Impression they may have received from an imperfect account of the matter."[15]

Johnson's reply was not optimistic. He assured Penn that he would "use every argument with the Six Nations" to dispel "the unfavourable ideas which they must certainly entertain of such a proceeding, as well [as] to satisfy them that your Government highly disapproves of it, & will severely punish the Offenders." But he warned him that the Iroquois were already deeply alienated and apprehensive as a result of the Conestoga massacres. The "friendly Indians in these parts," Johnson wrote, "may be induced to doubt our faith and sincerity towards themselves, from the unhappy fate of our late Friends in *Pennsylvania*, which will cause them to expect the same treatment whenever it is in our power to destroy them." These doubts, he feared, "may greatly check the Ardor They have lately expressed to me of assisting us against our Enemies, and even Spirit up many to obtain revenge within your Government." Johnson was also alarmed by rumors he had heard that "the Riotous parties" who had killed the Conestogas were planning to destroy the Indians "under the Protection of *Philadelphia*."[16]

These rumors had begun to circulate as early as December 27, the day of the Lancaster massacre. Edward Shippen reported that some eyewitnesses of that massacre heard the killers "declare they would proceed to the Province Island, and destroy the Indians there." Sheriff John Hay warned John Penn that the killers, "with a Superior Force intend an Attack on the Province Island, with a view to destroy the Indians there." Council member William Logan, a son of James Logan, reported that the "Irish rebels" who had killed the Conestogas, pleading "Scriptures a Duty for Exterpating the Heathen from ye Face of the Earth," now "threatened to come down to Province Island to kill the rest." Meeting with Penn in Philadelphia on December 31, the Council recommended that a company of fifty men be raised "to take post at the Province Island, and to keep sufficient Guards over the said Indians, Night and Day." As Philadelphians prepared to ring in the new year, the threat from the Paxton Boys was far from over.[17]

CHAPTER 15

PANIC IN PHILADELPHIA

When John Penn and his Council met on January 2, 1764, they had urgent business to consider. Edward Shippen had just forwarded an anonymous letter from Lancaster claiming that "many of the Inhabitants of the Townships of Lebanon, Paxton, and Hanover, in Lancaster County, were forming themselves into a Company of 200 Men, to March to Philadelphia, with a design to kill the Indians on the Province Island." Many of "the Farmers near the Mountain," Shippen's informant reported, "had contributed largely to defray the Expences of such of them as were not able to procure Horses, and pay their charges, &ca." Penn sent a message to the Assembly on January 3 warning that the killers of the Conestoga Indians "are making great addition to their numbers, and are actually preparing to come down in a large Body and cut off the Indians seated by the Government on the Province Island." The only way to stop the rebels would be to meet force with force, yet no funds were available for "levying men to strengthen the hands of Government, and protect the Indians." Penn therefore requested a bill furnishing him "with full powers to repel those bold Invaders of Law & Justice, & support the Honour & Dignity of the Government." With the existing provincial forces "engaged in the defence of our long extended Frontier," the Assembly agreed in principle to fund additional men for the defense of Philadelphia out of temporary funds, "till such a Bill as your Honour recommends, can be prepared and considered." These last words were ominous, given the long history of contention between the legislature and executive over supply bills.[1]

The Moravian Indians on Province Island, meanwhile, were increasingly eager to leave Philadelphia. Ever since their arrival in November 1763 many of them had been agitating to be removed to New York, where they believed Sir William Johnson would protect them. On January 4 the Council advised Penn to lose no time "in getting things ready for their departure early to-morrow morning." Captain Robinson and his Highlanders, who had been moved from Lancaster to Philadelphia after the second Conestoga massacre, agreed to escort the Indians as far as New York City. William Logan offered "to procure Passports for the Indians, & to do everything that might be necessary for their safe conduct thro' the Province of New Jersey." The Province Island Indians set out as planned on January 5. That evening John Penn wrote to Sir William Johnson, General Thomas Gage, and the governors of New York and New Jersey, informing them that the Indians were coming and suggesting that they might smooth relations with the Iroquois by explaining that the Paxton Boys had acted "in defiance of Government." Had Penn written these letters before allowing the Indians to depart he would have saved them a great deal of suffering.[2]

Governor Cadwallader Colden of New York refused to admit the Province Island Indians. His Council "expressed their surprize" that the government of Pennsylvania, without consulting New York, would "order so great a body of Indians, in number about one hundred & forty, to pass into this Province." Far from agreeing with Penn on the "mild and peaceable disposition" of the refugees, Colden insisted that the Indians "on the East side of the Susquehanna are the most obnoxious to the People of this Province of any, having done the most mischief." They consisted, he said, "of a number of rogues and thieves, runaways from the other Nations, and for that reason not to be trusted." Colden's Council believed that permitting them "to return to their Families on the Susquehanna, would be adding greatly to the strength of a people, from whom His Majesty's Subjects have already suffered so much." His government was "rather disposed to attack & punish, than to support and protect them, whom they still consider as their Enemy." The Moravian Indians had no choice but to turn back, escorted by the three companies of Royal Americans General Gage had promised to Penn. But what would happen once they returned to Philadelphia?[3]

During the Indians' three-week absence there had been no further word of a march from the frontier. "We hear nothing from our Frontier of our Hickory Boys as they call themselves but that they are often meeting in Taverns talking & threaten[g] what they intend to do," William Logan observed on January 21. But Logan knew as he was writing this letter that New York had turned back the Province Island Indians. He predicted, "If they return to Philad[ia.] & our People should Get mad again on our Frontiers & come down We shall certainly have many lives lost." The Moravian Indians arrived in Philadelphia on January 24 and were housed not on Province Island but in the more secure setting of the city barracks. And the mood on the frontier quickly turned ugly.[4]

Those who visited western Lancaster County in late January had alarming stories to tell when they returned to Philadelphia. All who journeyed to "these Parts," William Logan observed on January 28, "say That no person dare open his mouth in Condemnation of their Riotous Conduct without Risque of having his bones broke at least." In "the Back Parts," he observed, "our Rioters still continue mutinous, & say when they have compleated their Whole Companys they are determined to come down, & will stem all opposition." Benjamin Kendall, a Quaker merchant from Philadelphia who had just come back from a visit to Lancaster town, appeared before John Penn and the Council the same day to share "some Intelligence...concerning further Motions and ill designs of the Rioters in that County." On his return journey Kendall had met an acquaintance from Lancaster who informed him that "in ten days fifteen hundred Men would come down in order to kill the said Indians." If these 1,500 were not enough, this man added, "Five thousand were ready to join them." The insurgents, Kendall reported, were heavily armed and ready to kill all who stood in their way. Believing that "the Indians were put in small numbers into different Families in the City of Philadelphia, for Protection," they intended to burn the houses of all who did not cooperate.[5]

On January 29, alarmed by Kendall's testimony, John Penn ordered the British regulars in Carlisle to move to Lancaster for "the preservation of the Publick Peace." Writing to Captain William Murray, the commanding officer in Carlisle, Penn invoked General Gage's order allowing him to call on British troops to support his efforts to enforce the law. Penn told Murray that he had hoped not "to exert the power the General has put into my hands, but the Publick Security & the preservation of His Majesty's Peace" had left him no choice. Accordingly, he asked him to march with all his men to Lancaster "with the greatest Expedition." The Royal Americans would continue to guard the Moravian Indians at the barracks in Philadelphia.[6]

Meanwhile, in Paxton town the Rev. John Elder confirmed that the Paxton Boys were getting ready to march on Philadelphia and warned that it would be "in vain, nay even unsafe for anyone to oppose their measures." As was "well known," Elder continued, he had always used his "utmost endeavours to discourage these proceedings; but, to little purposes [for] the minds of the inhabitants are so exasperated against a particular set of men, deeply concernd in the Governm[t]." By this "set of men" Elder meant the Quakers of Philadelphia—from his perspective, an undifferentiated mass of self-interested pacifists. The Quakers, he complained, were infamous "for the Singular Regards they have always shown to Savages" and "the heavy burden" they "laid on the province in maintaining an expensive Trade & holding Treaties from time to time with Indians." They conducted their economic and diplomatic transactions to their own individual advantage, "without any prospect of advantage either to his Majesty or to the province."[7]

Although Elder saw all Quakers as the same, he bridled at those who returned the compliment by describing the Paxton Boys as typical Presbyterians. Some anti-Presbyterians, he protested, were claiming that the Paxton Boys embodied a spirit of intolerance and excess that marked the denomination as a whole. Pennsylvania's Presbyterians were "enraged at their being charged in bulk with these facts, under the name of Scotch Irish, and other ill natured titles." Some critics, he continued, were even comparing the events of December 1763 to the Irish Catholic massacre of several thousand Protestants in the 1640s, finding the killing of the Conestoga Indians "the most barbarous of either." The Paxton Boys, and by extension all Presbyterians, were being cast as even more barbaric than Irish papists—an especially galling comparison for any Ulster Presbyterian.[8]

With British troops stationed in Lancaster and Philadelphia, the provincial government began to make detailed preparations for a possible invasion by the "ill natured" frontiersmen. John Penn instructed the Royal Americans to protect the Moravian Indians at all times, "by Force, if necessary, against all Persons who shall come to molest, injure, or destroy them." If a body of armed men should arrive "with an Intent or suppos'd Intention to injure or Kill the Indians therein," the commanding officer on duty was to follow three clearly defined steps. First, he would "with great Moderation & Civility, address himself to the armed Persons and Multitude" and "forbid them to advance." If they advanced nonetheless, he was to repeat his order with a warning that he would "without any further Prohibition or request fire upon them." If they ignored that order and proceeded, "the commanding officer shall repel Force with Force, and take as many of the Party as you can Prisoners and secure them, to be dealt with according to law, by the civil Magistrates."[9]

As military preparations were getting under way, relations between the legislative and executive branches, already strained by Penn's failure to pursue the Paxton Boys, were once again deteriorating over the perennial question of how to fund military legislation. In a message to Penn dated January 20 the Assembly demanded more vigorous measures against the Paxton Boys. As local officials were making no progress, the assemblymen recommended that "the Sheriff & Coroner of Lancaster County, and the Magistrates of that Borough" be brought to Philadelphia for examination. On February 2 the Council advised Penn that this action "would be attended with many ill Consequences" and recommended instead that he instruct trustworthy justices in Lancaster County to examine the officials in secret, assuring them "that no Use shall ever be made of their Information so as affect themselves, nor their names be made public on the occasion." The assemblymen, however, had wanted an open hearing, and Penn's refusal to meet their request raised suspicions that he was sympathetic to the Paxton Boys, or at least unwilling to alienate them because he hoped to forge a political alliance with Presbyterians as a check to the Quaker party.[10]

Penn was unsure what measures to take next. He told the Assembly that he had "great difficulty in settling, on the Footing of Law, & on the principles of the English Constitution, the Orders proper to be given to the Commanding Officer of the three Companies" guarding the barracks. As their purpose was to protect the Moravian Indians, Penn was unsure if they could legitimately be used against "his Majesty's Subjects, though riotously assembled, with an intent to kill the Indians," at least before "the civil power has first been called in, & in vain endeavored to suppress the Tumult." On February 2 he requested from the Assembly a "short law" to temporarily "extend to this Province" the draconian riot act passed under George I in 1714. This measure would remove any constitutional doubts about using troops against the Paxton Boys if that became necessary. The Assembly presented a riot act for Penn's approval the next day.[11]

On Saturday, February 4, word arrived in Philadelphia that the Paxton Boys were expected to reach the city the following morning. According to this report, a "very considerable number of the people living on the Frontiers "of Lancaster County" were actually assembling themselves with an intention of coming to this City to put to death all the Indians in the Barracks under the protection of this Government." The "same Spirit & frantic Rage, which actuated those who lately put to death the Indians in Lancaster County, Still prevails among them," Penn informed the Assembly. "They have already given abundant Proof, that neither Religion, Humanity, or Laws, are objects of their consideration, or of sufficient Weight to restrain them." Their numbers were so great that the soldiers sent by General Gage would be insufficient to guard the Indians at the barracks, let alone defend the rest of Philadelphia. Other than the volunteers who patrolled the frontier, Pennsylvania had no defense force. Penn therefore requested an immediate militia law from the Assembly. But Philadelphia was by now in such disarray that the Assembly could not muster a quorum until February 10.[12]

Lacking a militia, Penn summoned the residents of Philadelphia to the State House on the afternoon of February 4 to prepare them to defend the city.

"Paxton Expedition, Inscribed to the Author of the Farce by HD." Cartoon by Henry Dawkins, 1764. Cartoon 1764 [Pax]/795.F.20a. #2. 66984.0.9. Courtesy of Library Company of Philadelphia.

Arrangements had already been made for civilian reinforcements to help guard the barracks overnight. A redoubt was built in the center of the parade ground and several cannon were placed in position. Spies were "dispatched up the different roads to observe the motions of the Rioters, & to bring intelligence of their Approach." When the people congregated at the State House at four o'clock a proclamation by Penn was read aloud, declaring that a march on the city would be considered an act of rebellion and that the riot act would be invoked against the offenders. Penn appointed Benjamin Franklin to organize a volunteer militia, and Franklin quickly assembled six companies of infantry, one of artillery, and two of cavalry. If, as expected, the Paxton Boys entered Philadelphia that night, the alarm would be sounded by the bells of the city ringing out.[13]

On Sunday, February 5, at about 2 a.m., the bells sounded the alarm. Watchmen spread the word that the Paxton Boys were coming, and the residents of Philadelphia assembled in the Council House square. "After two o'clock at night the watchmen began to cry, 'Fire!,'" the Lutheran clergyman Henry Muhlenberg recalled, "because the...backwoodsmen were approaching. Thereupon all the alarm bells began to ring at once and a drum was sounded to summon the inhabitants of the city to the town hall plaza. The ringing sounded dreadful in the night." It turned out to be a false alarm. By

Philadelphia State House, 1778 (later known as Independence Hall). Courtesy of the American Philosophical Society.

now, Muhlenberg wrote, rumors "were flying in every direction: The rebels had divided into three groups and were going to attack the open city in three places simultaneously; then they were near; then they were still far away; now they were coming from the east, then from the west, and so on." Hundreds or even thousands of frontiersmen were said to be marching on the city. Several more times during the night the bells rang out, but still the Paxton Boys did not come. In the morning men were sent out to bring the ferry boats to the Philadelphia side of the Schuylkill River to prevent the marchers from crossing. But one ferry was forgotten, and by the time the men reached it the rebels had crossed the river. On the afternoon of February 5 they reached Germantown, six miles northwest of the city.[14]

With the Paxton Boys set to enter Philadelphia, Israel Pemberton Jr. feared for his life. Although Sir William Johnson had silenced Pemberton at Easton in 1762, the Friendly Association remained active during Pontiac's War, assisting Indians who visited Philadelphia, distributing presents, and sending out teachers and missionaries. Pemberton embodied everything that frontier settlers hated about Quakerism. His older brother, James, was attending a meeting on February 6 when he heard that the Paxton Boys had "demanded my bro. Israel to be given up to them." Convinced that this was "a misapprehension,"

James rushed to Israel's house and "found he was preparing to depart the City having before Sent away part of his family." Israel was acting on "the earnest solicitations of some Gentlemen of the City," who had advised him that "he was particularly one Object of their Enmity against whom they had protested revenge."[15]

Most Quakers stayed in Philadelphia during the crisis, and a substantial minority took the fateful step of taking up arms in defense of the city. A young Quaker woman named Sally Potts noted that the Friends seemed "as ready as any to take up Arms in such a Cause to Defend the Laws and Liberty of their Country against a Parcel of Rebels." A prominent Philadelphia Quaker named Edward Pennington was said to have been "at the Head of a Company," Potts continued, "and I am apt to think 2 thirds of the Young Quakers in Town took up arms." The "big meeting-house on Third Day [i.e., Tuesday, February 7], instead of having youths' meeting, as was expected, was appropriated to the use of the armed men to shelter them from the rain." For a Quaker such as Sally Potts this was a bizarre spectacle to say the least: "The men were exercising and the colors flying in the gallery, from where there has so often doctrine been preached against that very thing of bearing arms."[16]

Muhlenberg took much pleasure in the idea of Quakers—and, by his account, Moravian pacifists—taking up arms in defense of Philadelphia. Some people "remarked concerning all this," he noted, "that it seemed

Philadelphia Courthouse and Quaker Meeting House. In John F. Watson, *Annals of Philadelphia and Pennsylvania, In the Olden Time. Vol. 1* (Philadelphia: E. L. Carey & A. Hart, 1830). Courtesy of Library Company of Philadelphia.

strange that such preparations should be made against one's fellow citizens and Christians, whereas no one ever took so much trouble to protect from the Indians His Majesty's subjects and citizens on the frontier." The "pious sheep" who had "such a tender conscience" during the French and Indian War, "and would rather have died than lift a hand for defense against the most dangerous enemies," were now suddenly "willing to put on horns of iron like Zedekiah, the son of Chenaanah (I Kings 22), and shoot and smite a small group of their poor, oppressed, driven, and suffering fellow inhabitants and citizens from the frontier!" For the present, however, the Paxton Boys remained at Germantown.[17]

FOUR

A WAR OF WORDS

CHAPTER 16

THE *DECLARATION* AND *REMONSTRANCE*

Founded by German settlers invited to Pennsylvania by William Penn, Germantown was renowned for its weaving and its manufacture of stockings, shoes, and paper. According to a report received by Philadelphia's Quaker Monthly Meeting, the number of Paxton Boys who entered Germantown did not exceed 300—far fewer than the 1,500 rumored to be marching from the frontier. Their arrival nonetheless caused a sensation. The town's most distinguished resident, David Rittenhouse, described how "about fifty of the scoundrels marched by my work-shop—I have seen hundreds of Indians travelling the country, and can with truth affirm, that the behaviour of these fellows was ten times more savage and brutal than theirs." The Paxton Boys, he claimed, paraded through the streets, "frightening women, by running the muzzles of their guns through windows, swearing and hallooing: attacking men without the least provocation; dragging them by their hair to the ground, and pretending to scalp them; shooting a number of dogs and fowls."[1]

Rittenhouse was not alone in comparing the Paxton Boys to Indians. An anonymous Quaker noted matter-of-factly, "This formidable body of forces consisted principally of a set of fellows, dressed in blanket coats and moccasins, like our Indian traders, or back-country wagoners." They "were armed with rifles and tomahawks, and some of them had a brace of pistols besides." Few of the rebels, he observed, "were men of any property, but had been hired or persuaded to the under taking, by persons, whose views and designs may, perhaps, in time, be disclosed." Unlike Rittenhouse, this Quaker observer found that "they behaved with great civility to those they conversed with—were surprised to hear that the citizens had taken up arms to oppose them." They declared "that they had no intention of injuring any one, and only wanted satisfaction of the Indians, as some of them had been concerned in the murder of their friends and relations." These words were at odds with his description of the

Paxton Boys' physical appearance—and given the events of December 14 and December 27 they were quite implausible.[2]

For Pennsylvania's German population, the Paxton Boys' choice of Germantown as a place to break their march was unfortunate. Germans, both rural and urban, were already under suspicion for their possible role in the Paxton affair. The most detailed account of their actions during the crisis came from the Lutheran minister Henry Muhlenberg. Confined to bed with illness when the city's bells sounded the alarm early on the morning of February 5, he asked a German neighbor to "go to the town hall and bring me news of what was happening there." This man reported "that the market place was crowded with all sorts of people and that arms were being distributed to those who would take them. He had not, however, seen many Germans." Nor had many of Philadelphia's Germans volunteered to join Benjamin Franklin's militia. Were they secretly on the side of the rebels? And what about the Germans of Lancaster County?[3]

The only known German contribution to Philadelphia's defense, as recalled by an anonymous Quaker, was less martial than farcical. Early on the afternoon of February 5, this observer recalled, "there was a general uproar—they are coming! they are coming! Where? Where? down Second street!" This time the alarm was justified: a "troop of armed men, on horseback, appeared in reality coming down the street." Members of Franklin's militia "grounded their fire-locks" and prepared to fire. At the last moment they noticed that the horsemen were not Paxton Boys but, instead, "a company of German butchers and porters" who had come to volunteer their services.[4]

Muhlenberg believed that Germans responded so tepidly to Philadelphia's needs because they sympathized with the Paxton Boys' grievances, though not their methods. They believed "it could be proved that the Indians who had lived among the so-called Moravian Brethren had secretly killed several settlers." Many Germans were also convinced that Quakers and Moravians had bribed Indians with presents and used them as spies. They objected to the idea that they "should enlist to fight, resist, or even kill their own flesh and blood, their fellow citizens and fellow Christians, and seek to protect the lives of the Bethlehem Indians!" Pennsylvania's Germans were loyal subjects of the Crown and would "gladly pour out their possessions and their blood for our most gracious king," Muhlenberg concluded, but they would not "wage war against their own suffering fellow citizens for the sake of the Quakers and Herrnhuters [Moravians] and their creatures or instruments, the double-dealing Indians."[5]

On the morning of Monday, February 6, John Penn invited the Lutheran leader Dr. Carl Wrangel to explain why "few or none of our German church people had reported on Saturday or last night to take up arms against the rebels." Wrangel assured Penn that Germans were loyal and that he would urge those "who had stood idly in the market place to take up arms." He dispatched a Swedish Lutheran pastor, Paul Brycelius, to Germantown to "warn the elders of our congregation there not to join the approaching rebels, but rather to stand on the side of the government." The elders of the Lutheran congregations in Germantown told Brycelius "they had not seen nor did they know anything of the so-called rebels." Within a few hours German craftsmen had "gathered together, formed themselves into a small mounted company furnished with proper arms, sounded the trumpets, and made a several hours' tour in and around the city." These valiant artisans, however, were as hapless as the German butchers in Philadelphia. "They were almost shot by inadvertence," Muhlenberg noted, "for cannons loaded with small balls had been placed here and there and the ignorant *constable* was just on the point of blazing away at them because he thought they were rebels."[6]

On his way back to Philadelphia on the evening of February 6 Brycelius "suddenly and unexpectedly ran into the vanguard" of the Paxton Boys. "He realized his mistake and was about to turn and flee," Muhlenberg wrote, "but was stopped and ordered to remain with them." Finding them "respectable," Brycelius "struck up a conversation with several of them, Irishmen and Englishmen." The pastor informed them "that he had formerly spent time in Dublin...and thus cherished a love for the Irish nation." Brycelius did not say what impression this news made on the rebels; the "Irish nation" he had encountered in Dublin would have been Protestant, but of the Anglican rather than Presbyterian persuasion, and hence scarcely to the taste of the Paxton Boys.[7]

When Brycelius "innocently asked" the Paxton Boys "what was the purpose of their coming," they gave him a detailed answer. "They replied that it was not their intention to do any injury to the least child of their fellow inhabitants nor to anyone else." They wanted "custody of the Bethlehem Indians, not to kill them, but only to conduct them out of the province"—an outlandish claim given what the Paxton Boys had done to the Conestoga Indians. People in and around Philadelphia, the rebels continued, "lived a pleasant, protected life and had no feelings for the great need and tribulation which the poor settlers on the frontier had to endure." Brycelius reported that he told the Paxton Boys "they would not achieve their purpose" because the Moravian Indians were guarded by a large company of royal soldiers. He also informed them that John Penn "had on the past Saturday publicly proclaimed that this was a case of illegal assembly and...that if they did not desist they would be declared outlaws." Brycelius therefore advised the Paxton Boys not to proceed to Philadelphia armed, "inasmuch as this would cause a great and horrible blood-bath." Instead they should "send their most intelligent men into the city" with a list of grievances that could be peacefully remedied.[8]

This account claims a lot for Brycelius, who, as the Quaker assemblyman Samuel Foulke noted, was only one of several clergymen sent to Germantown by John Penn "to meet the Insurgents or Lawless banditi." Among these clergymen, reportedly, were the Presbyterian evangelist Gilbert Tennent and Dr. Daniel Roberdeau of the Anglican Church. According to Foulke, when these ministers told the Paxton Boys about "ye preparations the Governm't was making for their reception & punishm't," the rebels decided "to Halt, and proposed to Extenuate ye Enormity of their Crime by laying before ye Legislature Certain Grievances for which they demanded redress." The Quaker pacifist James Pemberton noted that the rebels claimed "they did not know, the Indians were under the Protection of the Kings Forces otherwise [their] Loyalty would not permit them to have undertaken this Expedition." Foulke, however, found this "a very poor thin Guise." The Paxton Boys had, after all, openly defied government authority by slaughtering the Conestogas and admitted at Germantown that "they had set out, with full purpose to kill Every Indian in ye Barracks." In halting their march at Germantown when they learned of the military presence in Philadelphia, they had merely revealed themselves, in the eyes of Foulke and others, as the cowards that they were.[9]

After sending the ministers to warn the Paxton Boys, Penn appointed Benjamin Franklin to lead a high-level delegation to Germantown to negotiate with the rebels. The delegation included the speaker of the Assembly, Joseph Galloway; the attorney general, Benjamin Chew; William Logan of the Council; and Mayor Thomas Willing of Philadelphia. On February 7, after a day of negotiations at Coleman's tavern, the Paxton Boys agreed to discontinue their march on Philadelphia and to write down their grievances instead. The main body of rebels went home, leaving (as Foulke maliciously put it) "two of their Chiefs to draw up & lay before ye Governm't their pretended Grievances." The first of these "chiefs" was Matthew Smith, one of the commanders of the Paxton Boys' expedition against Wyalusing in October 1763 and a leader of the attack on Lancaster workhouse on December 27. The second was James Gibson, about whom virtually nothing is known.[10]

Before leaving Germantown the Paxton Boys requested and received permission for some of "their Shabby Gang," as Foulke described them, to enter Philadelphia and "inspect the Indians in the hope of finding some who had been hostile to the whites." On February 8 a small party of Paxton Boys set out for the city, accompanied by John Armstrong and Joseph Shippen. But as Foulke recalled, they "were seen on ye Road by some weak person," who was thrown into a panic, rode into Philadelphia, and announced "that four Hundred of the rebels were Comming all arm'd within 2 miles of ye City." Philadelphians rushed to arms one last time and prepared for the worst. In the end, however, only about thirty frontiersmen entered Philadelphia. Armstrong and Shippen "conducted them by a back way into Town to shun ye fury of ye disturbed populace," and the visit passed without incident. The Paxton Boys recognized none of the inmates at the barracks "and soon left for their homes." Their supporters later charged that Quaker sympathizers had concealed the guilty Moravian Indians. With the Paxton Boys dispersed, Philadelphia was tranquil once again. "At present," Franklin observed on February 11, "we are pretty quiet, and I hope that Quiet will continue."[11]

The Paxton Boys submitted two documents to the provincial government, the *Declaration* and the *Remonstrance*. According to James Pemberton, the *Declaration* was delivered to John Penn as early as February 6, on the eve of the negotiations at Coleman's tavern, "by one of the Country members of Assembly who had received it from the Rioters about 25 miles from the City, before they turned off for Germantown." In the *Declaration*, which Foulke described as "a kind of manifesto" written "in ye most audacious, daring, Insulting Language that can be imagined," the Paxton Boys offered an unvarnished justification of their actions. The killing of the Conestogas, they argued, was both necessary and just. Far from defying authority, they were loyal servants of the Crown, opposing the king's enemies, "whether openly avowed or more dangerously concealed under a Mask of falsely pretended Friendship, and chearfully willing to offer our Substance and Lives in his Cause." The false "friends" in question, as the play on words suggested, were the Quakers of Pennsylvania.[12]

According to the *Declaration* the Conestoga Indians were anything but innocent victims. They were "known to be firmly connected in Friendship with our openly avowed imbittered Enemies." Some of them had "by several Oaths, been proved to be Murderers." Well acquainted with "the Situation and State of our Frontiers," they were more capable than other Indians "of doing us Mischief," and yet they were "cherished and caressed as dearest Friends."

This favoritism was "but a Part, a small Part of that excessive Regard manifested to *Indians* beyond his Majesty's loyal Subjects, whereof we complain." The many conferences where Indians received "exorbitant Presents" and were treated with "great Servility," the Paxton Boys complained, "have long been oppressive Grievances we have groaned under."[13]

The favoritism had continued during Pontiac's War, providing "still more flagrant Reasons of Complaint." The assemblymen declined Jeffery Amherst's repeated calls to assist Henry Bouquet when he was proceeding toward Fort Pitt in the summer of 1763, but immediately granted requests for assistance by Indians. Among the Indians who received assistance were some "known to be his Majesty's Enemies," who fought against Bouquet at Bushy Run in August 1763 and were then "reduced to Distress by the Destruction of their Corn at the *Great Island*, and up the East Branch of *Susquehanna*." Pretending to be friendly Indians in need of subsistence, they were "openly caressed, and the Publick, that could not be indulged the Liberty of contributing to his Majesty's Assistance, obliged, as Tributaries to Savages, to support those Villains, those Enemies to our King and our Country."[14]

Content to watch the frontier bleed, the Quaker Assembly bestowed every hospitality on the Moravian Indians, housing them on Province Island and then in the city barracks. The "publick Money [was] lavishly prostituted to hire, at an exorbitant Rate, a mercenary Guard, to protect his Majesty's worst of Enemies, those falsely pretended *Indian* Friends." Even as these Indians enjoyed the Assembly's largesse, "hundreds of poor distressed Families of his Majesty's Subjects, obliged to abandone their Possessions, and flee for their Lives... were left to starve neglected." Receiving nothing from the government, they had to rely on "what the friendly Hand of private Donations has contributed to their Support." The Paxton Boys charged that the Quakers, "who are most profuse toward Savages, have carefully avoided any Part" in that charitable enterprise. "Hungry Christians," in other words, were left to suffer as Indians prospered on idle land.[15]

The Paxton Boys were also angry at the provincial government for failing to provide scalp bounties during Pontiac's War. Pennsylvania had introduced premiums for killing and capturing Indians in 1756, but these were discontinued when the fighting ended in 1758. Not only did the provincial government fail to reintroduce scalp bounties with the outbreak of Pontiac's War, but it offered bounties for the capture of the Paxton Boys instead. Their conduct, the *Declaration* protested, was "painted in the most atrocious Colors, while the horrid Ravages, cruel Murders and most shocking Barbarities committed by *Indians* on His Majesty's Subjects are covered over and excused under the charitable Term of this being their Method of making War."[16]

Was it any surprise, the Paxton Boys concluded, that such treatment "should awaken the Resentment of a People grossly abused, unrighteously burdened, and made Dupes and Slaves to Indians?" The killers of the Conestoga Indians deserved sympathy rather than censure, for at "their own great Expence and Trouble," they had attempted to rescue "a labouring Land from a Weight so oppressive, unreasonable and unjust." And they would continue their efforts. They assumed this burden "with great Reluctance," but they had no choice in the matter, such was their loyalty to their province and to the Crown, and such was their antipathy to "the Villany, Infatuation and Influence" of the Quaker faction that "have got the political Reigns in their Hand and tamely tyrannize over the other good Subjects of the Province!"[17]

After the negotiations in Germantown, Matthew Smith and James Gibson composed—or, at any rate, submitted over their signature—a second, more formal statement of the Paxton Boys' grievances, known as the *Remonstrance*. Although the *Declaration* and *Remonstrance* presented similar concerns and accusations, the *Remonstrance* was notably more formal in tone and systematic in presentation. The differences between the two documents led several contemporaries to believe that the Paxton Boys received some assistance in drawing up the second. Muhlenberg, for example, wrote that Smith and Gibson "requested that Mr. Francklin and City Mayor Willing help them get their *gravamina* on paper, which request was granted." According to James Pemberton, Smith and Gibson initially asked Franklin and Willing "to assist them in drawing up their remonstrance, to which they on terms consented," but the Paxton Boys "soon found assistance of persons more suitable to their purpose."[18]

The strongest grounds for suspecting external assistance lay in the broad sectional grievances with which the *Remonstrance* began, which stood in sharp contrast to the *Declaration*'s rehearsal of local defeats and frustrations. The *Remonstrance* claimed to speak on behalf of "his Majesty's faithful and loyal Subjects, the Inhabitants of the Frontier Counties of *Lancaster, York, Cumberland, Berks,* and *Northampton*." The three eastern counties, along with the city of Philadelphia, held twenty-six of the thirty-six seats in the Assembly, an imbalance the *Remonstrance* found "oppressive, unequal and unjust." As "Free-Men and *English* Subjects," the Paxton Boys claimed, "we have an indisputable Title to the same Privileges and Immunities with his Majesty's other subjects, who reside in the interior Counties of *Philadelphia, Chester* and

Bucks, and therefore ought not be excluded from an equal Share with them in the very important Privilege of Legislation." The *Declaration*, by contrast, made no mention of political representation, nor had any of the petitions from the western counties to the legislature in the 1750s and 1760s.[19]

Subsequent champions of the Paxton Boys in the nineteenth century (and well into the twentieth) cast them in the role of frontier democrats doing battle against Quaker oligarchy and proprietary privilege. But only one of the nine grievances presented in the *Remonstrance* referred to political representation; frontier settlers were concerned with more basic issues of land and security, and all the grievances except the first dealt with Indian matters. And there was another reason why politics was absent from the *Remonstrance, Declaration*, and most petitions from the frontier: broad-based representative democracy was not a feature of political life in this period, and Pennsylvania's system was actually more egalitarian than most. It was designed in large part to keep power in the hands of an elite, but the franchise qualifications were generous by the standards of the time. Nor was the disparity between east and west as great as the Paxton Boys and their apologists claimed. About half the population of Pennsylvania lived in the eastern counties and Philadelphia in 1763, while the other half lived in the new western counties. But easterners, being richer than westerners, paid higher taxes to their counties and, during wartime, to the provincial government. Aware of this disparity, James Pemberton thought that easterners rather than westerners deserved more representation.[20]

After the opening reference to political representation, the *Remonstrance* concentrated on issues of more direct relevance to the Paxton Boys. These had to do with the appropriate form of trial for settlers who killed Indians, government favoritism toward Indians, the exclusion of Indians from Pennsylvania during wartime, care for the wounded, scalp bounties, redemption of captives, and the practice of distributing presents at Indian conferences. The sectional imbalance in the Assembly interested the Paxton Boys only insofar as it had a bearing on these more fundamental questions.

The Paxton Boys, as might be expected, were very concerned with the question of where settlers charged with killing Indians ought to be tried. They objected to a bill currently before the Assembly providing "that such Persons as shall be charged with killing any *Indians* in *Lancaster* County, shall not be tried in the County where the Fact was committed, but in the Counties of *Philadelphia, Chester, or Bucks*." According to "the well known Laws of the *British* Nation," they insisted, defendants deserved a trial "by their Equals in the Neighborhood where their own, their Accusers, and the Witnesses Character and Credit, with the Circumstances of the Fact are best known." If the western counties had been "equally represented in Assembly," the *Remonstrance* added, no such measure would have been proposed.[21]

The Paxton Boys flatly rejected the distinction between "friendly" and "enemy" Indians, asserting that all Indians were perfidious and deserving of annihilation during wartime. The Moravian Indians, the *Remonstrance* insisted, were enemies of Pennsylvania, who should be punished rather than protected. Living "amongst us under the Cloak of Friendship," they "carried on a Correspondence with our known Enemies on the *Great-Island*." Some of these "savages" were Wyalusing Indians, whom the Paxton Boys had intended to attack in October 1763. The Indians' protectors in Philadelphia claimed "that altho' the *Wyalusing* Tribe is at War with us, yet that part of it which is under the Protection of the Government may be friendly to the *English*, and Innocent." The Paxton Boys dismissed this argument as absurd. "Who ever proclaimed War with a part of a Nation," they asked, "and not with the Whole?"[22]

In the course of this discussion the *Remonstrance* proudly recalled how the Paxton Boys had murdered three Indians while returning from their first expedition in August 1763. These three Indians, they claimed, were "going from *Bethlehem* to the *Great-Island*, with Blankets, Ammunition and Provisions; which is an undeniable Proof, that, the *Moravian Indians* were in confederacy with our open Enemies." Charles Read, a justice of the New Jersey Supreme Court who published a pamphlet attacking the Paxton Boys, described the incident rather differently as "the destroying in cold Blood [of] three Indian Guides, who undertook to pilot the Paxton Voluntiers (who were starving when they met with them) to Fort-Augusta, and by whose Assistance the whole Party were undoubtedly saved from perishing by Famine." According to the *Remonstrance*, the Paxton Boys were "filled with Indignation, to hear of this Action of ours, painted in the most odious and detestable Colours, as if we had inhumanly murdered our Guides, who preserved us from perishing in the Woods." After all, they had "only killed three of our known Enemies, who attempted to shoot us when we surprized them." The government's policy of protecting the king's enemies, they concluded, "is sufficient to make us mad with Rage, and tempt us to do what nothing but the most violent Necessity can vindicate."[23]

Moving beyond the Moravians, the *Remonstrance* pushed the logic of dispossession to its ultimate form, demanding the removal of all Indians from the frontier in time of war. "We humbly conceive that it is contrary to the Maxims of good Policy and extremely dangerous to our Frontiers," the Paxton Boys announced, "to suffer any *Indians* of what Tribe soever, to live within the inhabited Parts of this Province, while we are engaged in an *Indian* War; as Experience has taught us that they are all Perfidious." To grant so-called friendly Indians "Freedom and Independency" under government protection merely allowed them to "act as Spies, to entertain and give Intelligence to our Enemies, and to furnish them with Provisions and warlike Stores." "To this fatal Intercourse between our pretended Friends and open Enemies," they claimed, "we must ascribe the greatest Part of the Ravages and Murders that have been committed in the Course of this and the last *Indian* War." As a remedy for some of the damage caused by these attacks, the *Remonstrance* made three demands: better care of the wounded, restoration of scalp bounties, and redemption of captives.[24]

Like the *Declaration*, the *Remonstrance* closed with a forthright denunciation of the Quakers: "We complain that a certain Society of People in this Province in the late *Indian* War and at several Treaties held by the Kings Representatives, openly loaded the *Indians* with Presents." In a thinly veiled reference to Israel Pemberton Jr., the Paxton Boys protested that "a Leader of the said Society, in defiance of all Government not only abetted our *Indian* Enemies, but kept up a private Intelligence with them, and publickly received from them a Belt of Wampum, as if he had been our Governor or authorized by the King to treat with his Enemies."[25]

Thus concluded the *Remonstrance Of the distressed and bleeding Frontier Inhabitants Of the Province of Pennsylvania*. Dated February 13, 1764, the *Remonstrance* was submitted to John Penn the following day and, along with the *Declaration*, was read before the Assembly on February 17. Incensed by the charges made against them, the assemblymen proposed to Penn that Matthew Smith and James Gibson be summoned to appear before the Council and the Assembly in a joint session. The Assembly's intention, as James Pemberton noted, was that the legislative and executive branches "should unite in an examination of the Remonstrants in hopes by that means to be able to make some discovery of the promoters of the Insurrection & bring to Justice the perpetrators of the Murders."[26]

Penn rejected the Assembly's request. Although he would "with great pleasure, take every legal and constitutional Measure which had a Tendency to promote the Publick Peace & Harmony," he gave two reasons for declining the request. First, he found it "unbecoming the Honour and Dignity of the Government...to enter into any Argument or Justification with the Petitioners, on the subject of the matter of their Complaints." Second, it was the function of the Assembly alone to respond to such petitions, when appropriate to do so. The second argument, concerning constitutional responsibilities, was the important one. According to Penn it was essential to maintain the separation of powers between the executive and legislative branches of government, which "the Petitioners have in this case very injudiciously blended together." The Paxton Boys had already broken the law; now they were seeking to undermine the provincial constitution. Penn's refusal to consider the Assembly's request for a joint hearing, however, forestalled efforts by the provincial government to pursue the Paxton Boys more vigorously. Critics began to ask if he had a secret agenda.[27]

On February 21 the Assembly dispatched a clerk to Matthew Smith and James Gibson, curtly informing them that other business took precedence over theirs and that they need not wait around in Philadelphia. According to Samuel Foulke, the Assembly told them it would "take into consideration such parts of their s'd remonstrance as related to this branch of ye Legislature." Smith and Gibson "appeared to be satisfied," Foulke noted, "but were observed on going out of Town to shew some marks of Disgust, probably occasion'd by Conversation with some State Incendiaries in the city."[28]

Foulke hinted frequently at a conspiracy among Philadelphia's Presbyterians, and several Quaker leaders shared his sentiments. James Pemberton told the London Quaker James Fothergill that there were "many Circumstances to confirm the General Suspicion that the Scheme has been enabled by some & Countenanced by others." He was especially struck by the "Supineness of the Magistrates in Lancaster in omitting proper measures to prevent the murder of the Indians in that Burrough, & the Neglect of them & other Justices of the County of Sending intelligence of the motions of the Rioters afterwards tho' Some of them must be acquainted therewith." At Germantown, Pemberton claimed, many of the rioters "openly acknowledged...that they had received repeated invitations" from residents of Philadelphia "to prosecute y.ˢ Scheme of destroying the Indians." Their plan, he said, was to surprise the inhabitants by claiming that "at least four hundred of their brethren" in the city would join them when they entered Philadelphia. Pemberton noted suspiciously that "Presbyterians had no worship at their houses" on the morning of February 6, when the Paxton Boys were due to enter Philadelphia, though he was unsure whether that "was owing to their knowledge of the Scheme or the absence of some of their Preachers."[29]

Despite all of this innuendo, no plausible evidence emerged of a conspiracy in Philadelphia. The Paxton Boys do seem to have received assistance in drafting the *Remonstrance*, but Philadelphia's Presbyterians certainly did not rally to their cause during the February crisis. In the highly charged atmosphere of early 1764, however, it was all too easy to place credence in rumors of this sort. And while the city's Presbyterians had not taken up arms in support of the rebels, they were already rallying to their defense in words as part of a pamphlet war unprecedented in American history.

CHAPTER 17

A PROPER SPIRIT OF JEALOUSY AND REVENGE

When the Paxton Boys agreed to write down their grievances rather than proceed with their march on Philadelphia, daily life in the city returned to its normal busy but well-ordered state. Politically, however, all was in ferment; instead of a war of weapons, a war of words ensued. As the anonymous author of *The Apology of the Paxton Volunteers* put it, "Our late Conduct at the Conestogo Mannor & Lancaster has occasioned much Speculation, & a great Diversity of Sentiments in this & the neighbouring Governments; some vindicating & others condemning it; some charitably alleviating the Crime, & others maliciously painting it, in the most odious & detestable Colours." The debate went far beyond the immediate issue of the Conestoga massacres to address the fundamental question of how Pennsylvania ought to be governed. Sixty-three pamphlets dealing with the Paxton affair, either exclusively or as part of a larger debate on government, were published in Philadelphia in 1764, along with ten political cartoons.[1]

Benjamin Franklin published the first pamphlet. His *Narrative of the Late Massacres* appeared on January 30, 1764, six days before the conference with the Paxton Boys at Germantown. Franklin had a characteristically high opinion of this work, which he believed had a decisive influence in mobilizing the people of Philadelphia against the Paxton Boys. Enclosing a copy of the pamphlet in a letter to the London lawyer and politician Richard Jackson on February 11, he noted that his intention had been to check the spirit of rebellion "and strengthen the Hands of the Government by changing the Sentiments of the Populace." The pamphlet barely had "time to circulate in this City & Neighbourhood," he told Jackson, "before we heard that the Insurgents were on their March from all Parts." "It would perhaps be Vanity in me to imagine so slight a thing could have any extraordinary Effect," Franklin conceded. "But however that may be, there was a Sudden and very remarkable Change; and above 1000 of our Citizens took Arms to Support the Government in the Protection of those poor wretches."[2]

Franklin's *Narrative* did not rally Philadelphians to the extent he claimed, but it did serve as a catalyst for the pamphlet war over the Paxton Boys. Printed by a handful of Philadelphia publishers in the area around Market and Second Streets, the pamphlets were sold and read aloud in the taverns and coffee shops concentrated in this section of the city, several of which were owned by the publishing houses. Most of the authors wrote anonymously or under pseudonyms, though their identities were often well known in Philadelphia. A few published under their own name, including the Rev. Thomas Barton and Benjamin Franklin, who respectively wrote the most important pamphlets for and against the Paxton Boys.[3]

Because Franklin was so well-known and his pamphlet came out so early, the pro-Paxton authors directed much of their animus against him. They

"Indian Squaw King Wampum Spies." Cartoon by Henry Dawkins, 1764. An "Indian Squaw" notices a Quaker named "King Wampum" and, taking advantage of his "lustful passions," steals his gold watch. In the center of the picture, Quaker dogs prepare to go to war against Indian bears. "When Dangers threaten 'tis mere Nonsense / to talk of such a thing as Conscience," the text beneath the image reads. "To Arms to Arms with one Accord / The Sword of Quakers and the Lord." A serenely self-interested Benjamin Franklin observes the action from the right, willing the actors on: "Fight Dog, Fight Bear, / You're all my Friends / By you I shall attain my ends / For I can never be content / Till I have got the government. / But if from this Attempt I fall / Then let the Devil take you all." Cartoon 1764/795.D.216. Courtesy of Library Company of Philadelphia.

"German Bleeds & Bears Ye Furs." Cartoon by Henry Dawkins, 1764. A Quaker rides on the back of an Ulster Presbyterian, who is holding a rifle, ready to fight for his new master. Behind them an Indian wielding a tomahawk rides on a blind-folded German. The Indian is wearing a bag emblazoned with the letters "IP," evidently intended to hold gifts from Israel Pemberton Jr. The dead bodies of settlers litter the foreground, a cabin burns in the background, and Benjamin Franklin looks dispassionately ahead. The caption reads, "The German bleeds & bears ye Furs / of Quaker Lords & Savage Curs / The Hibernian frets with new Disaster / And kicks to fling his broad brim'd Master / But help at hand Resolves to hold down / The Hibernian's Head or tumble all down." Cartoon 1764/66984.0.9. Courtesy of Library Company of Philadelphia.

focused less on the intellectual merits of the *Narrative*, which was written to provoke an emotional response rather than to persuade through rigorous argumentation, than on Franklin's reputation as the consummate politician and diplomatist. From his enemies' perspective, Franklin's political acumen epitomized the cold-hearted, self-serving duplicity they attributed to the Quaker party in general. Although Franklin was not a Quaker, pro-Paxton authors cast him as the embodiment of Quaker vices. Several cartoons portrayed him as a self-centered schemer whose only goal was to perpetuate his own power. In pursuit of this end he was prepared to support or sacrifice his Quaker allies as circumstances demanded.[4]

Franklin was a man of strong dislikes, and of no people did he hold a dimmer opinion than of Presbyterians. He was critical of Pennsylvania's

German population, but his dislike of Presbyterians amounted to hatred, much of it stemming from his early years in Boston. For Franklin, New England Congregationalists and Ulster settlers in Pennsylvania belonged to a larger body of intolerant, uncharitable fanatics whom he once described as "zealous Presbyterians." Several of his allies in the pamphlet war made the same equation, citing the intolerance of seventeenth-century New England as typical of the Presbyterian ethos. In seeking allies against the Presbyterians, Franklin could not rely on the Anglicans, who dominated the college he had helped found in Philadelphia. He had long since broken with the college's provost, William Smith, who, like all of Pennsylvania's Anglican clergymen, supported their coreligionist Thomas Penn.[5]

The Rev. William Smith, the most formidable of the Anglican apologists, happened to be in England in 1764 raising money for the college, leaving the Rev. Thomas Barton of Lancaster as the main spokesman for the proprietary interest. Barton's *Conduct of the Paxton-Men, Impartially Represented* responded directly to Franklin's *Narrative*. "A mighty Noise and Hubbub has been made about killing a few Indians in Lancaster-County," Barton wrote, "and even *Philosophers* and *Legislators* have been employed to raise the Holloo upon those that killed them." These learned men had been sent "to ransack *Tomes* and Systems, Writers ancient and modern, for Proofs of their Guilt and Condemnation!" Yet all they had demonstrated was that the people of Paxton and Donegal "have violated the Laws of Hospitality!" This conclusion, Barton observed, was so deeply unsurprising that he could "sincerely assure the ingenious and worthy Author of the NARRATIVE, that a Shock of *Electricity* would have had a much more sensible Effect upon these People than all the Arguments and Quotations he has produced." Barton claimed to have heard from "sundry of their nearest Neighbours in the *Conestogoe Manner*," that the Indians there "were a *drunken, debauch'd, insolent, quarrelsome* Crew; and that ever since the Commencement of the War, they have been a Trouble and Terror to all around them." The "Guilt and Treachery" of "*Will Soc* and his Brother" was not in question. The Conestogas, in short, deserved their fate.[6]

The pro-Paxton pamphleteers appealed to their readers' sympathies by describing the horrors of Indian warfare in overblown, sentimental language. Tracing the origins of the Conestoga massacres directly to the impact of the French and Indian War on frontier settlers, the anonymous *Apology of the Paxton Volunteers* noted that, with the onset of Indian attacks, "all their fair Prospects were suddenly exchanged for Scenes of the most melancholly

Distress & Horror." With the "breaking out of an Indian War, the state of four Frontier Counties in this Province became wretched & deplorable beyond Description." The Indians set fire to houses, barns, and crops, "in short to every thing that was combustible; so that the whole Country seemed to be in one general Blaze and involved in one common Ruin." Large numbers of settlers "were murdered, scalped & butchered in the most shocking manner, & their dead Bodies inhumanly mangled." Some had "their Ribs divided from the Chine with the Tomahawk," while others were "left expiring in the most eguisite Tortures, with Legs & Arms broken, their Skulls fractured, & the Brains scattered on the Ground." Children, according to the *Apology*, were "either spitted alive & roasted or covered under the Ashes of a large Fire, before their helpless Parents Eyes. The Hearts of some taken out & eaten reeking hot, while they were yet beating between their Teeth and others, where Time & Opportunity would admit of it were skinned, boiled & eaten." Hundreds more were carried off into captivity and tortured.[7]

Language of this sort was designed to persuade the reader that the Paxton Boys were provoked by Indians whose brutality greatly exceeded their own. Barton's *Conduct of the Paxton-Men* included scene after grisly scene drawn from Indian massacres in Cumberland County. In contrast to this barbarity, the Paxton Boys' violence was presented as sharply focused and efficient. In *The Quaker Unmask'd* David James Dove emphasized this distinction between humane and savage forms of brutality. "None of those killed at Lancaster were by Design kept one Moment in Torment," he wrote, "whereas many of our Frontier Inhabitants have been wantonly kept whole Days and Nights in exquisite Tortures," never knowing when their captors would "vouchsafe to give the merciful finishing Blow!"[8]

Those, like Barton, who defended or sympathized with the Paxton Boys pursued a number of common themes. As well as emphasizing Indian "savagery" as a way of diminishing the Paxton Boys' brutality, these pamphleteers blamed the Quakers for the government's failure to provide adequate frontier defense, which forced the Paxton Boys to act as they did. They ridiculed those Friends who had taken up arms to defend Philadelphia and argued that all Quakers were unfit to be in government. The pro-Paxton authors castigated the Assembly and the Quakers for refusing to help displaced settlers while dispensing aid to their enemies. Like the Paxton Boys in December 1763, they insisted that the distinction between "friendly" and "enemy" Indians was invalid. They praised the Paxton Boys for their Ulster pedigree and their loyalty to the Crown and defended their actions as an example of legitimate opposition to bad government.

From the pro-Paxton perspective, responsibility for the Conestoga murders rested firmly with that undifferentiated group, the Quakers. When the "*Dutch* and *Irish* were murder'd without Pity," Barton asked, did "we hear any of those Lamentations that are now so plentifully poured forth for the *Conestogoe Indians?*" Having long observed "the Distresses and Sufferings" of "the miserable Frontier People, who lately rose in Arms," he felt obliged to rescue them "from the Infamy and Odium thrown upon them, *by those* whose unfeeling Hearts have never suffered them to look beyond their own private Interest and Party." The Quakers had reduced the Paxton Boys "to the disagreeable Necessity of proceeding in the Manner they did." And having "made them Rioters," they now reproached them and demanded that "they may be *Shot* or *Hang'd* for being so."[9]

To discredit the Quakers the pro-Paxton authors concentrated on those who had violated the principle of pacifism in Philadelphia in February 1764. "Well Wisher," the anonymous author of a pamphlet titled *An Historical Account, of the late Disturbance*, noted that the defenders of Philadelphia included "the People call'd Friends, prepared with Arms like Spartans brave, striding forth with Gigantic Pace to defend their Laws and Liberty, more precious than Life." The most devastating attack came in Dove's *The Quaker Unmask'd*. When "their King and Country call them to Arms," Dove complained, the Quakers "plead Conscience, and will tell thee, with a pious Air, and meek Countenance, 'they would rather perish by the Sword than use it against the Enemies of the State.'" Yet this piety and meekness had dissipated the moment Philadelphia, rather than the frontier, came under threat. The march of the Paxton Boys had revealed the Quakers' true nature. When some of their "Fellow Subjects become obnoxious to their mild and peaceful Rage, by opposing any of their arbitrary Measures," Dove concluded, "we then see the Quaker unmask'd, with his Gun upon his Shoulder, and other warlike Habiliments, eagerly desiring the Combat, and thirsting for the Blood of those his Opponents."[10]

Popular songs lampooned the new Quaker militarism. One such number, "A Battle! A Battle! A Battle of Squirt, Where no Man is kill'd, and no Man is Hurt!," was especially merciless: "In Days of *Yore*, our Annals say, / The Saints would sit at home and pray, / But not vouchsafe to stir an Inch / Or lend Assistance at a Pinch; / Tho' for their King's and Country's good; / Stiff to their Text the Quakers stood." The Quakers had adhered to this policy all through the French and Indian War and Pontiac's War, the song continued, "For Feuds and Quarrels they abhor 'em, / The LORD will fight their Battles for 'em. / In this of late they were so stanch / As not to move against the *French*." Then in February 1764 everything changed, when Quakers for the first time found themselves in danger: "But now the Case is alter'd quite, / And what was wrong, is chang'd to Right. / These very Drones, these sluggish Cattle, / Prepare their Guns and Swords for Battle. / So Acts the sly perfidious Bat, / Sometimes for this side, sometimes that." With Quaker principles become so fickle, henceforth one might as well "let two and two make six, / Or any number you shall fix."[11]

The Rev. Thomas Barton combined his criticism of martial Quakers with vicious attacks on the Conestoga Indians. Philadelphia's Quakers, he wrote, "instead of *Resist not Evil*, attempt to *Resist Violence by Force*: and instead of *Give also thy other Cheek*, even plant Cannon (and surely not Spiritual Cannon) in Order to Strike again." In February 1764, Barton continued, they dug trenches and planted cannons "against a Handful of *Freemen* and the *King's Subjects*, who thought it their Duty to kill a Pack of villainous, faithless Savages, whom they suspected, and had Reason to believe, were Murderers, Enemies to his *Majesty*, his Government, and Subjects." These Quakers, Barton concluded, were more prepared "to see the Blood of 5 or 600 of his Majesty's Subjects shed, than give up, or banish to their native Caves and Woods, a Parcel of treacherous, faithless, rascally Indians, some of which can be proved to be Murderers."[12]

According to their critics, the Quakers had not only refused to assist frontier settlers, but had gone out of their way to help Indians. *The Quaker Unmask'd* claimed that every religious group in Philadelphia except the Quakers, "even the Roman-Catholicks, whom they so much despise," made "very generous and liberal Contributions" to assist the settlers. But the Society of Friends, "so easily affected with Pity for Indians, would not grant a single Farthing (as a Society)." Israel Pemberton Jr. and his Friendly Association were the worst offenders in this respect. Even as the frontier settlers were "abused, and thus stript of their *Birth-Rights*," Barton wrote, they "were permitted to lord it over the Land." In "Contempt of the Government, and the express Order of the Crown," they negotiated privately with Indians and showered them with gifts. Here, for Barton, lay the origins of the Paxton Boys' massacres. "Is it any Wonder then if the unhappy Frontier People were really *mad with Rage*, (as they express themselves) under such cruel Treatment?" he asked. "Shall *Heathens*, shall *Traytors*, shall *Rebels* and *Murderers* be protected, cloathed and fed? Shall they be invited from House to House, and riot at Feasts and Entertainments?"[13]

For defenders of the Paxton Boys "the horrid Doctrines of *Non-Resistance*," as Barton referred to them, rendered all Quakers unfit to participate in government. By equating the Quaker party with absolute pacifism Barton conveniently ignored that the last of the strict pacifists had resigned from the Assembly in 1756. To their critics, one Quaker was as bad as any other. Dove demanded to know how "a Person who declares that his Conscience by divine Inspiration forbids him to have any Hand in shedding Blood" could be considered fit to participate in government. How, he asked, could Quakers be trusted to represent frontier settlers, "who look on themselves to be obliged by the Laws of God, the Laws of Nature, and the Laws of their King and Country to take up Arms to defend themselves, and punish those who would deprive them of Life or Property"? It was an "an inexpressible Absurdity," he concluded, "that a war-like People should be governed by Persons of Quaker Principles, and especially in Time of War."[14]

The Quakers' pacifism, Barton argued, had utterly degraded their ability to govern. In the midst of "Desolation and Carnage," he wrote, "every publick Measure was clogg'd—the King's Demands for Men and Money procrastinated—unnecessary, or at least ill-timed Disputes, about *Proprietary Instructions and Taxes*, were brought upon the Carpet." The principal purpose of these maneuvers, he wrote, was "to divert the Reproach and Dishonour which the Province, thro' Quakers Measures, had incurr'd, and throw the whole Blame of the War at the Proprietary Doors." He and the other pro-Paxton writers, by contrast, placed all the blame for defense failures on the Quaker Assembly, ignoring the culpability of the executive branch.[15]

In the *Remonstrance* the Paxton Boys had insisted that it was impossible to distinguish between friendly and enemy Indians. Their supporters in the pamphlet war enthusiastically took up this theme. "We have long been convinced from sufficient Evidence," as the *Apology* put it, "that the Indians that lived as independent Commonwealths among us near our Borders were our most dangerous Enemies, both in the last & present War, altho' they still pretended to be our Friends." Years of experience had shown that the "Rum-debauched & trader-corrupted Thieves & Vagabonds that lived on Sesquehannah & Ohio are indesputably unfaithful & perfidious." Even as they concluded treaties, these Indians "were forming Schemes how they might destroy us, after they had received, Blankets, Ammunition, & other Presents from the white People."[16]

Not only did the Indians in these enclaves kill and capture frontier settlers, the *Apology* continued, but they "reported our weak & defenceless state to the

French together with all our Motions & Dispositions against them." While "wearing the Cloak of Friendship, they could readily obtain Provisions[,] Ammunition & warlike Implements to convey to our Enemies." Their "Claim to Freedom & Independency put it in their Power to harbour Spies & give Intelligence." They "asserted & exercised the Right of making War & Peace as independent Nations, never came under our Laws, nor acknowledged Subjection to our King & Government." Granted, "the little Commonwealth at Conestoga" had agreed that "if an Indian killed a White man, the Indian should be tried by our Laws." But the fact that the Conestoga Indians were empowered to make this concession merely confirmed their status as "a free & independent State." Frontier settlers knew full well that "no Nation could be safe especially in a Time of War, if another State or Part of a State be allowed to live among them, free & independent." Consequently, the *Apology* explained, "a Number of Persons living amongst us, who had seen their Houses in Flames, their Parents & Relatives butchered in the most in human Manner determined to root out this Nest of perfidious Enemies; & accordingly cut them off."[17]

In case there was any doubt about the Conestogas' guilt, the *Apology* presented evidence "by Persons of undoubted Probity & Veracity, to prove this Point." This evidence included the affidavits taken in Lancaster at the end of February 1764 concerning alleged visits by Conestoga Indians to the Delaware town of Kittanning, Will Sock's alleged murder of Chagrea, and his supposed involvement in the murder of an old man near Fort Augusta. The *Apology* expanded the number of Sock's victims to six, though without citing any evidence. The Conestogas, this pamphlet claimed, were "as much Enemies as any other Tribe of Indians on the Continent." They communicated with French-allied Indians, and because they lived among the frontier settlers they had the "Power to be a more dreadful Enemy than any other Tribe that consisted of no more Persons." "What then means all the malicious Clamour against us, as if we had murdered our innocent Friends?" the *Apology* concluded. "Are we not justifiable in cutting off this Tribe of Enemies as any other? Can their living amongst us justify their Perfidy, or entitle them to commit Ravages upon his Majesty's loyal subjects with Immunity?" The massacres of December 1763, in other words, were a justified act of war.[18]

According to their defenders, the Paxton Boys were the most loyal of all British subjects in Pennsylvania. They defended the province militarily, while Quakers hid behind the smokescreen of piety and principle. The people of the frontier, as Barton put it, "have suffered and bled in the Cause of their Country, and have done more to protect it from the Violence of a rapacious

Enemy than any others in the Province." Born to "Liberty, and all the glorious Rights and Privileges of BRITISH SUBJECTS," they were denied protection by the heartless Quaker government "at a Time when the Cries of Murder and Distress might have made the very Stones relent."[19]

The *Apology* likewise bridled at "the unjust Charge of Disloyalty to our gracious King, whom we have faithfully served with Success thro the late & present Indian Wars." Because the Conestogas had lived under the protection of the government, the Paxton Boys were accused of "flying in the Face of lawful Authority to kill these Indians, especially such of them as were in the Work-House in Lancaster." The *Apology* countered this accusation with a tortured but original argument on legitimate opposition to government. Although the Conestogas were in the workhouse "by the Consent of the Magistrates of Lancaster," this argument ran, they were not, and could not have been, "under the Protection of the Government." No administration had the constitutional power "to protect its Enemies, that is, to ruin itself," and no branch of that administration was authorized to preside over the government's dissolution.[20]

To "grant protection" to Indians during wartime, therefore, was not only unwise, it was literally impossible, as all Indians were real or potential enemies. The magistrates in Lancaster may have provided accommodation to the fourteen surviving Conestogas, but they "neither had nor could have a Power by Virtue of their Commissions, to *protect* these Enemies of his Majesty against the Resentments of his injured Subjects." This line of reasoning produced a grim explanation for why nobody had come to the Conestogas' aid when the Paxton Boys attacked. The Lancaster magistrates must have known "that their Commissions did not authorize them to protect these Indians for they never attempted to defend them," the *Apology* argued. "Indeed the very attempt would argue either Ignorance of their Office or Rebellion against his Majesty, neither of which can be justly laid to their Charge." Just as the magistrates had violated no law by their inaction, the *Apology* concluded, the Paxton Boys had "insulted no lawful Authority, nor flew in the Face of Government, but acted as loyal Subjects of his Majesty when we cut off these his Enemies." If the magistrates had mistakenly tried to stop them, the Paxton Boys would have been justified in resisting.[21]

The Paxton Boys, in short, had protected the interests of the Crown by striking its enemies, whom the provincial government had perversely insisted on sheltering for seventy years. Many of the pro-Paxton pamphlets reiterated this idea of killing Indians as a form of loyal opposition to bad government. According to *The Quaker Unmask'd*, "any candid Person" seeking to explain the actions of the Paxton Boys "will certainly admit such an Apology for their Extravagancies as the wise SOLOMON suggests, that 'Oppression will make a Wise Man mad.'" The Glorious Revolution of 1688, which secured civil and political rights for English Protestants, was "a striking Instance of this known truth." Thomas Barton, the most learned of the Paxton Boys' defenders, sprinkled his *Conduct* with classical as well as contemporary allusions to legitimate political opposition. "It has, indeed, been always thought highly imprudent, not to say dangerous, to resist the Groans of the People," he observed. The need to listen to the Paxton Boys was all the greater, as "nine Tenths of the Inhabitants of the Back-Counties either tacitly, or openly, approve and support them."[22]

Despite the well-established English tradition of resisting political oppression, Barton continued, the Quakers had been prepared to kill the Paxton Boys if they entered Philadelphia in pursuit of their rights. Their "violent Proceedings" against the frontier protestors were consistent neither "with the Principles which *Quakers* have professed to the World" nor with "the Lenity and Mercy of an *English* Constitution." Such conduct would "never do with a free People, who conceive themselves oppressed." Barton took pains to explain that he had "as great an Aversion to Mobs, and all riotous Proceedings, as any Man can have, as any Man ought to have." But he was equally opposed to "sacrificing the Lives and Liberties of a free People to the Caprice and Obstinacy of a destructive Faction." Loyal opposition, he insisted, was essential to the proper functioning of society: "A proper Spirit of JEALOUSY, and REVENGE too, in a People who are oppress'd and injur'd, is a politick and commendable Virtue; without which they will never be valued or respected."[23]

Several pro-Paxton authors pointed to sectional imbalance in political representation as an example of bad government. Barton claimed that the five "Frontier Counties, altho' a great Majority," had for eight years lain "at the Mercy of a cruel Savage Enemy and an unrelenting Quaker Faction." In a pamphlet titled *The Plain Dealer*, the Presbyterian pastor and professor of mathematics, Hugh Williamson, declared that the only hope for Pennsylvania was to cast off Quaker rule. "For God's sake," he exclaimed, "are we always to be slaves, must we groan for ever beneath the yoke of three Quaker counties?" Williamson hoped that the proprietary party might form an alliance with Pennsylvania's two Presbyterian constituencies, those living in the western counties and those in Philadelphia, thereby breaking the power of the Quaker party in the Assembly. But the Quaker leaders, led by Benjamin Franklin, were determined to resist this plan.[24]

CHAPTER 18
CHRISTIAN WHITE SAVAGES

Critics of the Paxton Boys challenged all of the arguments advanced by their apologists. At the most basic level, Benjamin Franklin and his allies demanded concrete evidence supporting the contention that the Conestogas had been in league with enemy Indians. They countered the assertion that all Indians were the same by pointing to the profusion of different Indian nations in Pennsylvania and elsewhere. Skin color, they argued, was irrelevant in judging people's character and allegiance. The true "savages" in this case were the Paxton Boys rather than their victims. The anti-Paxton authors lampooned the supposed bravery of the men who had slaughtered the Conestoga Indians, characterizing them as cowards, bigots, traitors, and zealots. And, neatly reversing the accusation that Quakers were unfit to govern, they identified a long Presbyterian tradition of subversion and fanaticism dating back to the English civil wars.

Franklin was the first to demand proper evidence of the Conestogas' supposed complicity with hostile Indians. "I call thus publickly on the Makers and Venders of these Accusations to Produce their Evidence," he wrote in his *Narrative*. "Let them satisfy the Public that even *Will Soc*, the most obnoxious of all that Tribe, was really guilty of those Offences against us which they lay to his Charge." Even if Sock was guilty, Franklin asked, "ought he not to have been fairly tried?" Like all the Conestoga Indians, he "lived under our Laws, and was subject to them; he was in our Hands, and might easily have been prosecuted." The same applied to "Shehaes [Sheehays], the women, and the boys and girls hatcheted in their parents' arms." If there was evidence that they had done something wrong, they ought to have been treated within the framework of the law.[1]

Franklin cleverly refuted the central pro-Paxton argument that all Indians were the same by applying it to Europeans. "If an *Indian* injures me," he asked, "does it follow that I may revenge that Injury on all *Indians?* It is well known that *Indians* are of different Tribes, Nations, and Languages, as well as the White People." If the French, "who are White People," should injure the Dutch, Franklin asked, should the Dutch take revenge on the English "because they too are White People?" The Conestogas had committed no crime other than having "a reddish brown Skin, and black Hair; and some People of that Sort, it seems, had murdered some of our Relations." By the Paxton Boys' logic, if a man "with a freckled Face and red Hair"—the stereotypical Ulster complexion—should kill Franklin's wife and child, it would be right for him "to revenge it, by killing all the freckled red-haired Men, Women and Children" he could find. Several other anti-Paxton authors followed Franklin's lead on this point.[2]

From this perspective, the Paxton Boys rather than their Indian victims were the true "savages." The massacres, Charles Read lamented, "can only serve to convince the World, that there are among us Persons more savage than *Indians* themselves." Franklin denounced the Paxton affair as a "Horrid Perversion of Scripture and of Religion!" The people of Pennsylvania "pretend to be Christians," he wrote in the *Narrative*, "and, from the superior Light we enjoy, ought to exceed Heathens, Turks, Saracens, Moors, Negroes and Indians, to the Knowledge and Practice of what is right." Citing numerous "Examples from Books and History," he concluded that the Conestoga massacres could have been perpetrated "by no civilized Nation in *Europe*." "Do we come to *America*," he asked, "to learn and practise the Manners of *Barbarians?*" The Conestogas had always been friends to Pennsylvania. "Their Fathers received ours, when Strangers here, with Kindness and Hospitality." Pennsylvania had offered them protection in return, but "the mangled Corpses of the last Remains of the Tribe" demonstrated "how effectually we have afforded it to them!" The Conestogas "would have been safe in any Part of the known World," Franklin concluded, "except in the Neighbourhood of the CHRISTIAN WHITE SAVAGES of *Peckstang* and *Donegall!*"[3]

The Paxton Boys, who claimed to epitomize martial prowess, were highly vulnerable to charges of cowardice. "*Cowards* can handle Arms, can strike where they are sure to meet with no Return, can wound, mangle and murder," Franklin observed, "but it belongs to *brave* Men to spare, and to protect." The Paxton Boys, he concluded, were "Unmanly Men! who are not ashamed to come with Weapons against the Unarmed, to use the Sword against Women, and the Bayonet against young Children." Isaac Hunt, the author of the two most philosophically substantial anti-Paxton pamphlets, *A Looking-Glass for*

Presbyterians, made the same point satirically. "As to their Bravery no Body will ever dispute it, that has heard of their gallant and loyal Behaviour at *Lancaster*," he wrote, "where only fifty of them compleatly arm'd were able to vanquish a numerous Company of eight Men and Women, and seven small Children, all disarm'd and coop'd up in Goal [jail]."[4]

A fictitious dialogue between two Ulster Presbyterians, "Andrew Trueman" and "Thomas Zealot," pursued this theme satirically. "WHAR ha'you been aw this Time, *Tom*?" Trueman asks. "Whar I have been!" Zealot replies. "Whar you should ha' been too, Andrew, fecthing [fighting] the Lord's battles, and kill-ing the Indians at *Lancaster* and *Cannestogoe*." When Trueman asks how many they killed at Conestoga Indiantown, Zealot replies, "Ane and Twunty." But "there were but twunty awthegether," Trueman protests, "and fourteen of them were in the Goal." Zealot insists that his count is correct: "I tell you, we shot six and a wee ane, that was in the Squaw's Belly; we sculped three; we tomhawked three; we roasted three and a wee ane; and three and a wee ane we gave to the Hogs; and is not that ane and is not that ane and twunty you Fool." Zealot and his comrades proceeded to Lancaster, where they "kilt them aw, men women and weans," though by then he had lost count of the number.[5]

Awestruck by Zealot's valor, Trueman asks, "Were you not frechtened to facht so mony Indians?" "Indeed were we," says Zealot, "But we did no' let them fecht Us. We kilt them at the Mannor just as they getting out of their Beds in the Morning." And when the remaining Indians were removed from Conestoga Manor, "the Gued Folks of *Lancaster* had taken away aw the Guns, Tomhawks, and long Knives, from they that were in the Goal." Zealot claims that there were 1,500 Paxton Boys in Lancaster town on December 27, with another 5,000 ready to join them "that would ha' foucht the *Quackers*, as well as the Heathens." When Trueman expresses concern about the killing of "the Women and the Weans," Zealot reassures him that, the night before the massacres, "auld Saunders Kent" had resolved any lingering doubts by sing-ing Psalm 137. Saunders Kent is well-known to both of them, Zealot reminds Trueman, for "he has been an Elder this thirty Year."[6]

The reference here, suggested by the play on words, was almost certainly to the Rev. John Elder, pastor of Paxton Presbyterian Church since 1738. In Zealot's account, he "sung the 137 *Psalm*, where it says, 'happy surely shall he be, they tender little ones, who shall lay hold upon, and them shall dash against the Stones.'" Saunders Kent also "read the 15. *Chapter* of I *Samuel*," wherein Samuel conveyed to Saul the Lord's command to "go and smite Amalek, and utterly destroy all that they have, and spare them not; but slay both man and woman, infant and suckling, ox and sheep, camel and ass." Such, according to their critics, were the biblical inspirations of the Paxton Boys.[7]

A second satirical dialogue, this one between "Positive" and "Zealot," made similar fun of the Paxton Boys. Defending the *Declaration* and *Remonstrance* against charges that they were rebellious, "false, foolish, or impertinent," Positive insists that "all the witty Politicians and great Geniuses in the Province" should instead be celebrating the Paxton Boys' military prowess. He expresses wonder that they have not yet "employed their Pens in applauding our never-to-be-forgotten Action at Lancaster; where we bravely conquer'd, our Eye not pitying, nor our Hand sparing either Age or Sex." Positive asks Zealot to talk to him no more "of Cassius, Brutus, Caesar, Pompey, or even Alexander the Great! We! We Paxton Boys have done more than all, or any of them!" In killing the Conestoga Indians they not only won a battle, they "Slaughter'd, kill'd and cut off a whole Tribe! a Nation at once!"[8]

The most substantive question in the debate over the Paxton Boys was how Pennsylvania ought to be governed. While the pro-Paxton authors insisted that the Quakers' pacifism and cold-hearted self-interest made them unfit to rule the province, the anti-Paxton authors responded by arguing that it was Presbyterians who should be disqualified from governing. Isaac Hunt, in his two *Looking-Glass for Presbyterians* pamphlets, made the principal arguments in this respect. He conceded "that according to the strict Rules of *Quaker Principles*," members of the Society of Friends were "not qualified to govern in Time of War." But he reminded his readers that strict pacifist Quakers had been absent from the Assembly for almost a decade and that pacifist principles were therefore irrelevant to the question at hand. What really mattered was the innumerable benefits Quaker rule had brought to Pennsylvania. The "present amazing Perfection" of the province, which had arisen "in so short a Time, both in Riches, Trade and Commerce," resulted from the Quakers' "wise and prudent administration." They had encouraged "Emigrents of all Nations to settle here," granting them "Liberties both civil and religious in the most ample Manner." Among these emigrants, Hunt reminded his readers, were tens of thousands of Ulster Presbyterians.[9]

Hunt's principal tactic was not to praise Quaker virtues but to castigate Presbyterian extremism. Most of the first *Looking-Glass* pamphlet consisted of a historical explanation of why Presbyterians "are by no Means proper Men to hold the Reigns of Government, either in War or Peace." If "a firm Attachment to the KING, and the Laws of our Country, be necessary Ingredients in a representative of the People," Hunt argued, "a *Presbyterian* can lay no claim to them; and consequently ought not to be elected." Throughout history, "*Presbyterianism* and *Rebellion*, were twin-Sisters, sprung from Faction, and their Affection for each other, has been ever so strong, that a separation of them never could be effected." Given the Paxton Boys' proclamations of loyalty to the Crown, Hunt and other anti-Paxton pamphleteers paid special attention to the antagonistic relationship between Presbyterianism and monarchy. Their gravest accusation was regicide: Presbyterians took over England in the 1640s, executed Charles I, and installed Oliver Cromwell, "a Tyrant, chosen from the very Dreggs of the People, upon the Throne." From the English civil wars to the present, Hunt concluded, Presbyterians had embodied the spirit of rebellion and regicide.[10]

No doubt aware that Presbyterians would find comparison between them and Irish Catholics especially galling, Hunt and several other anti-Paxton authors took pains to draw just this analogy. Their point was not to defend Catholicism but to argue that the Presbyterian "kirk" (the Scottish word for church) was just as bad as the Catholic Church and perhaps even worse. "The Success that attended the one in behalf of the *Kirk*," as Hunt put it, "encourag'd the other to pursue the same Steps in Favour of the *Mass*." The fanatical Scottish Presbyterians who rebelled against Charles I, in other words, had caused Irish Catholics to launch a rebellion as well, and Hunt wondered "whether all the innocent Blood that was shed in that horrid Massacre, may not be justly laid to their Charge." His *Looking-Glass II* opened with a vicious epigraph by Jonathan Swift: "The Pope and Calvin, I'll oppose, / Because I think them both our Foes. / The Church and State have suffer'd more / By Calvin than the scarlet Whore." Yet, Swift concluded, although both "Popish and Presbyterian Zeal" were threats to "Britain's Weal," Catholicism was the lesser of the two evils: "The Pope wou'd of our Faith bereave us. / But still our Monarchy would leave us. / Not so the Presbyterian Crew / That ruin'd Church and Monarch too."[11]

The long Presbyterian tradition of disloyalty, Hunt continued, persisted after the Glorious Revolution, through the Scottish Jacobite rebellions of 1715 and 1745, to the summer of 1763, when thousands of Presbyterian "Oakboys" in the north of Ireland took up arms to protest local taxes and the tithes exacted by the established Anglican Church. Like the Paxton Boys, the Oakboys proclaimed their loyalty to the Crown, but according to Hunt both belonged to the same fanatical and bigoted tradition. The Oakboys, he marveled, simultaneously invoked the "Glorious Memory of King William the Third, who delivered us from Popery, Slavery, Bribery, Brass Money and Wooden Shoes," and the "Martial Brave Actions of Oliver Cromwell, our First Deliverer." Hunt could see no affinity between Cromwell the republican dictator and William the constitutional monarch; Presbyterians were rebels through and through. Although the Oakboys declared in an anonymous letter that they were "ready to fight for King and Country" and signed off as "Reformers of Abuses in Church and State," Hunt dismissed Presbyterians' claims of loyalty, on both sides of the Atlantic, as masks for fanaticism. Their quarrel was "not with a bad King, more than a good one," he concluded, but with monarchy itself.[12]

The anti-Paxton authors found further proof of Presbyterian intolerance in the history of New England. Like Franklin, Hunt made no distinction between Presbyterianism and Congregationalism. "Let the righteous Blood of the *Quakers* unjustly shed in *New England*, purely for Conscience Sake," he wrote, "warn the Inhabitants of *Pennsylvania*, from trusting *Presbyterians* with Power, least the same mournful Tragedies should be acted over again!" An anonymous pamphlet titled *The Quakers Assisting*, written in part as a response to David James Dove's *The Quaker Unmask'd*, lamented that the Boston Quakers "were used in the most cruel Manner, that the Serpentine Nature in Man could invent; they bore cruel Whippings, cutting off their Ears, and several were murdered, and for no other reason, then for their faithful obedience to CHRIST." All of this was done by the "*Unmasker's* dear Brethren, *viz.* Envious, Malicious, Hard-hearted *Presbyterians*."[13]

How could such a people be considered fit to govern Pennsylvania? Alluding to the Paxton massacres as the acme of Presbyterian excess, Hunt warned "of Men who wou'd cram Laws down your Throats with Muskets, Daggars, Tomahawks and Scalping-knifes." Pennsylvanians must protect their civil and religious liberties, which were "the most extensive ... of any People in the World." In *Looking-Glass II* Hunt offered a parody of what a Presbyterian Assembly would do if voted into power. It would enact bills "exempting the Proprietries from all Taxes forever," "establishing *Synods, Presbyteries,* and *Kirk Sessions,*" and "rating every Taxable of whatever Denomination towards the supporting *Presbyterian Ministers* and their poor Widows." It would also pass a bill "obliging every Body to attend *Presbyterian Meetings*, under Pain of Corporal Punishment for the first Offence, and Hanging for the second." For other first offenses the guilty would pay a fine, "and for the second Offence Excommunication from the Conversation of all Mankind, and to be given over to *Satan* to be buffeted, till absolv'd by the Kirk."[14]

Pennsylvania's Quakers were by now deep into their gravest crisis since William Penn had established the Peaceable Kingdom. The pro-Paxton authors were attacking them relentlessly, and although the anti-Paxtonites launched a robust defense, the Quakers had serious questions to answer. The Philadelphia Monthly Meeting responded to the charges made in the *Declaration* and *Remonstrance* by presenting a written *Address* to John Penn on February 25. Having "perused and considered" the "two Papers presented to thee by some of the Frontier Inhabitants on the 6th and 13th Instant," the Quaker leaders declared their innocence against these "false Charges and unjust Insinuations thus invidiously propagated against us." They began by reminding Penn that, although they had suffered persecution in the past, they were "never concern'd in promoting or countenancing any Plots or Insurrections against the Government," the implicit comparison being with Presbyterians. On the contrary, the inhabitants of Pennsylvania had lived in "Tranquillity and Peace" until the 1750s, with people of all denominations "protected in Person and Property and in the full Enjoyment of religious and civil Liberty."[15]

The *Address* refuted the specific "Insinuations and Slanders" made in the *Declaration* and *Remonstrance*. The efforts of the Friendly Association in the 1750s "to promote Reconciliation with the Indians," the Quakers insisted, were intended to restore peace and win the release of captives, not to succor the enemy. The accusation in the *Declaration* that Quakers contributed nothing to the relief of distressed families on the frontier was manifestly untrue. The accusation in the *Remonstrance* of "abetting the Indian Enemies, and keeping up a private Intelligence with them," was "altogether False and Groundless."[16]

Pennsylvania's Quakers had to respond to transatlantic as well as local critics. The Philadelphia Friends were in frequent contact with their brethren in London, on whom they relied for spiritual guidance and approval. The London Meeting had long accepted the idea of providing funds for defensive war, but taking up arms, as Quakers had done in Philadelphia in February 1764, was another matter. So forthright a challenge to the principle of nonviolence threatened to rupture Quaker unity, which in the absence of theological doctrines or formal devotional rituals depended on consistency of practice. Following the march on Philadelphia, the Monthly Meeting set up an investigative commission that eventually interviewed 140 Friends, asking them to account for their actions. Most who had taken up arms admitted that their actions were inconsistent with Quaker principles and recanted; a minority, however, insisted that their actions were not only necessary but morally justified under the circumstances. The result was a crisis in Pennsylvania Quakerism.[17]

In the course of the investigation the Philadelphia Meeting corresponded regularly with its London counterpart. "The Commotions which have been in this Province for some time past," the Philadelphia Quakers wrote to the London Meeting on the day they submitted their *Address* to John Penn, had "affected the minds of the sober and considerate part of the People, & particularly our Religious Society." The "Enemies of Truth" had availed themselves of "the Opportunity to vilify and calumniate" against the Quakers. In writing to the London Meeting, the Philadelphia Quakers did not seek to explain or defend the breach in unity. For the present they merely described what had happened and invited guidance.[18]

James Pemberton, brother of Israel, wrote in his own behalf to the London Quaker leader, Dr. James Fothergill. Pemberton was greatly troubled by "the Anarchy & Confusion" in Philadelphia. Although John Penn and the proprietary party were responsible for the crisis, Quakers were bearing the brunt of the blame. If Penn "had the Integrity, understand[in]g & application of his Grand father," Pemberton wrote, "he might be instrumental in improving peace and appeasing in some measure the present discontents, but it is obvious he is too inactive & liable to be imposed upon by the few with whom he converses." Pemberton saw the discrediting of Quakers as an opportunity for Presbyterians to expand their influence in Pennsylvania. New England was already "well known to be chiefly inhabited by the People of that Society," he wrote, and "they are also numerous in New Jersey. Our Frontier Counties are mostly settled by them." Presbyterians controlled the College of New Jersey (later renamed Princeton University) and "most of the Tutors in this city." Their "priests" were being "appointed as missionaries to the Indian country," and now they were pleading "the Authority of the Scripture for exterminating" those same Indians. They were stirring up "a Spirit of Enmity amongst the people by propagating the most absurd falsehoods" about the Society of Friends.[19]

The London Quakers replied to the letter from the Philadelphia Meeting in April. They recommended compassion and emphasized the healing power of faith, but they insisted on the need for consistent practice. Those who had taken up arms must recant "and chearfully submit to the righteous Judgment of Truth." They would be welcomed back into the Quaker fold, but only if they acknowledged their transgression. For the sake of its own survival, the Society of Friends must ensure that nobody could accuse it of being "one thing in Principle, & another in Practice."[20]

An influential minority of Quakers disagreed with the Philadelphia and London Meetings on this point. Foremost among these dissidents was the merchant Edward Pennington. Thirty-seven years old at the time of the march on Philadelphia, Pennington had been a strict pacifist and a trustee of Israel Pemberton's Friendly Association in the 1750s, but he did not take his seat in the Assembly until 1761. Consequently he did not have to take a stance during the French and Indian War, when strict pacifists resigned their seats to protest the pro-war Quaker pragmatism of the majority, led by Isaac Norris. Pennington finally made up his mind on the question of violence in February 1764, with the Paxton Boys approaching Philadelphia, when he took up arms and headed a company of men to defend the city.[21]

Pennington was convinced that what he had done was right. In a letter to the Philadelphia Meeting he self-confidently explained why he had "borne arms, contrary to the professions of the Society of which I am a member." He did so to prevent further violence and to defend his city, which he saw as an obligation rather than a transgression. The Paxton Boys had killed the Conestoga Indians "in defiance of Government" and were on their way to the Philadelphia barracks to kill the Indians there. Many Quakers "who were friends to good Government" desired that "those disturbers of it's peace should be brought to Justice, or at least prevented from committing further acts of violence." But who would perform this task, given the Friends' scruples on bearing arms? Pennington had thought hard about this question and concluded that it was his duty "to prevent these people from executing their bloody purposes." No government "could long exist," he observed, "while large bodies of men were suffered to commit the most horrid crimes with impunity."[22]

Here was the Quaker dilemma in a nutshell. "To prevent bloodshed and preserve good order in Civil Society," Pennington declared, "was my design in bearing Arms." If he had done wrong he hoped God would "open" his "understanding"; otherwise, he hoped God would help him to live up to what he was "convinced" was his "duty." Pennington concluded his letter to the Philadelphia Meeting by expressing his desire to be "continued as [a] member of this Society, and in Such unity as the nature of the cases will admit." Although he had "deviated from the professions of Friends," he was "fully convinced of the truth of their principles in general." In an effort to resolve the contradiction in these words, he ventured the opinion that "a good degree of unity may be maintained in a Society whose members do not think alike in every respect."[23]

This was a highly subversive opinion for an eighteenth-century Quaker to hold. The inner light, simplicity, and modesty—all were essential, but intangible, characteristics of Quakerism. What mattered most was an individual's actions in the world and how these actions conformed to core principles. Among the actions proscribed by the core teachings of Quakerism was bearing arms. If nonviolence became peripheral to Quakerism, what was left? Conversely, if men like Edward Pennington were excluded from Quakerism, could the Society of Friends survive in Pennsylvania? Quaker unity disintegrated over these issues in 1764. The Philadelphia and London Meetings tried and failed to resolve the dilemma. In the end, the Philadelphia Meeting took no action against Pennington or the other Quakers who had taken up arms. The crisis in Quakerism put paid to what was left of Pennsylvania's pacifist tradition, with grave consequences for the province's Indians, who had few protectors beyond the Society of Friends.[24]

With the Quakers divided, and Philadelphia still recovering from the shock of the Paxton Boys' march, Pennsylvania's political system was in disarray. Other than exacting retribution against the Conestoga Indians, the Paxton Boys had failed in all of their goals. Yet the December massacres, the march on Philadelphia, and the pamphlet war that followed had destabilized the provincial government to an extent the Paxton Boys could never have imagined possible. By the spring of 1764 the executive and legislative branches were reeling under the severity of each other's attacks. Each side, according to the other, was responsible for the crisis. The proprietary party was forging links with Presbyterians, both in Philadelphia and in the western counties, with a view to bringing the Assembly to heel at last. But Benjamin Franklin and the Quaker party responded with an audacious plan of their own. They wanted the king to abolish proprietary government in Pennsylvania and place the province under direct royal rule.

CHAPTER 19

UNDER THE TYRANT'S FOOT

"To govern is absolutely repugnant to the avowed principles of *Quakers*," wrote the author of a minor pamphlet in 1764. "To be govern'd is absolutely repugnant to the avowed principles of Pr[esbyteria]ns." What hope was left, then, for Pennsylvania? Supporters of the Paxton Boys blamed the Conestoga massacres on the Quaker party's inability or unwillingness to provide adequate defense, an elementary obligation of any government. Critics of the Paxton Boys, by contrast, saw the massacres and the march on Philadelphia as proof of proprietary incompetence and Presbyterian fanaticism. For Benjamin Franklin and his allies the solution was to place Pennsylvania under direct royal government. The stage was set for a political showdown.[1]

The anti-Paxton pamphleteer Isaac Hunt recommended royal government as the only way "to stem the Torrent of *Presbyterianism*, which is pouring down upon us." Under continued proprietary rule, he predicted, Presbyterians would "with more than *vandalic Barbarity*, bury us, our Religion and Liberties, in one general Inundation." If the government of Pennsylvania were freed from the control of the Penn family, the province could be placed under the enlightened rule of the Crown. But Presbyterians were mobilizing in opposition to this goal, Hunt warned, led by three of their most prominent ministers: Gilbert Tennent, Francis Alison, and the vehemently pro-Paxton John Ewing, who declared that only Quakers felt "that the Lancaster Indians have suffered any thing but their just desserts." These ministers circulated a letter accusing the Assembly of proposing royal government as "an artful scheme to *divide* or *divert* the Attention of the injur'd Frontier Inhabitants from prosecuting their Petitions, which very much alarm them." Hunt dismissed this letter as a "treacherous Jesuitical Presbyterian *Bull*" and "a *circular Apostolical* Letter wrote by the Presbyterian Pope in *Philadelphia*, and his two *Cardinals* to all the inferior Brethren and

John Ewing (1732–1802). Portrait painting by Edward D. Marchant, from an original by Charles Wilson Peale, 1779. Record ID 20040220008. Courtesy of Collections of the University of Pennsylvania Archives.

their Flocks throughout the Province, in order to deter them from becoming immediate Subjects of *King George*."[2]

Samuel Foulke left a detailed account of the antiproprietary sentiment within the Assembly. He sensed "a patriot spirit in ye House which breathed forth the Genuine principles of Freedom." This new spirit was directed at proprietary rule, "that Monster of arbitrary power swell'd to an enormous size by ye possession of immense wealth." Instead of protecting the people, the Penn family was "with unrelenting Cruelty preying upon the vitals of that excellent & salutary consti-tution of Government establish'd by their Father, Our first worthy Proprietor." Pennsylvania, it seemed to Foulke, must remain "under the Tyrant's foot...untill it shall please Our Gracious Soveraign to interpose & take the Government out of ye Hands of the Proprietaries into his own, which I believe is the wish of every one who retains a Just sense of Freedom."[3]

Relations between the two branches of government by this time had once again bogged down in the perennial disputes over power and money. On February 1, 1764, the Assembly passed a supply bill appropriating £50,000 to fund a 1,000-man force that Pennsylvania had agreed to raise for imperial defense. The money was to be raised by "a Tax on all Estates, Real and personal." Back in 1760 Thomas Penn had conceded that his estates could be taxed, but a sharp dispute now arose over the appropriate rate of taxation. According to some vaguely worded instructions issued by the Privy Council that year, "the Located uncultivated Lands belonging to the Proprietaries shall not be assessed higher than the lowest Rate at which any located uncultivated Lands belonging to the Inhabitants shall be assessed." This language lent itself to contrary interpretations. The Assembly took it to mean that the proprietaries' uncultivated lands, which varied in quality, should not be taxed at a rate *lower* than that charged on land of equivalent quality. The Penns, however, insisted that their uncultivated lands could not be taxed at a rate *higher* than that charged on the poorest wasteland in the province. Insisting that the Assembly's position violated the Privy Council's instructions, John Penn vetoed the supply bill. This decision reinforced a widespread perception that his uncle Thomas was a skinflint and a tyrant.[4]

On February 11 the Assembly passed the militia bill John Penn had requested when the Paxton Boys were approaching Philadelphia the previous week. The militia bill raised a further set of issues, of a nonmonetary kind, which divided the executive and legislative branches. Benjamin Franklin predicted, correctly, that Penn would insist on controlling the appointment of officers, the Assembly would resist, and "so the Bill will probably fall through." Penn returned the bill unsigned on March 12, demanding, as Foulke noted, that "the proprietaries by their Deputy must have ye nominating and appointing all ye officers of the Militia." He also insisted that the militia bill provide for courts-martial empowered to inflict the death penalty. With both the supply bill and the militia bill rejected, Franklin moved to bring the political crisis in Pennsylvania to a head.[5]

Franklin had detested Thomas Penn since meeting him in England in 1757 while working as the Assembly's agent. His antipathy to the proprietary family was heightened by John Penn's arrival in Philadelphia in 1763. The Assembly, he told Dr. John Fothergill, had "receiv'd a Governor of the Proprietary Family with open Arms," offered him "sincere Expressions of Kindness and Respect," and cooperated with him during the Paxton crisis. But Penn, it seemed, was on the side of the Paxton Boys: he had dropped "all Enquiry after the Murderers" and was "answering the Deputies of the Rioters privately." He was busy "Insulting the Assembly without the least Provocation," refusing "several of their Bills, or proposing Amendments needlessly disgusting." As a result, "all Regard for him in the Assembly is lost; all Hopes of Happiness under a Proprietary Government are at an End." Unless the Assembly could secure royal government, Franklin concluded, "we shall soon have no Government at all."[6]

In mid-March the legislators returned the supply bill to Penn unaltered except for an unexplained increase of £5,000. Penn once again rejected the bill, disagreeing with the Assembly over the rate at which proprietary estates would be taxed. Explaining the executive's position, Attorney-General Benjamin Chew bluntly reiterated that the proprietary's uncultivated lands must be assessed at a rate no higher than the rate levied on the poorest lands in the province. Incensed by Chew's intervention, the Assembly appointed a committee to draw up a series of resolves stating the case for royal government. The committee, chaired by Franklin, reported back to the Assembly on March 24 with twenty-six "Resolves," which presented in one document all the Assembly's grievances against the proprietaries—some of long standing and others of recent vintage, some highly specific and others addressing the fundamental question of how Pennsylvania ought to be governed.

The "Resolves" began with an argument that Franklin apparently regarded as the most important issue at stake. It is "the Opinion of this House," the assemblymen stated, "that the Proprietaries of this Province, after having delegated their Powers of Government, can be justly or legally considered in no other Light than as private Owners of Property, without the least Share or constitutional Power of Legislation whatever." In other words, because Thomas Penn was an absentee proprietor who had chosen to rule through deputies, he had relinquished his power to control the legislature, and his lieutenant governors had (or ought to have) full discretion over legislative matters. By prevailing constitutional norms, however, this idea was little more than wishful thinking. To give it some substance, the "Resolves" argued that Penn had caused the "Obstructions and Delays" that hampered Pennsylvania during the French and Indian War and Pontiac's War. It was a "high Presumption in any Subject to interfere between the Crown and the People," they observed, yet "by his private Instructions to a Deputy Governor, enforced by penal Bonds," Penn had prevented "the Crown's receiving, and the Peoples granting, the Supplies required, and necessary for the Defence of His Majesty's Province."[7]

The assemblymen, aware that the Paxton Boys blamed them for the lack of frontier defense, argued that the true fault lay in proprietary land policy. Every time the Penns purchased land from Indians they "located and surveyed the best Tracts of Land for themselves and their Dependants, to lie waste in great Quantities for a future Market." As a result, the frontier was "thinly and scatteringly settled" and "the poor Inhabitants there have been rendered less able to defend themselves, and become a more easy Prey to the small skulking Parties of the Enemy." When the proprietaries made these lands available for purchase they did so "at exorbitant Prices." This policy had driven thousands of families out of Pennsylvania into Maryland, Virginia, and the Carolinas. The ruinous impact of this land policy, the "Resolves" continued, made it all the more unreasonable for the proprietaries to object to paying fair taxes on their land. Again, this was not an especially strong argument; proprietary greed explained frontier settlers' suffering only to a limited extent.[8]

The "Resolves" concluded by addressing the militia bill. The assemblymen denounced John Penn's amendments to the bill, especially his claim to "sole Appointment of the Officers," as arbitrary, unnecessary, and unacceptable. They might be willing "to comply with the same under a Royal Government," but to do so now "would be an Addition to the Proprietary Power, that by no Means can be safely trusted by the People in their Hands." The proposed fines for offenses in the militia, moreover, were "enormously high, and calculated to enslave the good People of this Province." Likewise, Penn's desire to march "any Number of Militia to any Part of the Province, and keeping them there during any Time, at Pleasure," was a power too great to "safely be trusted in the Hands of the Proprietary Governor." And the proposed courts-martial might be used as "a destructive Engine of Proprietary Power."[9]

The answer to Pennsylvania's problems, according to the "Resolves," was royal government. Otherwise the proprietaries' control over executive power and landed property would eventually "become as dangerous to the Prerogatives of the Crown as to the Liberties of the People." The Assembly therefore recommended that Pennsylvania's government "be separated from the Power attending the immense Property, and lodged, where only it can be properly and safely lodged, in the Hands of the Crown." Franklin's *Pennsylvania Gazette* printed the "Resolves," along with the recent exchanges between the Assembly and John Penn. Franklin arranged for the publication and distribution of an additional 3,000 copies of the "Resolves" along with his broadside *Explanatory Remarks on the Assembly's Resolves*. On March 24, having approved the "Resolves," the legislators adjourned for seven weeks "in order to consult their Constituents." Their ostensible purpose was to decide whether the Assembly should send a petition to the king asking him to take over the government of Pennsylvania. But that was a foregone conclusion by now. In reality, Franklin and his supporters were launching a political campaign that would culminate in the October elections, which served in effect as a referendum on the question of royal government.[10]

The Paxton crisis produced some strange political alignments in Pennsylvania. On one side was the Quaker party in the Assembly, led by the non-Quaker Benjamin Franklin. On the other was the largely Anglican proprietary or "gentleman's" party, which found itself in uneasy alliance with an emerging Presbyterian faction based in the western counties and Philadelphia. John Penn's critics saw in this "new ticket" a possible explanation of why he was so timid in his pursuit of the Paxton Boys. The members of the Quaker party, meanwhile, condemned by their Presbyterian critics as a self-interested oligarchy, presented themselves as the people's champions against proprietary tyranny and greed. Yet their proposed solution, monarchy, was a more ancient and powerful form of hereditary privilege. Two of the Quaker party's leaders, moreover, John Dickinson and Isaac Norris, opposed the movement for royal government, as did Israel Pemberton Jr. They were afraid that under monarchical rule Pennsylvanians might lose the religious and civil liberties guaranteed by the Charter of 1701.[11]

On April 12 Franklin published his principal contribution to the debate, *Cool Thoughts on the Present Situation of Our Public Affairs.* Along with the "Resolves," *Cool Thoughts* was the most influential argument published in favor of royal government. Franklin set out to explain the advantages that would come with monarchical rule and to dispel the doubts of those who were ambivalent. Proprietary government in itself, and not just the officials who happened to administer it in Pennsylvania, was the problem. "Disputes of the same Kind have arisen in ALL Proprietary Governments," Franklin noted, "and subsisted till their Dissolution." Among the many problems he saw as inherent to proprietary rule, the corruption of public responsibility by private gain was foremost. "Proprietaries must have a Multitude of private Accounts and Dealings with almost all the People of their Provinces, either for Purchase-money or Quit-rents," Franklin wrote. "Dealings often occasion Differences, and Differences produce mutual Opinions of Injustice."[12]

For Franklin nothing demonstrated the bankruptcy of proprietary rule better than the Paxton affair. "The Government that ought to keep all in Order, is itself weak, and has scarce Authority enough to keep the common Peace," he

wrote. "Mobs assemble and kill (we scarce dare say *murder*) Numbers of innocent People in cold Blood, who were under the Protection of the Government."
Proclamations against the perpetrators were "treated with the utmost Indignity
and Contempt. Not a Magistrate dares wag a Finger towards discovering or
apprehending the *Delinquents*, (we must not call them *Murderers*)." When the
Paxton Boys assembled and marched on the capital, the government called
"aloud on the sober Inhabitants to come with Arms to its Assistance," yet
those who rose to this challenge—Franklin had in mind men like the Quaker
dissident Edward Pennington—were "daily libell'd, abus'd, and menac'd by its
Partizans for so doing."[13]

Franklin's *Cool Thoughts* offered reassuring words to those who feared royal
government was too drastic a proposal. Pennsylvanians, he insisted, would not
lose their "Liberty of Conscience and the Privileges of Dissenters." Royal rule
would not entail Anglican bishops and tithes, or a standing army, all of which
were more likely to be introduced under the present system of proprietary government. "The expression, *Change of Government*, seems, indeed, to be too
extensive; and is apt to give the Idea of a general and total Change of our Laws
and Constitution," Franklin wrote. "It is rather and only a *Change of Governor*,
that is, instead of self-interested Proprietaries, a gracious King!" Franklin ended
his *Cool Thoughts* with a novel call for unity, given his long record of hostility
to Presbyterians and Germans. "We are chiefly People of *three Countries*," he
wrote: English, Irish, and German. Pennsylvania's English population, originating in a land marked by liberty, "can no longer bear the Treatment they have
received," and "the Irish and Germans have felt too severely the Oppressions of
hard-hearted Landlords and *arbitrary Princes*, to wish to see, in the Proprietaries
of Pennsylvania, both the one and the other united."[14]

The Assembly's six-week recess came to an end in mid-May. For ten days,
the legislators considered petitions in favor of royal government from various
inhabitants of Pennsylvania. On May 23 they appointed a committee to draw
up a petition from the Assembly for presentation to the king. The committee
was well balanced, with representatives from seven of the eight Pennsylvania
counties (all except York). Franklin, representing the city of Philadelphia, wrote
the first draft of the petition with assistance from his friend Joseph Galloway,
who represented Philadelphia County. They faced strong opposition within the
Quaker party from John Dickinson, who delivered a long written speech arguing his case that royal government would endanger the religious and political
liberties long enjoyed by Quakers and other residents of Pennsylvania. Galloway
delivered a rejoinder in defense of the committee's petition.[15]

John Dickinson (1732–1808). Portrait by Horace Carpenter, 1922, after an original by Charles Wilson Peale, 1770. Courtesy of Dickinson College.

Isaac Norris, speaker of the Assembly for the previous fourteen years, also disagreed with Franklin's plan. Like Dickinson, he believed royal government would endanger religious liberties; he also feared it would undermine the powers William Penn had granted to the Assembly. On the eve of the vote on whether to submit the Assembly's petition to the king, Norris requested and received permission to express his opinion and have it entered into the minutes the following day. Overnight, however, he decided to resign on grounds of ill health. "Be pleased to inform the House," he instructed the clerk of the Assembly, "that my Attendance through this and the last Week has proved

Isaac Norris (1701–1766). Portrait. Record ID 20040427003. Courtesy of Collections of the University of Pennsylvania Archives.

too much for my Constitution, and particularly the long Sitting of Yesterday, and the bad Night I have had in Consequence of it." Norris announced his indefinite withdrawal from the House, and the Assembly unanimously chose Franklin to replace him as speaker.[16]

With Franklin in the chair, the Assembly approved a petition for royal government in Pennsylvania. The petition paid more attention to the breakdown of social and political order due to the Paxton affair than to any other issue. The lack of respect for proprietary rule "in the Minds of the common People," it stated, rendered the current government "unable to support its own

Authority in a Degree sufficient to maintain the common internal Peace of the Province." The incompetence of the Penns had encouraged the recent "Great Riots," with "armed Mobs marching from Place to Place, and committing violent Outrages and Insults on the Government with Impunity to the great Terror of your Majesty's Subjects." The Assembly therefore requested that the Crown "resume the Government of this Province." The petition was signed by Benjamin Franklin.[17]

Franklin soon became the target of an unprecedented smear campaign. His enemies accused him of more than the usual vanity, ambition, and self-promotion. They mocked his humble beginnings, belittled his scientific accomplishments, and accused him of corruption and venality in his role as the Assembly's agent in England. They claimed he had a secret agenda to install himself as the first royal governor of Pennsylvania. They unearthed some criticisms of Germans he had written back in 1751. And in a relentless attack on his personal morality and sexual proclivities, they repeatedly brought up the matter of his illegitimate son.[18]

One of the most extreme attacks came from Hugh Williamson, author of the pro-Paxton pamphlet *The Plain Dealer*. Williamson's *What is sauce for a Goose is also sauce for a Gander* took the form of an eight-page "Epitaph," laid out in the form of words on a tombstone, for the "the much esteem'd Memory of B———F———Esq." Franklin had once published a piece complaining, as Williamson put it, " 'That so many *Palatine Boors* are suffered to swarm into our Settlements, and by *herding* together establish their Language and Manners.' " If his tyrannical plan to topple the government was accomplished, this bigoted principle might be extended to "dispossess the People of / Their CHARTER RIGHTS, / And inestimable Privileges." Williamson concluded with a vicious attack on Franklin for his treatment of his illegitimate son's foster mother. Anti-Paxton pamphleteers occasionally responded in kind, with Isaac Hunt's *A humble attempt at scurrility* being especially vituperative. Their efforts, however, did little to help Franklin's cause.[19]

Franklin was worried about the October elections. His *Narrative*, as he noted on September 1, had produced a vast "Number of bitter Enemies" among "the Irish Presbyterians." If the proprietary party emerged victorious in October, Franklin concluded, "Behold me a Londoner for the rest of my Days." Although there had been no Indian raids in Pennsylvania for almost a year, Pontiac's War was still in progress. Pennsylvania declared war on the Delawares and Shawnees on July 7, 1764, which helped the proprietary party. As a wartime leader John Penn could present himself as champion of the frontiersmen's interests. The declaration of war included bounties for Indian scalps—the only grievance of the Paxton Boys redressed before the American Revolution.[20]

Franklin's worst fears about the elections came true. With heavy Ulster Presbyterian and German support, the "new ticket" won eleven of the thirty-six seats in the Assembly. The Quaker party retained all sixteen seats from Bucks and Chester Counties, and five of the eight for Philadelphia County, but Franklin and Galloway lost their seats. On October 26 the Assembly voted to send Franklin to London to present the petition for royal government. The new ticket proved short-lived, but Presbyterians had become an important force in Pennsylvania politics. They consolidated their position in 1765 by opposing the Stamp Act, while the Quaker party, including Franklin from afar, once again misread the political climate. The Quaker party remained resilient, however, with Galloway defeating Dickinson in the Assembly elections in Philadelphia County in 1765 and serving as speaker of the Assembly for the next ten years. Franklin presented the Assembly's petition for royal government in November 1765, but the Privy Council dismissed it the same month. Thereafter an emerging Presbyterian party led by Dickinson and Charles Thomson constituted the main opposition in the Assembly. By the end of the decade it had eclipsed both the Quaker party and the proprietary party. Thomson's faction of the Presbyterian party led the movement toward independence in Pennsylvania in the early 1770s. When Benjamin Franklin returned to Philadelphia at the outbreak of the American Revolution he found himself with some unexpected political allies.[21]

FIVE

UNRAVELING

CHAPTER 20
KILLERS

In the aftermath of the Paxton affair social order on the Pennsylvania frontier disintegrated. With no effective means of law enforcement much of the frontier was ungovernable. Indian affairs were in disarray. The boundary line set by royal proclamation in 1763 had little effect in stemming the westward tide of migration and the seizure of Indian lands. The provincial government had lost control over the aggressive vanguard of Ulster settlers in the lower Susquehanna Valley. In the Assembly, leaders of the still dominant Quaker party insisted that the chaos on the frontier arose directly from John Penn's failure to pursue the Paxton Boys. They had not been investigated, let alone arrested, tried, or punished; they were free, it seemed, to do as they pleased, and the lesson was not lost on other western settlers.[1]

The breakdown in social order was nowhere more evident than in the "Black Boy" disturbances that began in March 1765, when a group of vigilantes attacked a wagon train carrying goods from Philadelphia to Fort Pitt. The incident took place at Sideling Hill, in the part of southwestern Cumberland County where squatters were evicted in 1750 and Shingas launched a devastating attack in 1755. The region had long been marked by antipathy to Indians and to the provincial government. The goods intercepted at Sideling Hill were being shipped by the Philadelphia firm of Baynton, Wharton, & Morgan for use in the Indian trade. They included "blankets, shirts, vermillion, lead, beads, wampum, tomahawks, scalping knives," and liquor. Because the attackers blackened their faces, they became known as the Black Boys. They were led by James Smith, who had been captured by Delaware Indians in 1755 while participating in Braddock's march. When Smith returned to his home in the Conococheague Valley in Cumberland County after five years in captivity, he recalled in his memoir, the people "received me with great joy, but were surprized to see me so much like an Indian, both in my gait and gesture."[2]

European settlers, having been driven out by the French and Indian War, returned to the Conococheague Valley in the early 1760s, only to be forced out again by Pontiac's War. Despairing of receiving assistance from the Assembly, a local committee took up a subscription and appointed James Smith captain of a company of Rangers. "As we enlisted our men," he recalled, "we dressed them uniformly in the Indian manner, with breech-clouts, leggins, mockesons, and green shrouds, which we wore in the same manner that the Indians do." The Rangers wore red handkerchiefs instead of hats and painted their faces "red and black, like Indian warriors." Smith participated in John Armstrong's raid against Great Island in October 1763 and fought against the Ohio country Delawares in 1764. The following year, with Pontiac's War at an end, he gathered ten of his "old warriors." They "blacked and painted" themselves "as usual" and attacked the wagon train at Sideling Hill.[3]

The day after the attack Lieutenant Charles Grant, the commandant of the 42nd Highland (Black Watch) Regiment at nearby Fort Loudoun, dispatched a patrol led by Sergeant Leonard McGlashan to salvage the remaining goods. About fifty frontiersmen surrounded McGlashan, demanding the release of two of their comrades who had been captured at Sideling Hill. McGlashan responded by taking several more of Smith's men prisoner and seizing eight rifles before returning to the fort. On March 9 the Black Boys marched on Fort Loudoun, demanding that the prisoners be released rather than transferred to Carlisle for trial, and captured several British soldiers outside the fort. Grant agreed to an exchange of prisoners, though he refused to return any weapons. After the Black Boys dispersed, a few arrest warrants were issued, but to no avail. Bills of indictment presented to the grand jury in Carlisle were returned for lack of testimony.[4]

The Black Boys resurfaced on a larger and more threatening scale in May. When a trader named Joseph Spears arrived at Fort Loudoun with goods and liquor to supply the garrison, James Smith suspected that some or all of these items were intended for the Indian trade. Spears deposited his stock at the fort, but as his drivers were leading their horses into the woods to forage "they were attacked by about thirty of the Rioters in disguise, with their faces blacked, who tied them up and flogged them severely, Killed five of their horses, wounded two more, and burnt all their Saddles." When Grant sent McGlashan and twelve soldiers into the woods to rescue the drivers, the Black Boys fired on the soldiers, who returned fire and wounded one of the "rioters" in the thigh. Smith's brother William, a justice of the peace, responded by issuing a warrant for McGlashan's arrest on charges of shooting a civilian.

In the coming weeks the Black Boys repeatedly demanded to inspect Spears's goods and Grant repeatedly denied their request. They warned that no future "Communication of goods would be safe unless it had their blessing."[5]

On May 28 five Black Boys led by Smith kidnapped Charles Grant as he "was taking the air on Horseback, and about half a mile from his post." When Smith ordered that they "shoot the Bougar...one of them fired at him, which frightned his horse, who run into the Bushes, & occasioned his being thrown upon the Ground." The Black Boys disarmed Grant, tied him to a tree, and threatened to leave him there to die unless he returned the weapons taken "from the first party of Rioters that appeared at his post" in March. Smith and his companions kept Grant in the woods overnight. The next morning the lieutenant signed a bond of £40 guaranteeing that he would return the Black Boys' muskets, a commitment he refused to honor when he returned to Fort Loudoun.[6]

The commander in chief of British forces in North America, Thomas Gage, was alarmed by the Black Boy disturbances. He wrote to John Penn from New York on June 2 "concerning the Proceedings of the Inhabitants of Cumberland County, who appear daily in Arms, and seem to be in an actual State of Rebellion." Gage warned that if the king's troops were fired upon and their forts threatened, the troops would retaliate and he would not "answer for the Consequences." The general also enclosed "a copy of a very singular Advertisement," posted by the Black Boys near Fort Loudoun, claiming that Penn was on their side. This "advertisement" called on all "our Loyal Voluntiers," and those not yet enlisted, to come "to our Town and come to our Tavern and fill your Belly's with Liquor and your Mouth with swearing, and you will have your pass, but if not, your Back must [be] whipt & your mouth be gagged." The Black Boys declared that even if they "Whip'd or Hang'd" Grant and the other officers at Fort Loudoun, Penn would pardon their crimes and the clergy would grant them absolution, "for we have Law and Government in our hands & we have a large sum of money raised for our Support." The notice ended with the belligerent coda, "God Bless our brave loyal Volunteers, and success to our Hellstown."[7]

Penn responded to Gage's warnings by issuing a proclamation condemning the Black Boys and proscribing unlicensed participation in the Indian trade. The royal proclamation of October 1763 required all Indian traders to receive a license from their colonial governor. Licenses were free but revocable if traders ignored or broke regulations. Penn's proclamation warned against disrupting authorized traders and condemned those men who "assembled themselves in armed Bodies on the Western Frontiers of this Province, and have, in a most riotous and illegal manner, presumed to interrupt the passage of all kinds of Goods to Fort Pitt, by which the Garrison there has been greatly distressed." As bands of these ruffians were reportedly planning another attack, he ordered that they desist and disperse, or they would "answer the Contrary at their peril." Penn instructed local magistrates and sheriffs to take measures to suppress "riots, tumults, and disorderly proceedings, tending to disturb the peace & quiet of his Majesty's Subjects" and to discover and arrest those involved.[8]

The proclamation had no effect. On June 27 Penn wrote to the magistrates of Cumberland County warning them that if they did not restore stability, he would "be under the disagreeable necessity" of applying for the assistance of British troops to enforce the law. That same day he wrote to Justice William Smith at Conococheague, informing him that he was accused of "having encouraged and protected the rioters in Cumberland County, in their illegal and disorderly proceedings" and of making his house "their place of Rendezvous." He ordered Smith to come to Philadelphia to answer these charges. And he wrote to Gage explaining his efforts to bring the Black Boys to justice and strenuously denying the "Villanously false & scandalous" accusations in the "Advertisement" the general had sent him, which he attributed to the machinations of the Quaker party.[9]

The Black Boys reemerged in an even more defiant mood in November 1765, when Smith and about 100 of his men surrounded Fort Loudoun in an attempt to capture Grant and McGlashan. They fired continuously at the soldiers inside the fort until Grant, lacking ammunition, agreed to their demands and turned over the weapons he had confiscated in March. On the following day the Black Watch Regiment was transferred from Fort Loudoun to Fort Bedford, defusing the animosity between Grant and Smith that lay at the heart of the dispute. The regiment's departure brought the violence to an end, though from Gage's perspective the matter was far from resolved: the Black Boys had attacked a British fort and must be held accountable. John Penn, all too aware of the sectional tensions in his province, was in no hurry to pursue them. At Gage's urging he issued a warrant for the arrest of James Smith, along with a writ to remove his brother William from office. But, like the Paxton Boys, none of the Black Boys was arrested or prosecuted.[10]

Having failed to act decisively in response to the Conestoga massacres in 1763 the Pennsylvania government had lost control over the frontier. Yet the chaos was not entirely to the disadvantage of the proprietary party. In the short term the collapse of order played into the hands of the squatters, contrary to the Penns' financial interests; in the longer term, however, the Penn family could only benefit from the presence of a vanguard of European settlers in the trans-Susquehanna west, provided that they did not provoke another Indian war. Penn worked hard at Indian diplomacy throughout the 1760s. But, though he went through the motions of condemning the Paxton Boys and the Black Boys, he did almost nothing to bring them to justice. During the crisis of 1764 the assemblymen feared that he was seeking to displace the Quaker party with an Anglican–Presbyterian alliance. A more plausible and troubling explanation is that the line between official and extralegal colonialism was at times paper thin. Throughout the 1760s the Assembly continued to criticize Penn strenuously for his failure to act against the Paxton Boys.[11]

After the Paxton Boy massacres Penn appointed a Mennonite farmer named Jacob Whisler to take care of Conestoga Manor. In January 1766 Whisler and his assistant, Thomas Fisher, were involved in an altercation with a group of about thirty Paxton Boys who had recently moved onto the Manor and erected makeshift cabins. A young man who called himself "the Captain" demanded "in a very angry, outrageous and menacing manner" to know by whose authority Whisler was acting. When the caretaker replied that "he had the Governor's Commission or Written Order to oversee and take care of the said Land," the young man and several others insisted on seeing these papers. Whisler invited a small delegation to his home, led by "the Captain" and "an Elderly Man."[12]

When the Paxton Boys had finished reading Whisler's papers, they declared that "the said Commission or Orders were good for nothing, and that the Governor had no power to give any such Orders." They insisted that neither John Penn nor the proprietary family had any right to Conestoga Manor "but that it belonged to the Indians who were killed there, and that they (meaning the said Company) had now the best right to it, and would have & keep it in spite of the Governor & the Proprietors." The Paxton Boys claimed the land by right of conquest: Conestoga Indiantown belonged to them because they had exterminated its Indian occupants. At the end of the meeting the "Elderly Man" called Whisler aside and "in a pretended friendly manner advised him by all means to have nothing more to do with the said Land but quit it intirely." If he "did concern himself any farther with it," or if he opposed "the said Company's taking & keeping Possession of it, he might depend upon it, they would do him some great Mischief." The authorities quickly ejected the Paxton Boys from the Manor and dismantled their cabins, but this sort of defiance was once again indicative of the collapse of government authority in the Susquehanna Valley.[13]

On September 23, 1766, seeking to restore some of this lost authority, John Penn issued a proclamation forbidding settlement on unpurchased Indian land. He had received information that "many ill-disposed persons, in express Disobedience of his Majesty's Proclamation and Royal Instructions, and regardless of the rights of the Proprietaries, or the Indians in Alliance with the English," had settled "without any Licence or Authority . . . upon Lands within this Province, not yet purchased of the Nations." This practice, Penn warned, "doth greatly tend to irritate the Indians and may again involve us in a War with them, if not put an immediate stop to." He instructed all persons who had made such settlements "immediately to evacuate & abandon them" and prohibited settlers from staking out rights "by marking Trees, or otherwise, beyond the Limits of the last Indian Purchase, within this Province, upon pain of the severest Penalties of the Law." Those who claimed land in this way—by tomahawk right—would be "excluded from the privilege of securing such Settlements, should the Lands, where they shall be made, be hereafter purchased of the Indians." The proclamation ended by singling out a German troublemaker named Frederick Stump, who had settled "beyond the Indian Purchase near to Fort Augusta" without warrant or authority. The proclamation said nothing more about Stump, but he would soon reenter the historical record in one of the most gruesome episodes in Pennsylvania's history.[14]

By January 1768 John Penn was worried that illegal settlers might provoke another Indian war. Declaring the Proclamation of 1763 ineffective, he requested legislation to remove squatters from Indian lands and prevent future unauthorized settlement. Reports were reaching him "from all Quarters (particularly from Sir William Johnson), of the dissatisfaction of the Indians, and their ill disposition towards us." There was "great reason to apprehend an immediate Rupture with them, unless some effectual Means are fallen upon to Pacify them." The assemblymen wanted to avoid an Indian war as much as Penn did, but they took issue with the idea that settlers' encroachments alone could explain the current problems. Several Seneca Indians had recently been murdered "on the Frontiers of this and the neighbouring Provinces," they informed Penn, bringing to mind "those flagrant Breaches of the Laws of Hospitality, and the horrid Acts of Barbarity committed in the Year 1763." The only way to stave off war, they insisted, was to finally bring the Paxton Boys to justice.[15]

For the Assembly, prosecuting the Paxton Boys was essential to the authority of government in Pennsylvania. It would provide "a favorable Opportunity of restoring the Government to its former Power and Dignity, lately so insolently trampled on, and of convincing those Offenders, that altho' Justice may sometimes *Sleep*, it can never *Die*." Only the "dread of exemplary Punishment" would deter others from committing such crimes in the future. But if "Crimes of the first Rank, of the deepest Dye, remain unpunished," frontier settlers would continue "to take Advantage of the Times and the Debility of Government, to commit the like, or other Crimes." The massacres of December 1763, after all, had taken place in open daylight in the presence of many spectators; the Paxton Boys had worn no disguises and their leaders were well known. They had escaped unpunished then, but they could easily be prosecuted now.[16]

With fears of a new Indian war intensifying, the timing of what happened next could not have been worse. On January 19 a magistrate named William Blyth appeared before John Penn and the Council and told them about an incident that had just taken place in Cumberland County. A party of four Indian men and two Indian women had visited Frederick Stump, the German settler cited by Penn in his proclamation in 1766, at his home on Middle Creek. Stump, becoming "apprehensive that they intended to do him some Mischief," waited for his visitors to become drunk and then killed all six. He dragged the bodies "down to a Creek near his House, made a hole in the Ice, and threw them in." The next day he traveled about fourteen miles up Middle Creek to the Indians' home, accompanied by a nineteen-year-old servant named John Ironcutter (Eisenhauer in German). There, in two cabins, they found "One Woman, two Girls and one Child," whom they killed "in order to prevent their carrying intelligence of the Death of the other Indians." They then set fire to the cabins with the four bodies inside. Stump freely admitted all of these details to Blyth.[17]

Penn ordered inquests "on the Bodies of all the said Indians that can be found," followed by proper burials. He issued a proclamation offering a reward of £200 for the arrest and conviction of Stump and wrote to Sir William Johnson, asking him to break the news of the Stump affair to the Six Nations in a way that distinguished between "the Acts of private Individuals and those of Government." He also sent messages to the relatives of the dead Indians, including some local Senecas and the Delawares at Wyalusing and Great Island, assuring them that Pennsylvania wished to "keep the Chain of Friendship entire and bright, notwithstanding this Accident." Penn's principal concern was that "so horrid a Crime," if left unpunished, would "certainly involve us again in all the Calamities of an Indian War."[18]

As the most powerful man in Carlisle, John Armstrong had a considerable stake in the Stump affair. Armstrong generally leaned toward the proprietary side, but he was no mere functionary of the Penn family. Although he had opposed royal government in 1764, he also insisted to an incredulous John Penn that nobody in Cumberland County was involved in the Conestoga massacres. Armstrong clashed frequently with Penn, and the Stump affair was no exception. On January 24, 1768, he reported a breakthrough in the Stump case, but he also sounded a note of caution. Stump and Ironcutter, he revealed, had been captured three days earlier by Captain William Patterson, who in 1763 had murdered three Moravian Indians in cold blood. Now, however, Patterson had assembled a posse of twenty paid men to capture the Indian killers Stump and Ironcutter, whom he turned over to Sheriff John Holmes in Carlisle. Stump readily admitted killing nine of the Indians and Ironcutter the tenth. Several settler families had already "fled the region for fear of Indian reprisals," Armstrong added, though he hoped the arrests would diminish the risk of enemy attacks. Yet the capture of Stump and Ironcutter, he warned, by no means guaranteed that they would be brought to justice. Western settlers were demanding that they be tried in Carlisle rather than Philadelphia.[19]

Like the Paxton Boys in 1764, frontier settlers in Cumberland County insisted that local trials were a basic right under English law. Armstrong also had a practical objection to sending Stump and Ironcutter across Pennsylvania, which he believed would invite their rescue and endanger the officials escorting them. The provincial authorities, on the other hand, regarded the risk of a rescue as much higher if the prisoners remained in Carlisle. Chief Justice William Allen issued a writ for their transportation to Philadelphia, along with instructions to county officials on the best procedure for transferring them across county lines. Armstrong refused to comply with this order and decided to keep Stump and Ironcutter in Carlisle jail.[20]

Penn was incensed at Armstrong's defiance. On February 2 he warned Sheriff Holmes of the consequences of not complying. The next day he wrote to Armstrong that he was "astonished at the impertinent insolence of those who have taken upon them to Suggest or even to suppose that the Government or Judges intended to do so illegal an Act as to Try the Prisoners in any other County or place than where the Fact was committed." If "inferior Officers of Government" were "with Impunity suffered to controul or counteract the Proceedings of their Superiors," he warned, "there will not only be an end of all Subordination and Order, but of Government itself."[21]

What Penn did not know as he was writing to Armstrong was that Stump and Ironcutter had already escaped. On the morning of January 29 a group of some eighty armed men broke into Carlisle jail and freed the prisoners. When he learned of the rescue from Armstrong, Penn sent a forceful reply. The sole purpose of bringing Stump and Ironcutter to Philadelphia, he insisted, was "that the Chief Justice himself might have the Examination of them in a matter of such Consequence." The government had never intended to try them outside their proper county. In Philadelphia the prisoners would have been "out of the Reach of any attempts to rescue them, which their Friends or Abettors might be disposed to make, till the Time of their Trial." Penn concluded by offering an olive branch: if the rescuers returned Stump and Ironcutter to custody and admitted their mistaken sense of the government's intentions they might still be treated leniently. If they resisted, Armstrong was to take all necessary measures against them. He and his fellow magistrates had witnessed the escape; they must know who was responsible, and they were obligated to avenge "this most daring Insult upon the Laws of the Country."[22]

The "Laws of the Country" were especially vulnerable to insult in Cumberland County at this time. The Assembly continued to insist that the root of the problem lay in Penn's failure to prosecute the Paxton Boys, which had given carte blanche to Indian killers. The only way to redress Indians' grievances, the assemblymen informed Penn, was to prosecute the culprits. All that Penn had done in the aftermath of the Conestoga massacres, they complained, was to write letters and issue proclamations, which were "treated with the utmost contempt." He had dismissed the Assembly's request that the local sheriff, coroners, and magistrates be brought to Philadelphia for interrogation. The legislators demanded that Penn reissue his proclamations against the Paxton Boys, increase the reward to £500 or more, call witnesses to Philadelphia, and thereby begin to restore the tattered reputation of government.[23]

Penn responded to this "indecent and unbecoming" message by insisting that the Paxton affair had no relevance to the current discontent, which he continued to blame on settlers' aggressive incursions onto Indian lands. He also claimed that any measures beyond the ones he had taken in 1763–1764 would have exceeded his executive powers. If these measures were the best the executive could do, the assemblymen responded, "every Impartial Person must be convinced that the Powers of Government, vested in the feeble Hands of a Proprietary Governor, are too weak to support Order in the Province, or give Safety to the People."[24]

Despite the vehemence of Penn's objections, there was undoubtedly a connection between the Paxton Boys and the wider pattern of violence on the frontier in the 1760s. Indeed, Penn himself left evidence to suggest that the Paxton Boys had not simply inspired the rescue of Stump and Ironcutter but had participated in the event. In March 1770, two years after the Stump affair, he told his uncle Thomas that some of "those who murdered the Indians at Lancaster" had "rescued Stump out of Carlisle Gaol." This admission, had Penn made it publicly, would have strongly reinforced the Assembly's position. But Penn included it only in a private letter and never publicly acknowledged a connection between the Paxton Boys and the wave of violence that followed his failure to pursue them. Nor did any corroborating evidence on this point survive.[25]

Throughout February 1768 Penn awaited word of Stump and Ironcutter. Seeking to explain why the prisoners had been freed, Armstrong informed Penn on February 7 that settlers in Cumberland County objected to a double standard. They believed the provincial government treated the murder of Indians with the utmost gravity but left the murder of settlers by Indians unpunished. They had freed the prisoners, Armstrong told Penn, because they opposed the idea that "White Men" should be executed for killing Indians "when War is expected." Armstrong reported that Stump had returned to his father's place at Tulpehocken, that Ironcutter might also be there, and that the pair were likely to flee to "some back part of Virginia" if they had not already done so. Penn issued a proclamation on March 16 offering a reward of £200 for the arrest and conviction of Stump and £100 for Ironcutter, but to no avail.[26]

Aware that the killers would probably not be captured, Penn had already summoned John Armstrong and John Holmes to Philadelphia to appear before the Council. The two men came to town in March to relate the circumstances of Stump's detention and escape. Finding some discrepancies between their stories, the Council ordered that they return in May with two additional magistrates. On May 12 these four men appeared before the Council. John Penn ruled that they had obstructed justice by jailing Stump and Ironcutter rather than conveying them to Philadelphia. But he conceded that they had done so because they feared the prisoners might be freed by a mob acting under the illusion that the trial would take place in Philadelphia. As their violation of the chief justice's instructions was therefore born of necessity rather than a desire to abet the prisoners' escape, Penn dismissed the four men with a mild admonishment that they confine themselves to matters within their own jurisdiction. With this slap on the wrist the Stump affair was closed.[27]

The Council's investigation of Armstrong and his fellow magistrates offered a partial response to the Assembly's accusations that the executive branch was indifferent or impotent in the face of frontier outrages. But John Penn was less concerned with mollifying the Assembly than with seeking conciliation on the larger stage of Indian diplomacy. On February 18 he wrote to Sir William Johnson apprising him of the measures he had taken in response to the Stump affair and informing him that Pennsylvania would provide £2,500 in condolence money for the Six Nations and the Ohio country Delawares and Shawnees. Johnson was to distribute some of these funds to the Iroquois at Johnson Hall, and his deputy, George Croghan, would distribute the rest to the Delawares and Shawnees at a conference at Fort Pitt.[28]

On February 22 Penn wrote to the Delawares, Shawnees, and Iroquois of the Ohio country about the Stump affair "and the regret of the Governor of his people therefore." He asked the Indians to "be sensible that there are bad and foolish Men of all Nations, whom at Times, the Evil Spirit gets the better of, and tempts to Murder their most intimate Friends, and even Relations, in order to disturb the Peace and Tranquility of their Neighbors." These men, he assured the Ohio country Indians, had no connection with the Pennsylvania government, which was determined to punish them severely. This letter was to be read aloud at the Fort Pitt conference in April.[29]

Penn also issued a proclamation, backed up by legislation recently passed by the Assembly, to further allay the concerns of the Ohio country Indians. The proclamation provided "immediate Measures for the removal of the Settlers on the Indian lands." As stipulated by the Assembly, all people settled on unpurchased Indian lands were required to evacuate; if they chose not to do so, or if they returned to land they abandoned and were "thereof legally convicted by their own Confession, or the Verdict of a Jury," they would "suffer Death without the Benefit of Clergy." Penn gave the settlers until May 1 to leave; those who remained on the land by the end of May would face the full penalty of the law. Two hundred fifty copies of this proclamation were printed, mainly for distribution in Cumberland County.[30]

Penn then turned his attention to the Iroquois, asking Sir William Johnson to meet with representatives of the Six Nations at Johnson Hall in March 1768. This meeting "produced a much more favourable Disposition" among the Iroquois, Johnson reported, even if it did not "remove their discontent totally." Johnson reminded the Iroquois that Penn had issued proclamations and offered rewards and that the Assembly had passed "some good Laws for your Benefit." He revealed that Pennsylvania had donated £2,500 by way of recompense and presented £1,300 of this sum "as a Testimony of their Love, to remove your Grief." Johnson then offered the Iroquois a belt of wampum sent by Penn that would bury "the Axe under the Roots of the Tree, clearing your Sight and your hearing, and removing all Cause of uneasiness from your Heart." This uneasiness, he acknowledged, had arisen not only "on Account of those lately Murdered," but also because of "those unhappy People who were murdered there 5 years ago," the Conestoga Indians. The Crown's superintendent of Indian affairs thereby confirmed the Assembly's position on a point that Penn stubbornly refused to concede.[31]

At Fort Pitt in April the Pennsylvania delegates John Allen and Joseph Shippen read aloud the letter Penn had sent to the Ohio country Indians, along with a second message from Penn stating that Johnson had already conferred with the Iroquois. Allen and Shippen presented a string of wampum to "gather up the Bones of all our dead Friends, and bury them in the Earth, that they may be no more seen." They then presented a large white belt "to clean the Blood off the Leaves and Earth whereon it was sprinkled, that the sweet Herbs which come through the Earth may have their usual Verdure, and that we may all forget the unhappy Accidents that have happened." To conclude the ceremony, they presented a belt of eleven rows, representing "the Chain of Friendship that Subsists between us." The Ohio country Indians, among them the Delaware leader Tamaqua, accepted the condolences and "rejoiced that the Chain of Friendship is now brightened by our Brother the Governor of Pennsylvania." By 1768, however, that chain was broken almost beyond repair. Pondering the condition of the frontier from Philadelphia, Penn's critics in the Assembly pinned their hopes on an imperial solution.[32]

CHAPTER 21

MERCENARIES

More than 2,000 representatives of the Iroquois, Delawares, Shawnees, and other Indian nations assembled at Fort Stanwix in New York at the end of October 1768. Sir William Johnson presided over the largest and most important Indian conference in American colonial history. Pennsylvania sent a high-powered delegation, including John Penn, Attorney-General Benjamin Chew, and former provincial secretary Richard Peters, whose knowledge of Pennsylvania's land transactions was unrivaled. The governments of New Jersey and Virginia also sent delegates. The resulting treaty, signed on November 5 by representatives of each of the Six Nations, pushed the boundary set by royal proclamation in 1763 considerably to the west. The Iroquois received land in New York in return; the Delawares, Shawnees, and Mingoes of the Ohio country, who lived in the territory ceded by the Iroquois, had no say in the matter. In a separate transaction Thomas Penn paid the Six Nations £10,000 for all land in his province not previously deeded to the proprietary family. Under the terms of this "New Purchase," he reacquired most of the Ohio country. Once again, the Indians who lived in the region were not consulted. After Fort Stanwix, European settlement formally penetrated beyond the Allegheny Mountains on a large and permanent scale.[1]

As part of the New Purchase, Thomas Penn also acquired the sacred lands in the Wyoming Valley and the Shamokin area that the Six Nations had vowed never to sell. The Penns moved quickly to develop the valley. In December 1768, while the Fort Stanwix conference was still in session, John Penn authorized the laying out of three new proprietary manors: Sunbury and Stoke in the Wyoming Valley and Pomfret in the Shamokin area. He hired two land speculators from New Jersey, Amos Ogden and Charles Stewart, who agreed to bring in settlers, run a trading post at Wyoming, and defend the valley against intruders from Connecticut, in return for generous land grants. Other speculators and proprietary favorites received similar rewards. Before opening the New Purchase to public sales in April 1769 the land office made forty-six grants in the Wyoming Valley, some of them for as much as 5,000 acres. This behind-the-scenes favoritism aggravated the perennially land-hungry settlers on the Pennsylvania frontier. Edmund Physick, the receiver-general of Pennsylvania, reported from Lancaster County that Ulster settlers in particular were angered by the allotment of large portions of the New Purchase to speculators and outsiders.[2]

The Penns believed that the Fort Stanwix settlement had resolved the Wyoming question, but the directors of the Susquehannah Company interpreted the treaty quite differently. By including Wyoming as part of the New Purchase, the Iroquois had once again repudiated the Susquehannah Company's claim to the valley, which was based on the fraudulent Lydius deed of 1754. But the Wyoming Valley, as the Company pointed out, stood well to the east of the revised boundary established in 1768. Sending settlers into the valley, therefore, would not violate the boundary line set at Fort Stanwix. Nor would it violate the boundary set by royal proclamation in 1763, the Company argued, as the treaty of 1768 had superseded this decree. The Company also claimed that the Fort Stanwix treaty had nullified the Privy Council's order of June 15, 1763, ordering the removal of Connecticut settlers from the Wyoming Valley. Meeting in Hartford at the end of December 1768, the directors therefore voted to send forty settlers to the valley by February, with 200 more to join them in the spring.[3]

At the end of March, just before the New Purchase was opened to the public, a group of Pennsylvania's "Back-Inhabitants" sent a petition to John Penn protesting the advance sales in the Wyoming Valley. The settlers reminded Penn that they had "long laboured under the great difficulty of a long tedious Indian War, being Fronteirs and straitly bounded, enjoying but small Tracts of land & mostly Barrening Ground." With the "late purchase made from the Indian Tribes" they had initially hoped that Providence had "opened a Door for the relief of the poor people." But now they had begun to realize that they would not benefit from the New Purchase, "as the whole of the best of the said purchase betwixt Military Officers and other private Gentlemen is wholly taken up." Among the sixty-three signatories was Lazarus Stewart, the ringleader of the Paxton Boys, who had not been heard from since leading the massacre at Lancaster workhouse in December 1763.[4]

Amos Ogden and Charles Stewart arrived in the Wyoming Valley early in January 1769. Together with Sheriff John Jennings of Northampton County, they took possession of the blockhouse and huts at Mill Creek left behind by Connecticut settlers and began to construct a more durable structure nearby, which became known as Fort Ogden. In February the first forty settlers authorized by the Susquehannah Company arrived. John Penn responded to the Connecticut incursion with a forceful letter to his counterpart in Hartford, William Pitkin. The "adventurers" sent out by the Susquehannah Company, he told Governor Pitkin, "have the Countenance of your Government in their very unjust and illegal Undertaking." The area they were seeking to settle lay within the charter of Pennsylvania, he insisted, and the Lydius purchase was spurious. "It is well known," Penn reminded Pitkin, "that the Indians never sell their Rights but in public Council, and it cannot be pretended that any Deeds made to the People of Connecticut were attended with that solemnity." The so-called purchase of 1754, he insisted, was "always looked upon by the Six Nations as private and fraudulent, and inconsistent with their prior Engagements to the proprietaries of Pennsylvania." It had provoked the eastern Delawares to attack Pennsylvania at the outset of the French and Indian War; with the diplomatic damage caused by the Frederick Stump affair barely contained, renewed incursions by Connecticut settlers could only antagonize the Indians once again.[5]

As the dispute between Pennsylvania and Connecticut intensified, both sides needed men on the ground to consolidate their claim. At a meeting in April the Susquehannah Company directors urged the 200 settlers authorized in December to proceed immediately to the Wyoming Valley. Charles Stewart wrote to John Penn from Stoke Manor on May 12, "One hundred and forty-six New England Men, and others, chiefly on Horseback, passed by our Houses, and are now encamped on the East Side of the River." At least as many more, Stewart reported, were expected the next day. Those he had seen that afternoon were "almost all armed and fit for Mischief." They planned to cross over to the west bank of the river's north branch, where Connecticut settlers had not yet established a foothold.[6]

The new wave of settlers was led by forty year-old Major John Durkee, a veteran of the French and Indian War and an influential figure in Connecticut politics. As a counter to Fort Ogden, the newcomers erected fortified log houses surrounded by a stockade, naming the compound Fort Durkee. They proceeded to lay out the town of Wilkes-Barré at the site of Teedyuscung's old home, Wyoming. On August 29, 1769, Durkee and 170 other residents of Wilkes-Barré signed a petition to the Connecticut legislature requesting the establishment of a new county in the Wyoming Valley.[7]

In November 1769 Pennsylvania launched a counterattack against the Connecticut settlers. Colonel Turbutt Francis, one of the proprietary favorites who received an early land grant in the Wyoming Valley, arrived in the valley on November 8 with twenty men and a four-pounder cannon to reinforce Amos Ogden and Sheriff John Jennings. On November 11 Pennsylvania forces captured a number of Connecticut settlers outside Fort Durkee, including John Durkee. When Ogden and Jennings approached the fort with a posse of as many as 200 men backed up by Francis's firepower, the Connecticut settlers agreed to sign articles of capitulation. Most of the settlers were expelled from the Wyoming Valley, though a few were permitted to stay pending a decision on the territorial dispute by the Privy Council in England. The Pennsylvania forces established themselves in Fort Ogden.[8]

These events might have terminated the Susquehannah Company's efforts to colonize the Wyoming Valley were it not for a new turn of events in Lancaster County, where resentment against the proprietary government was running higher than ever. Frontier settlers had an accumulation of grievances by this time: the draconian removal policy proclaimed on February 24, 1768; the botched attempt to bring Stump and Ironcutter to face trial in Philadelphia rather than Carlisle; the distribution of the New Purchase lands to favorites, speculators, and outsiders; and the lack of a response to the petition submitted by Lazarus Stewart and others in March 1769. Tapping into this discontent, the Susquehannah Company offered land in the Wyoming Valley to disaffected Pennsylvanians in return for their services. In September 1769 a group of Lancaster County settlers led by a man named Lazarus Young petitioned the Company for a six-square-mile township at a fair price without quitrents, promising to send fifty men to the valley immediately. In December Lazarus Stewart agreed to bring his Paxton Boys to the Wyoming Valley to fight on the Connecticut side.[9]

The Susquehannah Company sent two agents, Zebulon Butler and Ebenezer Backus, to Paxton and Hanover Townships in February 1770 to complete the arrangements with Lazarus Stewart and his men. Stewart's former comrade, Matthew Smith of Paxton town, opposed the initiative, but about forty Paxton Boys set out with Butler and Backus for the Wyoming Valley. They laid siege to Fort Ogden, driving out its occupants on February 23, and proceeded to plunder and destroy the houses of Pennsylvania settlers, including the proprietary agent Charles Stewart. "As I apprehended for a long while, so it has fallen out," John Penn informed his uncle on March 10, "that the Paxton Boys have joined themselves to the New Englanders, and are now in possession of your reserved lands at Wioming." Many of them, he believed, were drawn from the ranks of "those who murdered the Indians at Lancaster & Since rescued Stump out of Carlisle Gaol."[10]

Just across the Susquehanna River from the abandoned Fort Durkee, the New Englanders commenced construction of a more durable structure, which they called Forty Fort. Connecticut had once again taken control of the Wyoming Valley. Although the Pennsylvania authorities in Northampton County issued a warrant for the arrest of Lazarus Stewart, Lazarus Young, William Stewart, "and divers other evil disposed persons" for their participation in the events of February 23, there was little chance of this warrant being executed. Equally ineffective was a proclamation issued by John Penn on June 28 ordering all unauthorized residents of the Wyoming Valley to vacate their holdings and depart immediately.[11]

Nor did decisions made at the highest levels in far-away London have any practical effect. In 1763, when the Susquehannah Company made its previous attempt to settle the Wyoming Valley, the Board of Trade had ruled that the affair was intercolonial rather than imperial, that Pennsylvania and Connecticut should appoint commissioners to negotiate an agreement, and that Connecticut settlers should leave the region in the interim. By the time the two colonies were ready to negotiate, Teedyuscung's son, Captain Bull, had destroyed the Mill Creek encampment, terminating Connecticut settlement efforts. Lazarus Stewart and the Paxton Boys had discovered the remains of the massacre during their unauthorized expedition against the Delaware settlement of Wyalusing. In July 1770 the Board of Trade changed its position, declaring that the dispute was not between two colonies but lay entirely within the jurisdiction of Pennsylvania. This ruling validated Pennsylvania's ownership of the valley, but once again signified that the Crown wanted no involvement in resolving the dispute. Nor did the Board say anything about Connecticut settlers leaving the region. Pennsylvania would have to devise a solution on its own. But, for the present, physical possession of the valley was what really mattered, and Connecticut settlers were firmly in control.[12]

On September 15, 1770, Lazarus Stewart, back in Lancaster County for a visit, was arrested in the town of Lebanon on charges of arson, a capital offense. A local magistrate, John Philip De Haas, understanding that "the said Stewart was a dangerous, turbulent Man, & apprehending a Rescue might be attempted, employed three Men to assist the Constable to convey him down the Country, promising them a Reward of five Pounds to each of them if they accomplished it." A man named William Story delayed the group's departure, and he eventually "found means to intimidate the Persons employed to assist the Constable, so that they went away, leaving the Constable to do as he could." Stewart escaped with the assistance of one of Story's nephews, who furnished him with an axe handle. Stewart used this weapon to knock down the constable "& beat him in a Cruel and Unmerciful manner." When De Haas called on those who had witnessed the beating to assist him, nobody would cooperate, some being "Friends and abettors of Stewart, and the rest afraid." Stewart then stepped forward "with a Club in his Hand" and abused De Haas "in the most opprobrious Terms." Aware that "a Number of Stewart's Friends were expected from the Country, and apprehending from his Threats, that great Mischief and Disturbance would ensue," De Haas "thought proper to retire."[13]

About half an hour later a party of twenty armed men rode into Lebanon. Buoyed by these reinforcements, Lazarus Stewart, "with much Scurrility and Abuse, with a Pistol in one hand and a Club in the other," threatened De Haas for arresting him. De Haas "retired into his house and got his Pistols," and when Stewart and his men tried to follow him a family member fastened the door. Stewart stood outside, goading De Haas into trying to arrest him again in order to claim the reward offered after the massacres of 1763. Stewart then entered the tavern of Nicholas Hausaker and threatened that if he tried to assist De Haas he would tear him "to Pieces, and make a Breakfast of his Heart."[14]

John Penn and the Assembly agreed that a new reward should be offered for the arrest and conviction of Lazarus Stewart. The assemblymen, however, insisted that Stewart was "guilty of a Crime of a more atrocious Nature" than the one committed in Lebanon. If Stewart were arrested again, he should be tried not just for his current offenses but also for murdering the Conestoga Indians in 1763. As in the Frederick Stump case two years earlier, the assemblymen insisted that the root cause of the chaos on the frontier was Penn's failure to bring the Paxton Boys to justice. On October 3 Penn issued a proclamation for the recapture of Lazarus Stewart. It was "highly expedient for the Preservation of the Public Peace, and enforcing a due Execution of the Laws," Penn declared, that Stewart be brought to justice, both "for the Crime for which he was arrested, as for the daring Insult he has shewn to the Authority of Parliament." Penn's proclamation offered a reward of £50 for Stewart's arrest in connection with recent outrages, but it made no mention of his role in the Paxton Boys massacres of 1763.[15]

A second opportunity to bring Stewart to justice arose on October 23, 1770, when he was arrested while attempting to cross the Susquehanna River into York County. He was placed in York jail, but this time the outcome was farcical. Because he "was well known to be a principal Leader of the most lawless People in Lancaster County, who, on receiving an Account of his Imprisonment would take the most desperate measures to procure him his Liberty," the authorities in York County decided to send him to Philadelphia "in the most secret and expeditious manner." The sheriff of York County, assisted by a guard of three men, none of whom knew "the business he was going upon," set out with the "pinioned and handcuffed" prisoner around midnight. After traveling for fifteen miles they stopped to feed their horses and spend the night at Finley's Tavern, where Stewart "lay down by the Fire, handcuffed and tied with a Rope, which was also fastened to one of the Men that were to guard him." The sheriff, feeling unwell, went to an adjacent room to take a nap, leaving Stewart in the care of the other three men. Somehow, the report noted, "they all fell asleep, and the Prisoner got loose and made his escape, handcuffed and without his shoes." On November 2, believing that Stewart was still in York, several parties of Paxton Boys, "mostly dressed in blanket Coats and hunting Shirts, all armed with rifles and some having one and others two Case of Pistols," rode into the town with the intention of rescuing him.[16]

As Lazarus Stewart was making a mockery of the justice system in Lancaster and York Counties, Pennsylvania and Connecticut continued to do battle in the Wyoming Valley. On September 21, 1770, Amos Ogden's forces attacked Fort Durkee, capturing a number of Connecticut settlers, including Durkee once again. Most of the prisoners were confined in Easton jail, but Durkee and some others were transported to Philadelphia and imprisoned on charges of riot. Durkee remained in jail for almost two years, until John Penn freed him without prosecution. By November Penn could report triumphantly to his uncle, "We have seven of their people now in the gaol at Philadelphia, three of which are the head men amongst them." Pennsylvania had regained possession of Wyoming, and there was "pretty good reason to think the New Englanders will not make any further attempts there."[17]

Penn's confidence was misplaced. Following his escape in October, Lazarus Stewart made his way back to Wyoming with "a Body of Men from Hanover, in Lancaster County, armed with Guns and Clubs." At about three o'clock in the morning on December 18, Stewart's men recaptured Fort Durkee. A farmer named Aaron Von Campen, who was present in the fort that night, recalled that "they upon entering the Fort huzza'd for the Hanoverians [i.e., those who came from Hanover Township in Lancaster County] and King George, and immediately proceeded to break open the Doors of the Houses of the Fort." The Paxton Boys took Von Campen prisoner, "beat and abused him most unmercifully," and "proceeded in the same Manner through the Fort, breaking open Doors, beating and abusing the People, and making them Prisoners." Then they "ordered the People within the Fort to depart immediately, and would scarcely give them Time to collect a small part of their Effects to take with them." By Von Campen's estimate, the men who took the fort consisted of "twenty-three Hanoverians" and "Six New Englanders."[18]

Soon after this event Lazarus Stewart's proclivity for killing got the better of him. On January 18, 1771, Peter Kaechelin, the new sheriff of Northampton County, raised a posse and rode to Fort Durkee intending to arrest Stewart and several others on charges of riot. Stewart ordered Kaechelin "to depart, on Peril of his Life, at the same Time presenting a Gun towards him." Kaechelin had several more conversations with Stewart that day and the next, but "the said Stewart and most of his Party obstinately persisted in their Resolution to oppose him, and frequently threatened to fire" on the sheriff and his assistants. Amos Ogden's brother Nathan had the misfortune to be in Kaechelin's posse. On January 20 Stewart beckoned Ogden to come over to the fort, in what appeared to be a friendly manner. They chatted for a while and Stewart invited Ogden to come back the next day. When Ogden approached the fort the following morning, Stewart shot him dead. The Paxton Boys then started shooting from all corners, wounding several unarmed Pennsylvanians. Witnesses at the inquest confirmed that Stewart "did present his Gun through a Loop or Port hole in the Fort and saying that he would shoot the said Nathan Ogden did fire his Gun or Rifle." The inquest produced a "List of the rioters in the Fort at Wyoming" that included "Lazarus Stewart, the murderer," his cousin "Laz. Stewart, the younger," William Stewart, James Stewart, and forty-three other names.[19]

When they received a report of the events at Wyoming from John Penn, the assemblymen urged him to issue a new proclamation against Lazarus Stewart. As ever, their chief concern was his role in the Conestoga massacres. "This recent Instance," they wrote, "recalls to our Memory so many of the same kind in our back Counties, where Miscreants who have at once stained themselves with Sins of the deepest Dye, and have offered the highest Insults to Administration, have escaped with Impunity." Unless "some more successful Method of securing Criminals can be devised," they feared, such violent acts "will become equally common." At the assemblymen's urging, Penn issued a proclamation with a reward of £300 for the arrest of Lazarus Stewart and £50 for his accomplices. He also signed a new riot act presented by the Assembly.[20]

By this time, however, Lazarus Stewart was safely in Connecticut under the protection of the Susquehannah Company, which paid his expenses while he was there. Charles Stewart wrote to John Penn that not only had the killers abandoned the fort, but the other Connecticut settlers, fearing reprisals, had also left Wyoming. It was possible they would "return and endeavour to surprize us," but he was "of opinion they are gone for Ever." Amos Ogden, still mourning his brother, began construction of a more durable blockhouse, Fort Wyoming, adjacent to the abandoned Fort Durkee. But Pennsylvania's renewed control over the Wyoming Valley proved fleeting.[21]

Early in the summer of 1771 the Susquehannah Company sent Lazarus Stewart and the Paxton Boys back to the Wyoming Valley to launch a new offensive. On July 6 Colonel Asher Clayton, leading a force of 100 Pennsylvanians toward Fort Wyoming, was ambushed by Lazarus Stewart, his old comrade in the Paxtang Rangers. Clayton retired to Fort Wyoming with most of his men, and Stewart and Zebulon Butler laid siege. On August 15 Clayton signed articles of capitulation surrendering the fort and agreeing to return to Philadelphia with his men. Stewart and Butler regained possession of the Wyoming Valley for the Susquehannah Company and Connecticut finally established its first permanent settlement in Pennsylvania.[22]

CHAPTER 22
REVOLUTIONARIES

By the outbreak of the American Revolution, Connecticut was firmly in control of the Wyoming Valley. The settlers established five towns there in the early 1770s. Wilkes-Barré (formerly Wyoming town), Hanover (originally known as Nanticoke, but renamed in Lazarus Stewart's honor), and Pittstown stood on the east bank of the Susquehanna. Plymouth and Kingstown (where the settlers erected their strongest military outpost, Forty Fort) were on the west. Pennsylvania responded to the Connecticut threat by creating the county of Northumberland in 1772, hoping to consolidate its jurisdiction north of Fort Augusta. John Durkee countered this move the following year by sending another petition to Hartford seeking the creation of a county in the Wyoming Valley under Connecticut jurisdiction. Among the more than 220 signatories were the Paxton Boys Lazarus Stewart, William Stewart, and Lazarus Stewart Jr.[1]

The Connecticut legislature responded to the petition by setting up a township and eventually a county. The township of Westmoreland, established in 1774, was attached to the Connecticut county of Litchfield. Embracing all territory within the 42nd degree of latitude, from the Delaware River to a north-south line fifteen miles west of Wyoming town, Westmoreland covered an area almost as large as Connecticut itself. The residents divided the township into eight jurisdictional districts, and Lazarus Stewart was chosen as one of the selectmen, a position he declined in favor of "Sealer of Weights and Measures." Eventually, in October 1776, the Connecticut Assembly established Westmoreland County, coterminous with the township of the same name.[2]

The Connecticut settlers depended on the Paxton Boys' military prowess but found them cantankerous and divisive. They worried also about Lazarus Stewart's loyalty. Some suspected that Pennsylvania had offered to pardon "Capt Stuard and others of Paxtens" if they turned in the settlers' leader, Zebulon Butler. Others laid plans to betray Stewart and his men to Pennsylvania, but one of the Susquehannah Company's directors warned them that this course of action "must expose you in the highest degree to their resentment, and may possibly endanger your person." He added that he was "extreamly sorry" to hear of the plot, "as they (the Stewarts) have placed their confidence in ye Susquehannah Company & risqued their lives in what they have done for them." Meeting in Wilkes-Barré the following month, the Company reiterated its decision that "Cap^r Lazarus Stew[rt] & m^r William Stewart and their associates are Deserving the town of Hannover."[3]

Although tensions between the Paxton Boys and the Connecticut settlers persisted through the 1770s, Lazarus Stewart ultimately stayed loyal to the Susquehannah Company. "Great divisions have arisen at Wioming lately," a report to John Penn stated on December 16, 1775. "Lazarus Stewart...and his adherents are hourly wrangling with the Real Yankys." The Paxton Boys' leader was said to have made "repeated assurances of his neutrality," and it was rumored that he might even go over to the Pennsylvania side. But on the day this report was filed Stewart warned Butler that a party of men had assembled at Nescopeck, intending to rendezvous with a larger party coming from Shamokin. Their goal was to take back the Wyoming Valley for Pennsylvania.[4]

The attack came eight days later. Colonel William Plunket, a land speculator who was acting in concert with the proprietary government, arrived at the southwestern opening of the Wyoming Valley, just across the river from Hanover, on December 23. He was accompanied by several hundred men, some on horseback and others on foot. When Plunket's army attacked, Zebulon Butler turned them back. That night, as Plunket's men tried to cross the river by stealth, Lazarus Stewart drove them out of the valley. By this time the "Yankee" settlers in the Wyoming Valley had begun to refer to their Pennsylvania enemies as "Tories." The antagonism had much more to do with struggles over land than with abstract principles of liberty or patriotism. When the American Revolution came it offered an opportunity to settle long-standing local grievances.[5]

During the Revolution the Yankee settlers in the Wyoming Valley—including Stewart and his Paxton Boys—lined up squarely on the patriot side. The Committees of Correspondence appointed by the Westmoreland town meeting had a strongly punitive character. They were empowered to drive Pennsylvania settlers off disputed lands and to force all able-bodied men to undergo military training. Those who resisted were subject to fines, imprisonment, and even prosecution for treason. Most of the displaced "Pennamite" settlers moved farther up the north branch of the Susquehanna

THE WYOMING VALLEY IN THE 1770s

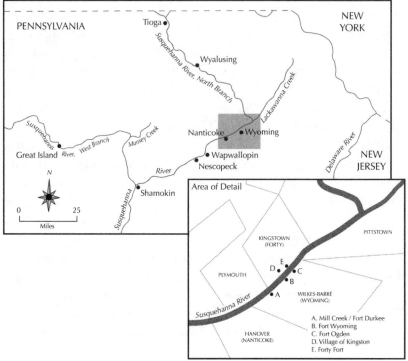

River, where they settled as tenants or squatters. A smaller number of "down-river Pennamites" settled in the Wapwallopin area, about halfway between Shamokin and Wyoming, where they endured harassment and intimidation by the Paxton Boys. Lazarus Stewart surveyed a tract of land there, but the Susquehannah Company stymied his aggression by ruling that the area lay outside its authority.[6]

Some of the displaced Pennsylvania settlers fled to Fort Niagara, where Colonel John Butler, a veteran of the French and Indian War, was assembling an army of frontier Rangers, American loyalists, and pro-British Cayuga and Seneca Indians. Many of the Pennamites at Fort Niagara agreed to join Butler's army in an expedition against the Wyoming Valley. This decision reinforced the perception that they were Tories, but they acted out of a desire to recover land, and to revenge themselves against the Paxton Boys, rather than a commitment to loyalist principles.

When Butler led his army into the Wyoming Valley at the end of June 1778 the Connecticut settlers were divided on how to respond. Nathan Denison,

"Massacre at Wyoming (Penn.)—Butler's raid, July 3 to July 4, 1778." Painting by Alonzo Chappel, 1858. Courtesy of Chicago History Museum.

a Westmoreland County magistrate, sent an eyewitness report to Governor Trumbull of Connecticut about what happened next. The news of Butler's arrival, he recalled, "alarmed the inhabitence so that Some Ware for Securing their famalies in our forts others for moveing out of the Settlement." On July 3 the settlers held a council of war at their stronghold, Forty Fort. Zebulon Butler urged caution; Lazarus Stewart recommended a surprise attack. Acting on Stewart's advice, "between three & four Hundred men" decided to "march out and attract the Enemy." After initially falling back, John Butler's forces counterattacked with devastating force. One list compiled shortly after the battle gave the Connecticut dead as 124, another as 157. Denison reported, "The Numbr Killed on our Sid Can not be Certing Knoon," but he believed it was "not far from two Hundred."[7]

Back at Forty Fort on the evening of July 3 all was chaos. Many settlers were fleeing, fearing a massacre. Denison reported that he "found numbr of Wimen & Children then in the Road Som Pushing out of the Settlement Some one Way & Some the other in the utmost Distres & Ankeiety indevering to make thire Escape from the Saveges." The following morning he surrendered Forty

Fort to John Butler, who ordered the destruction of all Connecticut forts in the Wyoming Valley, along with 1,000 dwellings. The terms of capitulation required that "the properties taken from the people called *Tories* be made good and they to remain in peaceable possession of their Farms and unmolested in a free Trade." The Pennamites would thereby retrieve the land they had lost to Yankee settlers. But in the turmoil of revolution this stipulation proved impossible to enforce.[8]

Immediately after the capitulation of Forty Fort rumors began to circulate of a terrible massacre by John Butler's Indian allies, featuring rapes and mutilation of women and children. Wildly exaggerated, these rumors became a rallying cry for patriots, who demanded vengeance against Indians as well as the British. Writing from the refuge of Paxton town, a settler named William Maclay, who had abandoned his home after the battle and brought his "Family by water to this Place," said that he had never seen "such Scenes of distress." He reported that "the River and the Roads leading down it, were covered with Men women and children flying for their lives, many without any Property, at all, and none who had not left the greatest part behind." Northumberland County "is broken up" and "Wioming is totally abandoned," Maclay continued, "and almost everyone is thinking of some place of greater security." Sunbury must be reinforced, he warned, or John Butler's army could "without difficulty penetrate to Carlisle."[9]

The scenes of flight and panic Maclay described were real, but the rumors of a massacre after the capitulation of Forty Fort were groundless. Everyone who died in Wyoming was killed on the battlefield. Among them was Lazarus Stewart. He died a patriot, of sorts; he did not care about theories of liberty or democracy but perished as he had lived, fighting Indians and Tories over land. His wife, Martha, fled the carnage and took their seven children—the last of whom was born on the day of the battle—down the Susquehanna River by raft to Paxton town.

The Paxton Boys sided with the patriots in the Revolution, but not for lofty reasons. John Elder and Matthew Smith rallied to the patriot cause in Lancaster County, as did John Armstrong in Cumberland County and Lazarus Stewart and his men in the Wyoming Valley. Most historians in the nineteenth century, and many in the twentieth, cast the Paxton Boys as harbingers of the American Revolution, frontier democrats fighting against the quasi-feudal privilege of the Penn family. The Paxton Boys did fight against proprietary privilege, but scarcely in the interest of liberty and equality for all.

What they wanted was land, personal security, and vengeance against Indians. Earlier historians made much of the western counties' underrepresentation in the Pennsylvania Assembly. The Paxton Boys included this issue in their *Remonstrance* in 1764, but all of their other grievances concerned Indians. Political representation was a mere abstraction compared to the more fundamental need for self-preservation. The Paxton Boys had the pleasure of seeing Pennsylvania's proprietary government toppled in 1776 and John Penn briefly imprisoned by American forces until he agreed to sign an oath of loyalty. But they played no part in that more familiar side of the Revolution. Their concerns remained, as ever, resolutely local.[10]

The idea that the Paxton Boys were precursors of republican revolution is brutally accurate in one sense. The American Revolution did more than destroy oligarchy and proprietary privilege in colonial Pennsylvania; it doomed the region's Indians. The Paxton Boys made no distinction between "friendly" and "enemy" Indians in 1763. They chose to kill the Conestogas precisely because they were peaceful and lived under government protection. They understood the symbolic significance of slaughtering Indians on government land and breaking open a county workhouse to kill their victims. They failed in their goal of acquiring land by right of conquest, but they openly challenged the authority of government, the government did not respond, and the long-term consequences for Pennsylvania's Indians were disastrous. During the pamphlet war of 1764 defenders of the Paxton Boys argued that killing Indians was a form of loyal opposition to bad government. This idea reached fruition during the American Revolution, when exterminating Indians became an act of patriotism. Unlike their counterparts in Virginia, revolutionary Pennsylvanians did not find the bedrock of white freedom in black slavery. Instead they built their new society by annihilating the Indians in their midst.[11]

Patriotic extermination reached its awful apotheosis at Gnadenhütten, Ohio, in 1782. Tragically, it involved some of the Moravian Indians who had been removed to Philadelphia almost twenty years earlier for protection against the Paxton Boys. When they were released from the city barracks in May 1765, after eighteen months in captivity, only eighty-three of the original 140 survived, the rest having fallen to dysentery, smallpox, and other diseases. Papounan led them back to Wyalusing, on the west branch of the Susquehanna River. But in 1771, with Lazarus Stewart entrenched in the Wyoming Valley and displaced Pennamites encroaching on their land, the Moravian Indians relocated once again, this time to the Ohio country. There they built a new mission, Gnadenhütten, which they named after the Moravian settlement destroyed during the French and Indian War. On March 9, 1782, Pennsylvania militiamen confined ninety-six Moravian Indians to their cabins and methodically bludgeoned them to death—twenty-eight men, twenty-nine women, and thirty-nine children. The commander of the expedition, Colonel David Williamson, was later elected sheriff of Washington County.

The Revolutionary War ended a year later with the declaration of American sovereignty over the vast territory stretching from the Floridas to Canada east of the Mississippi River. The United States acquired this territory by right of conquest over the British and their Indian allies, especially the once powerful Iroquois confederacy, four of whose six nations had taken Britain's side in the Revolution. Predictably, neither the Iroquois nor the other Indians who lived on the land in question were consulted. As the American commissioners put it to representatives of the Six Nations at Fort Stanwix in 1784, "The King of Great Britain ceded to the United States the whole, by the right of conquest they [the Americans] might *claim the whole*." If Indians wished to request allotments from this "whole"—the new national territory—they must first recognize the absolute sovereignty of the new American state.[12]

A combination of strong Indian resistance and scarce financial and military resources soon forced the American government to modify this hard-line policy. Washington and Jefferson backed away from the extreme logic of conquest to embrace a nonviolent, outwardly benevolent Indian policy, reminiscent of John Locke's idea of peaceful dispossession. Productive labor, Jefferson believed, was the basis of landed property. "Civilized" Indians therefore had a right to own land if they cultivated the soil. But they would not need much land for this purpose, leaving American farmers free to convert the rest from "waste" to private property. This approach to Indian affairs was certainly an improvement on the stark brutality of the Paxton Boys, yet in practice it presented few obstacles to the ongoing coercive dispossession of Indians. It also rested on a very narrow and one-sided understanding of land.

The U.S. Supreme Court revealed the limitations of this understanding in a set of legal cases involving the Cherokee Indians in the 1830s. One of the "Five Civilized Tribes" of the southeast, the Cherokees had their own form of constitutional government. The state of Georgia waged a campaign to drive them out, abolishing their political institutions and distributing their land to white citizens. The Court struck down these laws in the case of *Worcester v. Georgia* (1832), ruling that the Cherokees were a sovereign nation under the guardianship of the United States. Individuals or state governments could not confiscate the Cherokees' land or infringe on their government. The sovereignty of Indian nations was limited only by the federal government, which had sole authority in Indian affairs. And this sovereignty, Chief Justice John Marshall ruled, did not emerge from a Lockean social contract between property-owning individuals. Instead, it was grounded in territoriality—deep historical attachment to the land on which the Indians and their ancestors lived. The Supreme Court did not seek to enforce *Worcester v. Georgia*, however, fearing a showdown with the fiercely anti-Indian administration of Andrew Jackson.[13]

Throughout the nineteenth century Indians continued to endure the displacement and annihilation that had begun on the eastern seaboard in the colonial era. In 1838 the Cherokees were forcibly relocated, joining the other southeastern Indians on the "Trail of Tears" to the Indian Territory of present-day Oklahoma. *Worcester v. Georgia* did, however, provide an important precedent for the recognition of Indian national sovereignty in the twentieth century. William Penn had introduced a similar precedent with his "holy experiment," offering protection to the "independent commonwealths" of Indians living within his charter. But the Paxton Boys repudiated his vision and destroyed the remains of the Peaceable Kingdom.[14]

APPENDIX

IDENTIFYING THE CONESTOGA INDIANS AND THE PAXTON BOYS

Evidence from the Conestogas, Delawares, and Iroquois survives only in translation. Their words were recorded in the eighteenth century and collected by the Pennsylvania government from the 1850s onward in the multivolume *Pennsylvania Archives* and *Minutes of the Provincial Council*. Rendered into English and transcribed by officials who worked for the proprietary government, these sources were unusually biased from the start, and they were further distorted during the process of collation and publication. They must be read accordingly. Yet they include critical information on land purchases, Indian policy, and treaty conferences, without which the story in this book could not be told. As for visual sources, no contemporary likenesses of Teedyuscung, Pisquetomen, Shingas, or other Delaware leaders survive, let alone of Sheehays and the Conestoga Indians.[1]

The names of the twenty Conestoga Indians killed in December 1763, along with details of their effects and remains, can be found in a list sent by Sheriff John Hay to John Penn. Benjamin Franklin included some of this information in his *Narrative of the Late Massacres*. Some secondary sources, starting with Frank Eshelman's *Lancaster County Indians* (1908), suggest that two elderly Conestoga Indians survived the massacres. Eshelman told the romantic story of a reunion in 1907 of the Hershey family, famous for its production of chocolate and caramel, when the guests discovered "four stone markers set securely in the ground." Under these markers they found the remains of two Indians, Michael and Mary, "The Last Two Indians in Lancaster County."[2]

Milton Hershey, after leading a "prayer over the remains of these last Children of the Forest," read an order from John Penn to Edward Shippen dated August 17, 1764, concerning Michael and Mary. The order, which can be found in the *Pennsylvania Archives*, guaranteed protection to the two Indians, "who formerly resided with other Indians in the Conestogo Manor" and had "for upwards of fifteen months last past lived with Christian Hirshey." Penn ordered that they should be given "all necessary assistance" and allowed to live "without the least molestation or interruption." According to Eshelman, the two Indians spent the rest of their lives with the Hershey family.[3]

It is conceivable that Michael and Mary were the last of the Conestogas, and they may even have been "The Last Two Indians in Lancaster County" by the time they died. But they cannot have directly escaped the Paxton Boys because they had left Conestoga Indiantown well before the massacre there took place. Penn believed the two Indians had left more than fifteen months before he issued his order in August 1764, that is, at least seven months before the Paxton Boys struck. Yet the Moravian missionary Bernhard Adam Grube, who knew the Indians of the Susquehanna Valley better than most—and certainly better than Penn did—wrote that Michael and Mary had been living under the protection of a local Mennonite settler for fifteen *years*, not fifteen months, in December 1763. The Paxton Boys killed all twenty Indians they found. That was what they set out to accomplish, and that was why their actions were so brutally effective. Nobody escaped.[4]

There is a secondary question, concerning Michael and Mary's nativity. Penn initially believed they were Delaware Indians, despite their residence on Conestoga Manor. Grube was the first to identify them as Conestogas, when he met Mary in 1767. But regardless of their origin, they would both have been seen as Conestoga Indians if they had lived at Conestoga Indiantown for a substantial period, even if one or both of them belonged to a different Indian nation. "John Smith" (Saguyasotha), who settled on the Manor after marrying Sheehays's daughter "Peggy" (Cheenawan) and died with her at Lancaster, was a Cayuga Indian. The Cayugas laid claim to Conestoga Indiantown after the massacres, citing their kinship with Sheehays, perhaps on the basis of Smith's marriage to Peggy. Their kinsman John Smith has always been counted among the twenty Conestoga victims, despite his Cayuga origins; Mary and Michael would have been counted too, regardless of their origin, if they had been unlucky enough to be living on Conestoga Manor on December 14, 1763.[5]

As for the Paxton Boys, very little biographical information has survived, except on John Armstrong (1717–1795) and the Rev. John Elder (1706–1792), whose details can be found in this book. Once again no likeness is available for either man. The Cumberland County Historical Society holds a portrait of Armstrong's son, John Armstrong Jr., by Rembrandt Peale, which is sometimes mistakenly identified as the father. Concerning the other Paxton Boy leaders mentioned in the sources—Lazarus Stewart, Matthew Smith, and James Gibson—the evidence is scant and sometimes contradictory. Different sources give different accounts of Stewart's birth and lineage. Henry Blackman Plumb's *History of Hanover Township* states that he was born in Lancaster County in 1734, served in Braddock's march in 1755, commanded the Paxton Boys in 1763, and moved to the Wyoming Valley with his brother James and his cousin Lazarus Stewart Jr. in late 1769 or early 1770. According to Oscar Jewell Harvey's *History of Wilkes-Barré*, Lazarus Stewart was the second child of James Stewart and Margaret Stewart, who emigrated from Ulster to Pennsylvania with their families in 1729 and were married around 1731. Martha B. Clark, in her introduction to an unverified "Declaration of Lazarus Stewart," states that the Paxton Boys' leader was the son (rather than grandson) of Lazarus Stewart Sr. (d. 1744), who emigrated from Ulster in 1729 and settled along Swatara Creek in Lancaster County. According to Clark, Lazarus Stewart was born in Hanover Township, Lancaster County on May 16, 1733. Frank J. Cavaioli also states that Stewart was born in 1733. The Stewarts were members of Manada Presbyterian Church in Hanover Township, Lancaster County. Harvey's genealogy and Plumb's dates and life story seem the most reliable and have been relied on here.[6]

More information has survived on Lazarus Stewart's comrade, Matthew Smith. A biographical portrait of Smith by Frederic A. Godcharles states that Smith was born in Paxton in 1734, served under Colonel Henry Bouquet in the expedition against Fort Duquesne in 1758, and commanded the Paxtang Rangers in 1763. He was a member of Paxton Presbyterian Church. Godcharles denies that Smith was present in Lancaster on December 27, 1763, but most historians agree that he helped plan the Conestoga massacre and led the attack on Lancaster workhouse with Lazarus Stewart. In a first-person account published in a Lancaster newspaper in 1843, Smith readily admitted his participation in both massacres. But this account was fabricated. Smith's role as the Paxton Boys' spokesman at Germantown and the coauthor of the *Remonstrance* in February 1764, on the other hand, is undisputed. He appears to be the same Matthew Smith of Paxton who fought on the patriot side and played a prominent role in Pennsylvania politics during the Revolution. Smith died in Northumberland County in 1794.[7]

Almost nothing is known about Matthew Smith's collaborator at Germantown, James Gibson, who cosigned the Paxton Boys' *Remonstrance*. No details of his birth, career, or death survive. Cavaioli identified a James Gibson who owned several hundred acres in Lancaster County in 1771 and subsequently moved to Northumberland County, where he served as a "Frontier Ranger" during the Revolution. It is impossible to say if this James Gibson, who owned 400 acres in Northumberland County by 1794, was the signatory of the *Remonstrance*.[8]

The remaining fifty or more Paxton Boys who exterminated the Conestoga Indians, and the several hundred who marched on Philadelphia, will forever remain anonymous.

ACKNOWLEDGMENTS

This book has been a decade in the making. Along the way I have accumulated many professional and personal debts. My colleagues at Boston College provided a congenial atmosphere in which to write. Stephen Vedder, Michael Swanson, Kerry Burke, and Dan Thornbury lent their expertise to the task of illustrating the book. My research assistants Molly Whiteman and Yejin Lee helped me track down sources, checked the citations, and read several chapters. Morgan Adams read the full manuscript. Ian Delahanty helped correct the proof. Two sabbatical leaves from the College of Arts and Sciences at Boston College allowed me to finish the book. The Committee on Research and Publication of the University Research Council at Boston College funded the illustrations.

In writing this book I have been fortunate to receive the advice and assistance of some very knowledgeable archivists and librarians. I am especially grateful to the staff at the following institutions: the Albany Institute of History & Art, the American Philosophical Society, the Chicago History Museum, the Dauphin County Historical Society, Dickinson College Library, Haverford College Library, the Historical Society of Pennsylvania, the Historical Society of Western Pennsylvania, the John Carter Brown Library, the Library Company of Philadelphia, the Library of Congress, Paxton Presbyterian Church, the Pennsylvania Academy of the Fine Arts, the Pennsylvania Historical and Museum Commission, the Public Record Office of Northern Ireland, the University of Pennsylvania (University Archives, Office of the Curator, and Curator of Rare Books at the Annenberg Library), the William L. Clements Library at the University of Michigan, and the Reeves Center at Washington and Lee University. Above all I would like to thank Anne Kenny and Daniel Saulean at the O'Neill Library, Boston College.

At Oxford University Press, Susan Ferber offered expert guidance at every stage of the book's development. I signed with Oxford to get the benefit of Susan's extraordinary editing. She read every word of the manuscript twice, and her suggestions on what to add, cut, or clarify hit the mark with uncanny precision. I am very grateful to Susan, and I feel privileged to have worked with her. I would also like to thank my production editor, Joellyn Ausanka; my copy editor, Judith Hoover; and the anonymous readers who reviewed the proposal and manuscript for the press.

Rosanna Crocitto read the entire manuscript, offered many helpful criticisms, and showed me how to improve the writing.

Thank you, Rosanna, Michelino, and Owen for your love, laughter, patience, and support.

Owen has been waiting a long time for this book—as long as he's been with us.

Now, at last, it's his.

ABBREVIATIONS

APS	American Philosophical Society
BF	Benjamin Franklin
DCHS	Dauphin County Historical Society
HSP	Historical Society of Pennsylvania
JP	John Penn
MPCP	Commonwealth of Pennsylvania, *Minutes of the Provincial Council of Pennsylvania*, 10 vols.
PA	Commonwealth of Pennsylvania, *Pennsylvania Archives*, 9 series
PBF	*Papers of Benjamin Franklin*, ed. Leonard W. Labaree, 30 vols.
PG	*Pennsylvania Gazette*
PHMC	Pennsylvania Historical and Museum Commission
PJ	*Pennsylvania Journal*
PMHB	*Pennsylvania Magazine of History and Biography*
PP	*Paxton Papers*, ed. John Dunbar
PRONI	Public Records Office, Northern Ireland
PWP	*Papers of William Penn*, ed. Mary Maples Dunn and Richard S. Dunn, 4 vols.
SCP	*The Susquehannah Company Papers*, ed. Julian P. Boyd and Robert J. Taylor, 11 vols.
TP	Thomas Penn

NOTES

Introduction

1. BF, *A Narrative of the Late Massacres,* 58–59. The contemporary word "Indian" is used generically throughout this book in place of "Native American" or "Amerindian," which have certain merits but are of later vintage and can be awkward to use. Typically the various Indian nations are identified by name, for example, Delaware Indians or Conestoga Indians.
2. Rhoda Barber, "Journal of Settlement at Wright's Ferry on Susquehanna River," handwritten original, 1830, HSP Am.012. On the number of Conestogas living in December 1763, see the appendix.
3. BF, *Narrative,* 60; PHMC, RG-21, Records of the Proprietary Government, Provincial Council, Miscellaneous Papers, Item 262, Deposition: Jacob Whisler.
4. Isaiah 11:6–9; Penn used the term "holy experiment" in a letter to James Harrison dated August 25, 1681, *PWP,* 2:108.
5. Harper, *Promised Land,* 13–14; R. S. Dunn, "William Penn's Odyssey," 305–23.
6. Harper, *Promised Land,* especially 13–14, 27–34, 124–25, 130–32.
7. The term "frontier" is problematic, but European settlers used it all the time (as in the numerous examples cited in this work), and it is employed in this book mainly to express their perspective. Shorn of its intolerant underpinnings, the term is also used in these pages as a neutral way of describing the ever-shifting ground separating settlers and Indians.
8. James Logan to John, Thomas, and Richard Penn, February 17, 1731, HSP, James Logan letterbooks, vol. 3.
9. Locke, *Second Treatise of Government,* chapter 5, "Of Property," 18–19, 21, 23–24, 26. Locke was drawing on Genesis 1:28: "Be fruitful, and multiply, and replenish the earth, and subdue it."
10. Locke, *Second Treatise,* chapter 5, "Of Property," 23–24, 26.
11. Vaughan, "Frontier Banditti and the Indians."

12. Knouff, "Soldiers and Violence," 172, 188; Silver, *Our Savage Neighbors,* 229–32, 253–92; Griffin, *American Leviathan,* 152–72.

13. Thomas Barton to JP, HSP, Penn Add. Mss., Misc. Letters, II, in *SCP,* 4: v; Thomas Barton to Edmund Physick, December 18, 1770, "Notes and Queries," *PMHB,* 4.1 (1880): 119, 120; Russell, "Thomas Barton," 319; Franz, *Paxton,* 94.

14. M. Smith and Gibson, *A Declaration and Remonstrance.* These two documents were composed and submitted separately but later published together in a single pamphlet. The combined version, cited here, is in *PP,* 99–110.

15. The two principal pamphlets against and in favor of the Paxton Boys were, respectively, Franklin's *Narrative* and Thomas Barton's *The Conduct of the Paxton-Men, Impartially Represented.*

Chapter 1

1. *PWP,* 4:50–54; *MPCP,* 1:9–12; *MPCP,* 3:601–3 (quote, 601).
2. *MPCP,* 3:601–2.
3. *PWP,* 2:422; Jennings, *The Ambiguous Iroquois Empire,* 139–40, 145–50.
4. *PWP,* 2:422–25, 466–70, 479–83, 487–88; *PWP,* 3:477–78, 600–602; *MPCP,* 3:599–601, 603.
5. *MPCP,* 3:602. The boundary between Pennsylvania and Maryland remained contested until the drawing of the Mason–Dixon line in the 1760s.
6. *MPCP,* 3:602.
7. Anderson, *The War That Made America,* 9–10.
8. Clare, *A Brief History of Lancaster,* 4–5.
9. *MPCP,* 3:601–2.
10. *PWP,* 4:98–99.
11. *MPCP,* 9:102.
12. William Penn's first wife, Gulielma Springett, died in 1694; he married Hannah Callowhill in 1696.
13. Harper, *Promised Land,* 37–39.
14. Murphy, *Pennsylvania,* 97.
15. *MPCP,* 2:571. This is the earliest documentary reference to the Delawares' status vis-à-vis the Iroquois.
16. Harper, *Promised Land,* 13–14, 28.
17. Harper, *Promised Land,* 30–31; Treese, *The Storm Gathering,* 9; Shepherd, "The Land System," 117–18; Wing et al., *History of Cumberland County,* 18–19, 23.
18. Franz, *Paxton,* 99–102.
19. Shepherd, "The Land System," 117; *SCP,* 1: iv–xxxv; Treese, *Storm Gathering,* 9; Wing et al., *History of Cumberland County,* 18; Franz, *Paxton,* 220.
20. Treese, *Storm Gathering,* 9; Wing et al., *History of Cumberland County,* 18.

21. Clare, *Brief History*, 32; Kelker, *History of Dauphin County*, 1:16–17, 20; McAlarney, *History of the Sesqui-Centennial of Paxtang Church*, 335; Franz, *Paxton*, 106–8, 115–16. Paxton Township became part of Dauphin County in 1785.

22. James Logan to JP, October 18, 1728, HSP, James Logan letterbook, vol. 3; Clare, *Brief History*, 47–51, 65–66, 131; Mombert, *An Authentic History*, 413; Rupp, *History of Lancaster County*, 67–70, 131.

23. Brackbill, "The Manor of Conestoga," 17–18, 22–23.

24. *MPCP*, 3:45–49 (quote, 49); Brackbill, "Manor of Conestoga," 17–18, 22.

Chapter 2

1. Penn's four sons were William Jr. (1681–1720), John (1699–1746), Thomas (1702–1775), and Richard (1706–1771).

2. Tolles, *James Logan;* Jennings, "The Indian Trade."

3. Rupp, *History of Lancaster County*, 67–89, 268–69; Clare, *A Brief History of Lancaster County*, 120–23.

4. James Logan to the Proprietor, September 27, 1727, and "the next [undated] letter," Mrs. Logan's Copy Book, HSP, James Logan letterbook, vol. 4; *PA* 2, VII, 96.

5. William Smith to Archbishop Secker, November 27, 1759, in O'Callaghan, *Documents Relative to the Colonial History of New York*, 7:407; Mancall, *Valley of Opportunity*, 73.

6. Wing et al., *History of Cumberland County*, 17; Murphy, *Pennsylvania*, 90.

7. Proud, *The History of Pennsylvania*, 2:341–42, 345, 347–48; Rupp, *The History and Topography of Dauphin*, 211; Clare, *Brief History of Lancaster County*, 47–51, 65–66; Brackbill, "The Manor of Conestoga," 25, 29; Murphy, *Pennsylvania*, 90.

8. Proud, *History of Pennsylvania*, 2:351–52. John Huss was burned as a heretic in 1415.

9. BF, "Observations concerning the Increase of Mankind, Peopling of Countries, &c.," in William Clarke, *Observations on the late and present Conduct of the French, With Regard to their Encroachments upon the British Colonies in North America*, 53.

10. Boulter quoted in C. A. Hanna, *The Scotch-Irish*, 177–80; Franklin cited in Mancall, *Valley of Opportunity*, 73.

11. M. A. Jones, "The Scotch-Irish in British America," 293, 294; Klett, *Presbyterians in Colonial Pennsylvania*, 14–15; Leyburn, *The Scotch-Irish*, 236–43, 328 (Mather quote); Dunaway, *The Scotch-Irish of Colonial Pennsylvania*, 50–56; Dickson, *Ulster Emigration*, 223–26.

12. Landsman, "Presbyterians," 168; Klett, *Presbyterians in Colonial America*, vii–viii, 2–7, 116–26.

13. Klett, *Presbyterians in Colonial America*, 46–49.

14. McAlarney, *History of the Sesqui-Centennial*, 58–62, 73–74; H. B. Wallace, *Historic Paxton;* Downey, *History of Paxton Church*, 7–19; addresses by William Henry Egle, W. F. Rutherford, and A. Boyd Hamilton in *The Scotch-Irish in America*, 71–82, 219–26, 380–91.

15. Wallace, *Historic Paxton*, 20–33, 67–82, 99–102; Downey, *History of Paxton Church*, 7–19.

16. Samuel Evans, "Scotch-Irish Settlement of Donegal, Lancaster County, PA," in *Scotch-Irish in America*, 212–18; Rupp, *History and Topography*, 52; Shepherd, *History of Proprietary Government*, 50–51.

17. James Logan to John, Thomas, and Richard Penn, July 29, 1728, HSP, James Logan letterbook, vol. 4; James Logan to John Penn, September 11, 1728, HSP, James Logan letterbook, vol. 4; James Logan, "Instructions to Ja: Steel bound for Engl^d. Novr 1729 Prop^ty Affairs," HSP, vol. 10, p. 46 (another copy in James Logan to James Steel, November 18, 1729, HSP, Penn Mss., Off. Corr., vol. 2, p. 101).

18. Logan, "Instructions to Ja: Steel"; McBride, *The Siege of Derry*.

Chapter 3

1. Murphy, *Pennsylvania*, 91–92.

2. Murphy, *Pennsylvania*, 96.

3. Murphy, *Pennsylvania*, 92; Rupp, *An Account of the Manners,* 32 (originally published in the *Columbia Magazine*, 1789); Hooker, *The Carolina Backcountry*, 14.

4. *PA* 2, XVIII, 96–99; James Logan to TP, postscript, December 22, 1730, HSP, Penn manuscripts, official correspondence, vol. 2, p. 145; James Logan to John, Thomas, and Richard Penn, February 17, 1731, HSP, James Logan letterbook, vol. 3. Logan underestimated the size of Conestoga Manor by 1,000 acres.

5. James Logan to James Anderson, December 23, 1730, HSP, James Logan letterbook, vol. 4; James Logan to John, Thomas, and Richard Penn, February 17, 1731, HSP, James Logan letterbook, vol. 3; Shirk, "Wright's Ferry," 66–67.

6. Franz, *Paxton*, 96.

7. Lincoln, "Representation in the Pennsylvania Assembly," 23–34. William Penn's charter included three additional counties—Newcastle, Kent, and Sussex—on the lower Delaware River, which set up their own Assembly in 1704 and formed the state of Delaware in 1776.

8. *MPCP*, 3:343; Rupp, *History of Lancaster County*, 236–54; Shirk, "Wright's Ferry," 61–87.

9. Rupp, *History of Lancaster County*, 236–49; Rupp, *The History and Topography of Dauphin*, 53; Clare, *A Brief History of Lancaster County*, 125–55. Paxton and Derry Townships were incorporated into Dauphin County on its creation in 1785.

10. Rupp, *History of Lancaster County*, 236–54; J. H. Wood, *Conestoga Crossroads*; J. H. Wood, "The Town Proprietors of Lancaster"; Edgar J. McManus, "Hamilton, Andrew," *American National Biography Online*, www.anb.org/articles/01/01–00364.html?a=1&n=hamilton%2C%20andrew&ia=-at&ib=-bib&d=10&ss=1&q=3 (accessed October 16, 2007).

11. Wood, "The Town Proprietors," 353.

12. Wood, "The Town Proprietors," 351, 354; R. S. Klein, *Portrait of an Early American Family; PP*, 16, nn3, 4; Harris, *A Biographical History of Lancaster County*, 524. James Hamilton served as lieutenant governor in 1748–1754, 1759–1763, and briefly in 1771.

13. Hutson, *Pennsylvania Politics*, 63–66.

14. "Charter of Privileges Granted by William Penn, esq. to the Inhabitants of Pennsylvania and Territories, October 28, 1701," Avalon Project at Yale Law School, www.yale.edu/lawweb/avalon/states/pa07.htm (accessed April 24, 2008); Proud, *The History of Pennsylvania*, 2:284–89; *PP*, 4–5; Lincoln, *The Revolutionary Movement*, 42–46; Franz, *Paxton*, 18–30.

15. John C. Van Horne, "Peters, Richard," *American National Biography Online*, www.anb.org/articles/01/01–00722.html (accessed October 17, 2007); Tolles, *James Logan*.

16. Norman S. Cohen, "Allen, William," *American National Biography Online*, www.anb.org/articles/01/01–00017.html (accessed October 17, 2007).

17. K. Miller et al., *Irish Immigrants*, 487–99; University of Pennsylvania Archives, "William Smith (1727–1803)," www.archives.upenn.edu/histy/features/1700s/people/smith_wm.html (accessed May 4, 2005); R. G. Barton, "The Rev. Thomas Barton"; Russell, "Thomas Barton," 313–18; Harris, *Biographical History*, 29–38.

18. *MPCP*, 5:447; Clare, *Brief History*, 241; Berks County Historical Sites, Conrad Weiser Homestead, Conrad Weiser Biography, www.berksweb.com/conrad.html (accessed May 11, 2005); Historical Society of Berks County, "Conrad Weiser Homestead," www.berkshistory.org/articles/peacemaker_1960.html (accessed May 11, 2005).

Chapter 4

1. *MPCP*, 3:15–16, 19.

2. *MPCP*, 3:19–20, 45–47, and (for a similar meeting on June 15, 1722) 181.

3. Anderson, *The War that Made America*, 13–14; Jennings, *The Ambiguous Iroquois Empire*, 315–16.

4. *MPCP*, 3:197, 198, 201.

5. *MPCP*, 3:199–202, 10:255–56.

6. *MPCP*, 3:271, 273–74.

7. James Logan to Captain Civility, August 19, 1727, and James Logan to John, Thomas, and Richard Penn, February 17, 1731, both in HSP, James Logan letterbooks, vol. 3.

8. *MPCP*, 3:598–604 (quotes, 598, 599, 604).

9. *MPCP*, 3:435, 449 (full conference proceedings, 435–52); Jennings, *Ambiguous Iroquois Empire*, 314–16.

10. *MPCP*, 4:70, 83 (full conference proceedings, 80–95).

11. *MPCP*, 4:87–88, 93.

12. Harper, *Promised Land*, 39–40; Jennings, "The Scandalous Indian Policy," 28–32.

13. Harper, *Promised Land*, 40–41, 45, 49–51, 53, 57–58; Thomson, *An Enquiry*, 33–40; Jennings, *Ambiguous Iroquois Empire*, 320–46; Jennings, "Scandalous Indian Policy," 33–34; A. F. C. Wallace, *King of the Delawares*, 18–30.

14. Harper, *Promised Land*, 63, 67–68; Jennings, *Ambiguous Iroquois Empire*, 333–34, 336–37, appendix B, "Documents of the Walking Purchase," 388–97; Wallace, *King of the Delawares*, 26; Thomson, *Enquiry*, 47.

15. *MPCP*, 4:575–76.

16. *MPCP*, 4:579; Harper, *Promised Land*, 82.

17. *MPCP*, 4:579.

18. *MPCP*, 4:579–80. There is a sizable scholarly literature on the Delawares and womanhood. See, for example, Harper, *Promised Land*, 72, 82–85; Heckewelder, *History, Manners*, 57–58; Weslager, "The Delaware Indians as Women"; Speck, "The Delaware Indians as Women"; A. F. C. Wallace, "Women, Land and Society"; J. Miller, "The Delaware as Women"; Merritt, *At the Crossroads*, 219–23; Shoemaker, *A Strange Likeness*, 109–13.

19. Harper, *Promised Land*, 74, 75, 78, 103.

Chapter 5

1. *PA* 1, I, 629–30; *MPCP*, 5:446.

2. *MPCP*, 5:398–409, 447 (quote).

3. *MPCP*, 5:438–42, 447–48 (quote).

4. *MPCP*, 5:441–49, 442, 443, 444, 449; James Logan to John, Thomas, and Richard Penn, February 2, 1731, HSP, James Logan letterbook, vol. 3. Nearly all the squatters had recognizably Ulster Presbyterian surnames, such as McKeen, McClare, Kirkpatrick, Murray, Girtlee, and Kilaugh.

5. Kenny A. Franks, "Tanacharison," *American National Biography Online*, www.anb.org/articles/20/20–01693.html (accessed October 18, 2007).

6. Jennings, *Empire of Fortune*, 41.

7. Thomson, *An Enquiry*, 80 (citing Conrad Weiser's journal on Tanaghrisson's appraisal of Washington).

8. *MPCP*, 6:130–33.

9. A. F. C. Wallace, *King of the Delawares*; Jay Miller, "Teedyuskung," *American National Biography Online*, www.anb.org/articles/20/20–01006.html (accessed October 19, 2007).

10. O'Toole, *White Savage;* Francis Jennings, "Johnson, Sir William," *American National Biography Online,* www.anb.org/articles/01/01–00458.html (accessed October 19, 2007). Admiral Warren became famous for commanding the successful British assault on Fortress Louisbourg in 1745.

11. George Boudreau, "Norris, Isaac," *American National Biography Online,* www.anb.org/articles/01/01–00672.html (accessed October 19, 2007); Morgan, *Benjamin Franklin,* 315–16; J. A. Leo Lemay, "Franklin, Benjamin," *American National Biography Online,* www.anb.org/articles/01/01–00298.html (accessed October 19, 2007); Jennings, *Empire of Fortune,* 104.

12. Thomson, *Enquiry,* 82 (quote); Jennings, *Empire of Fortune,* 261, 325.

13. Jennings, *Empire of Fortune,* 104.

14. Thomson, *Enquiry,* 77.

15. Report of Richard Peters and JP, *SCP,* 1:123–27 (quotes, 125).

16. Wallace, *King of the Delawares,* 48.

17. Boyd, *The Susquehannah Company,* 3–8 (quote, 8); *SCP,* 1:iii–lxviii.

18. *SCP,* 1:lxxix–lxxxix, 101–16 (quotes, 102, 103), 124, 133; O'Toole, *White Savage,* 121, 124; Colonial Albany Social History Project, "John Henry Lydius," www.nysm.nysed.gov/albany/bios/l/jhlydius4615.html (accessed November 13, 2008); Boyd, *Susquehannah Company,* 10–13.

19. *SCP,* 1:131–32; *MPCP,* 6:248.

20. *SCP,* 1:137–38.

21. *MPCP,* 6:248–49, 259; Thomson, *Enquiry,* 78.

22. *MPCP,* 6:248–49, 276–93 (quote, 276–77).

Chapter 6

1. Paul E. Kopperman, "Braddock, Edward," *Oxford Dictionary of National Biography,* www.oxforddnb.com/view/article/3170 (accessed October 19, 2007).

2. Anderson, *The War That Made America,* 67.

3. Cummings, "The Paxton Killings," 222–23; J. Smith, *An Account.* On Stewart, see appendix. On the Black Boys, see chapter 20.

4. Francis Jennings, "Johnson, Sir William," *American National Biography Online,* www.anb.org/articles/01/01–00458.html (accessed October 19, 2007); Jennings, "The Indians' Revolution," 328–30.

5. Thomson, *An Enquiry,* 129.

6. Jennings, *Empire of Fortune,* 154–55.

7. Anderson, *Crucible of War,* 94–107; Jennings, *Empire of Fortune,* 157–60.

8. Faragher, *A Great and Noble Scheme.* Shirley was later appointed governor of Jamaica.

9. *MPCP,* 6:457–58.

10. *MPCP,* 6:459–60.

11. *MPCP*, 6:36–37.

12. *MPCP*, 6:155–56; Barr, " 'A Road for Warriors,' " 3, 15, 18–20.

13. *MPCP*, 6:645–48.

14. BF to Richard Partridge (draft and extract), *PBF*, 6:231; Barr, " 'Road for Warriors,' " 22–24.

15. *MPCP*, 6:646–48.

16. *MPCP*, 6:654, 655.

17. *MPCP*, 6:655.

18. *MPCP*, 6:658.

19. *MPCP*, 6:655–56.

20. *MPCP*, 6:656–59.

21. *MPCP*, 6:656–59.

22. Sipe, *The Indian Wars*, 1:204–54; *MPCP*, 6:707 (quote).

23. *MPCP*, 6:704–5.

24. W. F. Rutherford, "Old Paxtang Church," in *The Scotch-Irish in America*, 220–22; *MPCP*, 6:704–5, 763.

25. *MPCP*, 6:363; *PG*, December 18, 1755; Thomson, *Enquiry*, 83–87; A. F. C. Wallace, *King of the Delawares*, especially 56–86.

Chapter 7

1. In the War of the Austrian Succession (1740–1748), the North American phase of which was known as King George's War, the British fought Spain and its ally, France.

2. Davidson, *War Comes*, 49–63; Stephenson, "Pennsylvania Provincial Soldiers," 199–200; Dunaway, *The Scotch-Irish*, 154; Wing et al., *History of Cumberland County*, 58; J. W. Simonton, "History of Hanover Church and Congregation, Dauphin County, PA," in *The Scotch-Irish in America*, 238–39; Brumwell, *White Devil*.

3. T. Barton, *Unanimity and Public Spirit*; W. Smith, *A Brief State of the Province*; Russell, "Thomas Barton," 316; Morgan, *Benjamin Franklin*, 134–36; K. Miller et al., *Irish Immigrants*, 491–92; University of Pennsylvania Archives, "William Smith (1727–1803)," www.archives.upenn.edu/histy/features/1700s/people/smith_wm.html (accessed May 4, 2005).

4. Jennings, *Empire of Fortune*, 329.

5. Stillé, "The Attitudes of the Quakers," 285; Franz, *Paxton*, 24–26.

6. *MPCP*, 6:521, 524–32, 537–46; Bronner, "The Quakers," 12.

7. *MPCP*, 6:670–72, 682, 684–85.

8. *MPCP*, 6:702–3.

9. *MPCP*, 6:706, 729, 736–37; *PG*, January 8, 15, 1756; Hutson, *Pennsylvania Politics*, 25–26.

10. *MPCP*, 6:731–34 (quote, 731); Hutson, *Pennsylvania Politics*, 24, 26.

11. William Allen to Fernando Paris, November 25, 1755, quoted in Ketcham, "Conscience, War," 422; *MPCP*, 6:735.

12. "George Fox to Oliver Cromwell" and "The Time of My Commitments," in Peter Mayer, ed., *The Pacifist Conscience*, 90, 92.

13. Thayer, *Israel Pemberton;* Marietta, "Conscience," 12–13; Jennings, *Empire of Fortune*, 383; Woolman, *The Journal,* introduction, v–xi.

14. Jennings, *Empire of Fortune*, 334–35.

15. Windhausen, "Quaker Pacifism"; George Boudreau, "Norris, Isaac," *American National Biography Online*, www.anb.org/articles/01/01–00672.html (accessed October 22, 2007).

16. *The Humble Address of the People Called Quakers, residing in the city of Philadelphia, on behalf of themselves and many others,* in *MPCP*, 7:85, 86 (also in *PG*, April 22, 1756).

17. *MPCP*, 7:87–89; *PG*, April 22, 1756.

18. *PG*, April 22, 1756; *MPCP*, 7:84–85, 89–90.

Chapter 8

1. Thomson, *An Enquiry*, 88–90.

2. *PG*, July 8, 1756.

3. *MPCP*, 7:204–20; Jennings, *Empire of Fortune*, 275; Thayer, "The Friendly Association," 359–60.

4. Thayer, "The Friendly Association," 362.

5. Thayer, "The Friendly Association," 360, 362; Thomson, *Enquiry*, 98; A. F. C. Wallace, *King of the Delawares*, 105–13, 139.

6. Thomson, *Enquiry*, 91, 95, 96; *MPCP*, 7:213.

7. *MPCP*, 7:218.

8. *MPCP*, 7:297.

9. *PJ*, August 5, 1756.

10. *PA*, 1, II, 740.

11. *PA*, 1, II, 757; *MPCP*, 7:233–34; *PA*, 1, II, 758. Lord Loudoun (John Campbell) arrived in New York on July 23, 1756, replacing William Shirley.

12. *MPCP*, 7:234–36, 241–42; Anderson, *The War That Made America*, 94–95; Jennings, *Empire of Fortune*, 294–96.

13. *MPCP*, 7:242–43.

14. Report of John Armstrong to William Denny on the Kittanning expedition, in *MPCP*, 7:257–63; King, "Colonel John Armstrong"; Hunter, "Victory at Kittanning" (quote from Thomas Penn's testimony of 1775, 404); Myers, "Pennsylvania's Awakening." In 1775 Thomas Penn rewarded the "the hero of Kittanning" with a tract of land that included the abandoned site of the town.

15. *PG*, November 4, 1756; Jennings, *Empire of Fortune*, 277.

16. *MPCP,* 7:270 (quote), 305–338; Jennings, *Empire of Fortune,* 276–77.
17. *MPCP,* 7:320–21 (quote, 320).
18. Thomson, *Enquiry,* 48, 99–100; Wallace, *King of the Delawares,* 126–36.
19. Thomson, *Enquiry,* 101; Wallace, *King of the Delawares,* 246; Jennings, *Empire of Fortune,* 279–80, 386.
20. Stephenson, "Pennsylvania Provincial Soldiers."
21. *MPCP,* 7:247–56.
22. *MPCP,* 7:395–97, 401–3, 409–10, 412–16, 421–29, 437–53.

Chapter 9

1. *MPCP,* 7:465–66, 506–7; Thomson, *An Enquiry,* 106; Jennings, *Empire of Fortune,* 336–37; BF, *A Narrative of the Late Massacres,* 57.
2. *MPCP,* 7:7–8, 9.
3. *MPCP,* 7:465, 538; Jennings, *Empire of Fortune,* 336–37, 339.
4. *MPCP,* 7:521–22; Jennings, *Empire of Fortune,* 337–38.
5. *MPCP,* 7:649–714.
6. *MPCP,* 7:634–35.
7. Thomson, *Enquiry,* 110–12; Jennings, *Empire of Fortune,* 343; Boyd Stanley Schlenther, "Thomson, Charles," *American National Biography Online,* www.anb.org/articles/01/01-00886.html (accessed October 22, 2007).
8. Thomson, *Enquiry,* 115, 116–17; *MPCP,* 7:678.
9. Thomson, *Enquiry,* 114.
10. Thomson, *Enquiry,* 115, 118, 119; *MPCP,* 7:678.
11. *MPCP,* 7:700–701.
12. *MPCP,* 7:710.
13. "The Address of the Trustees and Treasurer of the Friendly Association," in Proud, *The History of Pennsylvania,* part II, appendix, 62–64.
14. Thayer, "The Friendly Association," 368–69; *PA* 8, VI, 4267; *PG,* September 22, 1757.
15. Hunter, "Thomas Barton,"435.
16. "Journal of Frederick Post's Journey from Philadelphia to Wioming, June the 20th, 1758," in *MPCP,* 8:142–45; Jennings, *Empire of Fortune,* 384–87.
17. Post, "The Journal," 132; Marston, *The French-Indian War,* 46; Jennings, *Empire of Fortune,* 364. In September 1758, after the campaigning season ended, Jeffery Amherst replaced Abercromby as commander in chief of British forces in North America.
18. Post, "The Journal," 132, 133, 136, 138.
19. Post, "The Journal," 137, 138, 140.
20. Post, "The Journal," 145, 147, 148.
21. Post, "The Journal," 151–52, 153, 154.
22. Thomson, *Enquiry,* 3, 48; Post, "The Journal," 155.

23. Post, "The Journal," 157, 162. Post did not support this assertion with evidence.
24. Post, "The Journal," 158–60, 161, 162, 163.
25. Post, "The Journal," 161, 162, 163.
26. Post, "The Journal," 166, 167–68, 170–71.

Chapter 10

1. "Extract of a Letter from Philadelphia, dated Dec. 10, 1758" and "Extract from a Letter from one of the Friendly Association in Philadelphia, dated Dec. 11, 1758," in Thomson, *An Enquiry*, 172, 173, 175, 183; *MPCP*, 8:203.
2. "Extract of a Letter from Philadelphia," 182.
3. Barr, "'A Road for Warriors,'" 27–32; Jennings, *Empire of Fortune*, 402.
4. "Extract of a Letter from Philadelphia," 182.
5. "Extract of a Letter from Philadelphia," 182.
6. Post, "The second journal," 2: appendix, 96–132 (quote, 97); Jennings, "A Vanishing Indian," 317–23.
7. Post, "The second journal," 99, 100–102, 103, 104, 105, 106; *MPCP*, 7:244.
8. Post, "The second journal," 109.
9. Post, "The second journal," 109–10.
10. Post, "The second journal," 111–12.
11. Post, "The second journal," 113, 114.
12. Post, "The second journal," 118, 120.
13. Post, "The second journal," 119, 120, 121, 125–32.

Chapter 11

1. A. F. C. Wallace, *King of the Delawares*, 245–51; Jennings, *Empire of Fortune*, 434–35; *SCP*, 2:xvii–xviii, xx, xxv; Boyd, *The Susquehannah Company*, 20–21.
2. *SCP*, 2:xii–xvi, xxv; Boyd, *Susquehannah Company*, 21; Wallace, *King of the Delawares*, 248; *MPCP*, 8:708; Jennings, *Empire of Fortune*, 436.
3. *MPCP*, 8:723–74; Wallace, *King of the Delawares*, 252–55.
4. *SCP*, 2:xxvi–xxvii; Boyd, *Susquehannah Company*, 21; Wallace, *King of the Delawares*, 254–61.
5. Boyd, *Susquehannah Company*, 24–26; *MPCP*, 9:60.
6. Peckham, *Pontiac*, 71–72, 92–111; Dowd, *War under Heaven*, 70–78; Dixon, *Never Come*, 74–84; Edward Shippen to Joseph Shippen, June 6, 1763, APS, Shippen Papers, Folder 314.
7. Peckham, *Pontiac*, 130–44, 156–70; Dowd, *War under Heaven*, 114–39; Dixon, *Never Come*, 106–33.

8. BF to Richard Jackson, June 27, 1763, APS, Franklin correspondence, letters by BF to Richard Jackson. For Indian raids in the Fort Pitt area in May, see *PG*, June 9, 1763.

9. *PJ*, June 30, July 7, July 21, 1763; *PG*, June 30, 1763.

10. Thomas Barton to Dr. Daniel Burton, June 28, 1763, HSP, Am. 813, "Copies of Letters from Rev. T. Barton, etc. to the Society for the Propagation of the Gospel in Foreign Parts (from originals in the possession of the Society)"; Thomas Barton to Richard Peters, July 5, 1763, HSP, Peters Papers, vol. 6, p. 10.

11. *PA* 8, VI, 5425–27 (also in *MPCP*, 9:31–33).

12. *MPCP*, 9:36.

13. Joseph Shippen to John Elder, July 12, 1763, DCHS, Elder Collection, MG70.

14. Thomas McKee to James Burd, July 9, 1763, HSP, Shippen Papers, vol. 6, p. 41; Edward Shippen to Joseph Shippen, July 13, 21, 30, 1763, APS, Shippen Papers, Folder 314.

15. Jeffery Amherst to Henry Bouquet, July 7, 1763, quoted in Parkman, *The Conspiracy of Pontiac*, 2:39; Bouquet to Amherst, July 13, 1763, and Amherst to Bouquet, July 16, 1763, in Jeffery Amherst, Official Papers, British Manuscript Project, Library of Congress, microfilm reel 34/40, postscript to item 309, and reel 34/41, postscript to item 114 (Stanford University Library, reels 32 and 33).

16. Jennings, *Empire of Fortune*, 447–48.

Chapter 12

1. *PJ*, July 21, 1763; *PG*, July 21, 1763; Thomas McKee to James Burd, July 9, 1763, HSP, Shippen Papers, vol. 6, p. 41.

2. *PG*, July 21, 1763, August 4, 1763.

3. John Elder to James Hamilton, August 4, 1763, DCHS, Elder Collection, MG70.

4. Elder to Hamilton, August 4, 1763.

5. *PJ*, August 18, 25, 1763, September 1, 1763 (quotes); *PG*, August 18, 25, 1763; Dowd, *War under Heaven*, 145–46.

6. John Elder to James Hamilton, August 24, 1763, DCHS, Elder Collection, MG70.

7. Edward Shippen to Joseph Shippen, September 1, 3, 1763, APS, Shippen Papers, Folder 314; "A Brief acct. of some Public Occurrences in the Province of Pennsylvania in the Administration of Governor John Penn" (undated, presumably by John Penn), HSP, Am.2016, Penn MSS, vol. 4, Indian Affairs, MS44.

8. Edward Shippen to Joseph Shippen, August 31, 1763, September 3, 26, 1763, APS, Shippen Papers, Folder 314; Franz, *Paxton*, 65; Merritt, *At the Crossroads*, 273.

9. *PJ*, September 15, 1763; John Elder to James Hamilton, September 13, 1763, DCHS, Elder Collection, MG70; Sipe, *The Indian Wars*, 2:450–63; *MPCP*, 9:42–43.

10. *MPCP*, 9:52–56, 64; Hutson, *Pennsylvania Politics*, 59–66, 70, 75 (quote, 61).

11. *PG*, October 27, 1763.

12. *PJ*, October 20, 27, 1763.

13. John Elder to James Hamilton, September 30, 1763, DCHS, Elder Collection, MG70; *PG*, October 13 and 27, 1763; *PJ*, October 20, 1763; "Brief acct. of some Public Occurrences"; Sipe, *Indian Wars*, 2:450–63.

14. *PJ*, October 20, 1763; *PG*, October 27, 1763; John Elder to James Hamilton, October 25, 1763, DCHS, Elder Collection, MG70; Joseph Shippen Jr. to James Burd, October 21, 1763, HSP, Shippen MSS, VI, 57 (in *SCP*, 2:276–77); John Elder to Joseph Shippen, November 5, 1763 (*PA* 1, IV, 132–33).

15. "Extract from a Letter from Paxton, Lancaster County, October 23," *SCP*, 2:277.

Chapter 13

1. *MPCP*, 9:62–63.

2. *PA* 8, VI, 5484–85.

3. *PA* 4, III, 235–36; Philip Carter, "Penn, John," *Oxford Dictionary of National Biography*, www.oxforddnb.com/view/article/21849?docPos=1 (accessed October 19, 2007); JP to TP, November 15, 1763, HSP, Penn MSS, Off. Corr., vol. 9, p. 208; Treese, *The Storm Gathering*, 26.

4. *PA* 1, IV, 135–36, 138.

5. *MPCP*, 9:88–89; Hunter, "Thomas Barton," 472 (on McKee).

6. *PG*, December 8, 1763; Calloway, *The Scratch of a Pen*, 92–100.

7. *PA* 8, VI, 5482–83; JP to TP, November 15, 1763, HSP, Penn MSS, Off. Corr., vol. 9, p. 208.

8. *PA* 8, VI, 5482–83; JP to TP, November 15, 1763, HSP, Penn MSS, Off. Corr., vol. 9, p. 208.

9. *MPCP*, 9:66–71, 77–79 (quotes, 67, 68); John Elder to JP, September 30, 1763, DCHS, Elder Collection, MG70.

10. *MPCP*, 8:116–23, 134–35 (quote, 135); deposition of John Hambright, in Anon., *The Apology of the Paxton Volunteers*, 198–99.

11. *MPCP*, 8:122, 457; BF, *A Narrative of the Late Massacres*, 57.

12. Anon., *Apology*, 195–96, 198–200.

13. BF, *Narrative*, 58–59.

14. Barber, "Journal of Settlement at Wright's Ferry," HSP.

15. Barber, "Journal of Settlement at Wright's Ferry," HSP; T. Barton, *The Conduct of the Paxton-Men*, 283; BF, *Narrative*, 59.

16. Edward Shippen to JP, December 14, 1763, in *MPCP*, 9:89–90, 102; Edward Shippen to Joseph Shippen, January 5, 1764, APS, Shippen papers, folder 314.

17. Affidavits reproduced in Barton, *Conduct*, 284–85.
18. Barton, *Conduct*, 283–84.
19. Proud, *The History of Pennsylvania*, 2:326–28. For the biblical allusions, see, for example, Deuteronomy 7:2, Joshua 6:17.
20. John Elder to JP, December 16, 1763, DCHS, Elder Collection, MG70 (a garbled copy can also be found in *PA* 1, IV, 148–49); Edward Shippen to John Elder, December 16, 1763, APS, Shippen Papers, Folder 314; *PA* 1, IV, 151–52.
21. *MPCP*, 9:92–93, 94, 95–96, 97.

Chapter 14

1. *MPCP*, 9:103–4; BF, *A Narrative of the Late Massacres*, 57–58. On mutilation, see the account by William Henry published in Mombert, *An Authentic History*, 185, quoted in *PP*, 29.
2. Foulke, "Fragments of a Journal," 66; Thomas F. Gordon, *The History of Pennsylvania, from its Discovery by Europeans to the Declaration of Independence in 1776*, 405; *Hazard's Register of Pennsylvania* 9 (January–July 1832), 115.
3. Edward Shippen to Joseph Shippen, Lancaster, January 5, 1764, APS, Shippen Papers, Folder 314.
4. Edward Shippen to Joseph Shippen, January 5, 1764.
5. Edward Shippen to Joseph Shippen, January 5, 1764.
6. Proud, *The History of Pennsylvania*, 2:329.
7. *PA* 4, I, 152.
8. *PA* 4, I, 155.
9. John Elder to JP, December 16, 1763, DCHS, Elder Collection, MG70; *PA* 1, IV, 151–52. On the Paxton Boys' leaders, see the appendix.
10. JP to John Elder, December 29, 1763, DCHS, Elder Collection, MG70.
11. *MPCP*, 9:107–8, printed in *PG*, January 9, 16, 1764, *PJ*, January 9, 16, 1764.
12. *MPCP*, 9:107–8; BF, *Narrative*, 63.
13. *MPCP*, 9:105.
14. *MPCP*, 9:105, 118.
15. Joseph Shippen Jr. to Colonel James Burd, January 3, 1764, HSP, Shippen Papers, vol. 6, p. 73; William Logan to John Smith, December 30, 1763, HSP, Am. 158, John Smith Correspondence; *MPCP*, 9:104–5, 106.
16. *MPCP*, 9:129–30.
17. *MPCP*, 9:100, 101, 103.

Chapter 15

1. *MPCP*, 9:108–10; Foulke, "Fragments of a Journal," 66–67.
2. *MPCP*, 9:110–13 (quotes, 111–12).
3. *MPCP*, 9:121–22; *PA* 1, IV, 157.

4. William Logan to John Smith, January 21, 1764, HSP, Am. 158, John Smith Correspondence.

5. Logan to Smith, January 21, 1764; *MPCP*, 9:126.

6. *MPCP*, 9:127–28.

7. John Elder to [unknown], February 1, 1764, DCHS, Elder Collection, MG70.

8. Elder to [unknown], February 1, 1764.

9. *PA* 1, IV, 161.

10. *MPCP*, 9:124, 128; *PA* 4, 1, 160.

11. *MPCP*, 9:128–29, 131–32; Foulke, "Fragment," 69.

12. *MPCP*, 9:132–34.

13. *PG*, February 9, 1764; *MPCP*, 9:132–33.

14. Muhlenberg, *The Journals*, 1:19; "Paxton Boys," *Hazard's Register of Pennsylvania* 7 (July 1833–January 1834), 11.

15. James Pemberton to Dr. James Fothergill, March 7, HSP, Pemberton Papers, vol. 34, pp. 9–10 (listed in the archive as pp. 125–28, but the pages are numbered 1–12, the sequence cited here); Thayer, "The Friendly Association," 373–75.

16. HSP, Society Collection, Letter of S. Potts to her sister, February 9, 1764; Pemberton to Fothergill, March 7, 1764, p. 12. Edward Pennington was descended from a prominent English Quaker family; the surname was originally spelled Penington.

17. Muhlenberg, *Journals*, 1:18–20.

Chapter 16

1. "Letters which passed between the Meeting for Sufferings in London and the Meeting for Sufferings in Philadelphia, 1757–1815," February 25, 1764 (copy provided by Haverford College Library), 39–40; David Rittenhouse, "A letter from Mr. Rittenhouse to the Rev. Mr. Barton, dated the sixteenth of February, 1764," in W. Barton, *Memoirs*, 148.

2. "Paxton Boys," *Hazard's Register of Pennsylvania* 7 (July 1833–January 1834), 11–12.

3. Muhlenberg, *The Journals*, 1: introduction, viii–ix, 19.

4. "Paxton Boys," *Hazard's Register of Pennsylvania*, 11.

5. Muhlenberg, *Journals*, 2:18, 19.

6. Muhlenberg, *Journals*, 2:20.

7. Muhlenberg, *Journals*, 2:20–21.

8. Muhlenberg, *Journals*, 2:21.

9. Foulke, "Fragments of a Journal," 70; *PP*, 43–44; "Paxton Boys," *Hazard's Register of Pennsylvania*, 11; "Letters which passed between the Meeting for Sufferings in London and the Meeting for Sufferings in Philadelphia,

1757–1815," February 25, 1764, Haverford College Library, 39–40; James Pemberton to Dr. James Fothergill, March 7, 1764, HSP, Pemberton Papers, vol. 34, p. 6 (listed in the archive as pp. 125–28, but the pages are numbered 1–12, the sequence cited here).

10. Foulke, "Fragments," 70–71.
11. Foulke, "Fragments," 71; "Paxton Boys," *Hazard's Register of Pennsylvania*, 12–13; BF to Richard Jackson, Philadelphia, 1764, APS, BJ85.j18, Franklin correspondence.
12. Pemberton to Fothergill, March 7, 1764, pp. 6–7, 9; Foulke, "Fragments," 70–72.
13. *Declaration*, in *PP*, 101–2.
14. *Declaration*, in *PP*, 102.
15. *Declaration*, in *PP*, 102–3.
16. *Declaration*, in *PP*, 102–3.
17. *Declaration*, in *PP*, 104.
18. Pemberton to Fothergill, March 7, 1764, pp. 6–7, 9; Foulke, "Fragments," 70–72; Muhlenberg, *Journals*, 2:23; Crowley, "The Paxton Disturbance," 319. An address submitted by Philadelphia Quakers to John Penn also gave the date of the *Declaration* as February 6 (*PP*, 103).
19. *Declaration*, in *PP*, 105. By "interior" the Paxton Boys, following contemporary usage, meant eastern Pennsylvania.
20. *PP*, 4–5; Pemberton to Fothergill, March 7, 1764, p. 6; *PBF*, 11: 82 n4; Lincoln, *The Revolutionary Movement*, 45–48; Thayer, "The Quaker Party," 28–31.
21. *Remonstrance*, in *PP*, 105–6.
22. *Remonstrance*, in *PP*, 107.
23. *Remonstrance*, in *PP*, 107; *PP*, 107, 108 n4; Read, *Copy of a Letter*, 77–82 (quote, 80). See chapter 12, pp. 125–26.
24. *Remonstrance*, in *PP*, 108–9.
25. *Remonstrance*, in *PP*, 109, 110; *PP*, 104 n2, 109 n5.
26. Pemberton to Fothergill, March 7, 1764, p. 7.
27. *MPCP*, 9:146–47.
28. Foulke, "Fragments," 72.
29. Pemberton to Fothergill, March 7, 1764, pp. 6–8; Foulke, "Fragments," 70, 72.

Chapter 17

1. Anon., *The Apology of the Paxton Volunteers*, 185–204 (quote, 185); Olson, "The Pamphlet War."
2. BF, *A Narrative of the Late Massacres*, 57–75; BF to Richard Jackson, Philadelphia, February 11, 1764, APS, Franklin correspondence, BJ85.j18.
3. Olson, "Pamphlet War," 34–35.
4. Olson, "Pamphlet War," 45, 54.

5. Buxbaum, *Benjamin Franklin*, 1–5, 186, 200.

6. T. Barton, *The Conduct of the Paxton-Men*, 265–98 (quotes, 282–83).

7. Anon., *Apology*, 185; Dove, *The Quaker Unmask'd*, 205–15.

8. Barton, *Conduct*, 293, 294, 295; Dove, *Quaker Unmask'd*, 208.

9. Anon., *Apology*, 187, 189; Barton, *Conduct*, 269, 281–82, 293, 294.

10. "Well Wisher," *An Historical Account*, 127; Dove, *Quaker Unmask'd*, 205–15.

11. Anon., "A Battle!" 175.

12. Barton, *Conduct*, 277, 278, 280.

13. Dove, *Quaker Unmask'd*, 208–9; Anon., *Apology*, 190–91; "Well Wisher," *Historical Account*, 128–29; Barton, *Conduct*, 272, 293.

14. Barton, *Conduct*, 270; Dove, *Quaker Unmask'd*, 211.

15. Barton, *Conduct*, 296.

16. Anon., *Apology*, 193.

17. Anon., *Apology*, 194.

18. Anon., *Apology*, 194–97, 199, 200.

19. Barton, *Conduct*, 271.

20. Anon., *Apology*, 200–202.

21. Anon., *Apology*, 203–4 (emphasis added).

22. Dove, *Quaker Unmask'd*, 209; Barton, *Conduct*, 278, 288–89, 297, 298.

23. Barton, *Conduct*, 278, 287, 296–97.

24. Barton, *Conduct*, 271–72; Anon., *Apology*, 188; Williamson, *The Plain Dealer...Numb. III*, 367–86 (quote, 384).

Chapter 18

1. BF, *A Narrative of the Late Massacres*, 71.

2. BF, *Narrative*, 63; Read, *Copy of a Letter*, 77, 80; Anon., *A Serious Address*, 93–94.

3. Read, *Copy of a Letter*, 79; BF, *Narrative*, 63–72 (quotes 63–64, 71–72).

4. BF, *Narrative*, 73, 74, 75; Isaac Hunt, *A Looking-Glass for Presbyterians*, 252–53.

5. Anon., *A Dialogue, Between Andrew Trueman, and Thomas Zealot*, 89.

6. Anon., *A Dialogue, Between Andrew Trueman, and Thomas Zealot*, 89.

7. Anon., *A Dialogue, Between Andrew Trueman, and Thomas Zealot*, 89; Psalm 137 (KJV): "Happy [shall he be], that taketh and dasheth thy little ones against the stones"; I Sam. 15.3 (KJV).

8. Anon., *A Dialogue, Containing Some Reflections*, 114.

9. Hunt, *Looking-Glass for Presbyterians*, 245, 246.

10. Hunt, *Looking-Glass for Presbyterians*, 246, 247, 248. Pointing to several massacres in Ireland in the 1640s, Hunt said that Presbyterians had been worse offenders than Catholics.

11. Hunt, *Looking-Glass for Presbyterians*, 248–49; Hunt, *A Looking-Glass, &c. Numb. II*, 301.

12. Hunt, *Looking-Glass for Presbyterians*, 249; Hunt, *Looking-Glass II*, 312, 314; anonymous letter from the "Hearts of Oak," July 1763, Wilmot papers, PRONI, T.3019/4672; the Rev. William Henry of Londonderry to the Archbishop of Canterbury, July 17, 1763, Alnwick papers, PRONI, T.2872/7; "A full and circumstantial account of what happened to me on the eighth of July 1763," by the Rev. Theodorus Martin, rector of Desertlyn, County Tyrone, G. M. Stewart MSS, PRONI, T.1442/6.

13. Hunt, *Looking-Glass for Presbyterians*, 250; "Philanthropos," *The Quakers Assisting II*, 392.

14. Hunt, *Looking-Glass for Presbyterians*, 250, 255; Hunt, *Looking-Glass II*, 305–6.

15. Anon., *The Address of the People call'd Quakers*, 133–34 (also in *PG*, March 1, 1764).

16. Anon., *The Address of the People call'd Quakers*, 134–37; M. Smith and Gibson, *A Declaration and Remonstrance*, 102–3, 109–10.

17. "Letters which passed between the Meeting for Sufferings in London and the Meeting for Sufferings in Philadelphia, 1757–1815," Haverford College Library; Sloan, "'A Time of Sifting'"; Sloan, "The Paxton Riots."

18. "Letters which passed between the Meeting for Sufferings," February 25, 1764, 36, 40–41.

19. James Pemberton to Dr. James Fothergill, March 7, 1764, HSP, Pemberton Papers, vol. 34, pp. 2, 3, 4–5 (listed in the archive as pp. 125–28, but the document is numbered pp. 1–12, which is the sequence followed here).

20. "Letters which passed between the Meeting for Sufferings," 41–42, 43.

21. HSP, Society Collection, Letter of S. Potts to her sister, February 9, 1764.

22. HSP, Pennington Papers (Edward Carey Gardner Collection), Box 26, Edward Pennington "To the Monthly Meeting of Friends in the City of Philadelphia," 1764 (in two pieces, one of which is a copy from the original).

23. Pennington "To the Monthly Meeting."

24. Sloan, "'A Time of Sifting,'" 5–6.

Chapter 19

1. "Philadelphiensis," *Remarks on the Quaker Unmask'd*, 227.

2. Hunt, *A Looking-Glass II*, 309, 311–12; "Dr. John Ewing, Philadelphia, 1764, to Mr. Reed, 1764," quoted in Jacobs, *The Paxton Riots*, 44–46.

3. Foulke, "Fragments of a Journal," 69, 73.

4. *PBF*, 9:205–7; Foulke, "Fragments," 69, 71–72; *MPCP*, 9:148–49; Hutson, *Pennsylvania Politics*, 58–62.

5. BF to Richard Jackson, Philadelphia, February 11, 1764, APS, Franklin correspondence, BJ85.j18; Foulke, "Fragments," 72–73.

6. Hutson, *Pennsylvania Politics*, 41–45; BF to John Fothergill, Philadelphia, March 14, 1764, in *PBF*, 11:104–5.

7. Pennsylvania, General Assembly, House of Representatives, *Votes and Proceedings 1763*, 72; Hutson, *Pennsylvania Politics*, 41.
8. Assembly, *Votes and Proceedings 1763*, 73.
9. Assembly, *Votes and Proceedings 1763*, 73–74.
10. Assembly, *Votes and Proceedings 1763*, 74; BF, *Explanatory Remarks on the Assembly's Resolves*, March 29, 1764, in *PBF*, 11:134–44.
11. Thayer, "The Quaker Party," 35–36; Hutson, *Pennsylvania Politics*, 110–13, 153–55; W. S. Hanna, *Benjamin Franklin*, 156–58.
12. BF, *Cool Thoughts on the Present Situation of our Public Affairs*, in *PBF*, 11:153–73 (quotes, 158, 159, 160).
13. BF, *Cool Thoughts*, 11:160–61.
14. BF, *Cool Thoughts*, 11:161–62, 168–73.
15. Assembly, *Votes and Proceedings 1763*, 80–84; *PBF*, 11:193–95.
16. *Votes and Proceedings 1763*, 84; *PBF*, 11:195–96.
17. *PBF*, 11:197–200.
18. Gleason, "A Scurrilous Colonial Election"; *PBF*, 11:370.
19. Williamson, *What is sauce for a Goose*, 2–3, 4, 5, 6; Hunt, *A Humble Attempt*, iii–v, 39–41. For the original version of the words Williamson attributed to Franklin, see BF, *Observations concerning the Increase of Mankind*, 53.
20. *PA* IV, 3, 290–93 (quotes, 291); *PP*, 20; O'Toole, *White Savage*, 245. After an expedition into the Ohio country led by Colonel Henry Bouquet, John Penn issued a proclamation declaring an end to hostilities with the Delawares, Shawnees, and Senecas on December 5.
21. BF to William Strahan, September 1, 1764, and BF to Richard Jackson, September 1, 1764, in *PBF*, 11:327, 329; BF to Lord Kames, June 2, 1765, in *PBF*, 12:158–65 (quote, 161); Thayer, "Quaker Party," 38–42.

Chapter 20

1. *MPCP*, 9:410–11; Vaughan, "Frontier Banditti," 2.
2. *MPCP*, 9:268–76, 292–93, 302–7; J. Smith, *An Account*, 120, 124; Wing et al., *History of Cumberland County*, 58, 70–71, 73–74; U. J. Jones, *History*, 165–70; Cutcliffe, "Sideling Hill Affair"; E. M. Webster, "Insurrection at Fort Loudoun." The Black Boys disturbances took place in a part of Cumberland County that is now in Bedford County (fd. 1771). Smith's birthplace is now in Franklin County (fd. 1784).
3. J. Smith, *An Account*, 121.
4. *MPCP*, 9:268–70, 276.
5. *MPCP*, 9:269–70.
6. *MPCP*, 9:268; J. Smith, *An Account*, 124–25.
7. *MPCP*, 9:267–68, 271.
8. *MPCP*, 9:234, 264–66.
9. *MPCP*, 9:272, 273, 274, 276.

10. *MPCP*, 9:292–93, 297.

11. On Quaker suspicions that the desire for a proprietary-Presbyterian alliance influenced John Penn's response to the Paxton Boys in 1764, see Hutson, *Pennsylvania Politics*, 110–13, 153–55; Hanna, *Benjamin Franklin*, 156–58. For the Assembly's criticisms of Penn later in the 1760s, see pp. 213–14, 222, 224–25 above.

12. PHMC, RG-21, Records of the Proprietary Government, Provincial Council, Miscellaneous Papers, Item 262, Deposition: Jacob Whisler.

13. PHMC, RG-21, Whisler Deposition.

14. *MPCP*, 9:327–28.

15. *MPCP*, 9:407, 409–10.

16. *MPCP*, 9:410–11.

17. *MPCP*, 9:414–15, 470, 489–90; Ries, "The Rage of Opposing Government"; Rowe, "The Frederick Stump Affair," 261.

18. *MPCP*, 9:416–17, 420, 422–23, 424–25, 428–30, 436–37; *PA* 4, III, 364.

19. *MPCP*, 9:444–45; Rowe, "Frederick Stump Affair," 262. On Patterson in August 1763, see chapter 12, pp. 125–26; Edward Shippen to Joseph Shippen, August 31, 1763, September 3 and 26, 1763, APS, Shippen Papers, Folder 314; "A Brief acct. of some Public Occurrences in the Province of Pennsylvania in the Administration of Governor John Penn" (undated, presumably by John Penn), HSP, Am.2016, Penn MSS, vol. 4, Indian Affairs, MS44.

20. M. Smith and Gibson, *A Declaration and Remonstrance*, 105–6; *MPCP*, 9:415, 463.

21. *MPCP*, 9:441, 446.

22. *MPCP*, 9:451–53, 488–89.

23. *MPCP*, 9:454–58 (quotes, 455).

24. *MPCP*, 9:454–58, 459–61, 473–80 (quote, 480).

25. *SCP*, 4:43.

26. *SCP*, 4:462–65, 484–85, 488–89.

27. *SCP*, 4:490–91, 510, 512–13.

28. *SCP*, 4:468–69.

29. *SCP*, 4:517–18.

30. *SCP*, 4:422–25, 481–82.

31. *SCP*, 4:495, 500, 501, 502.

32. *SCP*, 4:519–22, 525.

Chapter 21

1. McConnell, *A Country Between*, 248–54; Treese, *The Storm Gathering*, 106–7.

2. *SCP*, 3:xiv–xvii; Martin, "The Return of the Paxton Boys," 126–27.

3. *SCP*, 3:xxii–xxiii. For a succinct contemporary summary of the dispute (from the Pennsylvania perspective), see Richard Peters to Henry Wilmot, May 18, 1774, in *MPCP*, 10:177–79.

4. Petition of the "Back Inhabitants," HSP, Penn-Physick MSS, III, 18, quoted in *SCP*, 3: 103 n2.
5. *SCP*, 3:xxiv–xxvi; *MPCP*, 9:573–75.
6. *MPCP*, 9:583, 584.
7. *SCP*, 3:170–73.
8. *SCP*, 4:v–viii; Treese, *Storm Gathering*, 107; Rowe, "The Frederick Stump Affair," 282 n7.
9. *SCP*, 4:vi; Martin, "Return of the Paxton Boys," 128–29; Boyd, *The Susquehannah Company*, 29.
10. *SCP*, 4:42, 43, 45, 80; Martin, "The Return of the Paxton Boys," 129–30.
11. *SCP*, 4:51; *MPCP*, 9:679.
12. *SCP*, 4:xxxiii, 213.
13. *MPCP*, 9:682, 683.
14. *MPCP*, 9:683–84, 107–8.
15. *MPCP*, 9:685, 687–88.
16. *PA* 1, IV, 378–79.
17. JP to TP, November 25, 1770, HSP, Penn Papers, Off. Corr., X, 224, in *SCP*, 4:135; *SCP*, 4: xiv; *MPCP*, 10:52.
18. *MPCP*, 9:710–11.
19. *MPCP*, 9:711–13; *PA* 1, IV, 383, 385–92; *SCP*, 4:152–55.
20. *MPCP*, 9:714–17 (quote, 715).
21. *PA* 1, IV, 384; *SCP*, 4:153–54, 203–4.
22. *MPCP*, 9:767–73.

Chapter 22

1. *PA* 2, XVIII, 88–95; *SCP*, 5:81–86, 120–21, 142–46.
2. *SCP*, 6:144–46; Boyd, *The Susquehannah Company*, 37.
3. *SCP*, 5:9, 31, 51–52.
4. *SCP*, 6:412–14.
5. *SCP*, 7: xv; Boyd, *Susquehannah Company*, 42; Treese, *Storm Gathering*, 166.
6. Ousterhout, "Frontier Vengeance," 335–54 (especially 337, 344, 346, 347); *SCP*, 6:253; appendix.
7. *SCP*, 4:154–55; *SCP*, 7: xvin7, 47–48; *PA* 1, IV, 385–86; Ousterhout, "Frontier Vengeance," 351.
8. *SCP*, 7:48; Stefon, "The Wyoming Valley," 149–50; Knouff, "Soldiers and Violence," 183; Ousterhout, "Frontier Vengeance," 351, 354.
9. *SCP*, 7:46–47, 48; Stefon, "Wyoming Valley," 149–50; Knouff, "Soldiers and Violence," 183. On the history of the Yankee-Pennamite conflict after 1782, see Moyer, *Wild Yankees*.
10. Lincoln, "Representation in the Pennsylvania Assembly"; Hindle, "The March of the Paxton Boys," 462–63, 485–86.

11. Anon., *The Apology of the Paxton Volunteers*, 203–4; Dove, *The Quaker Unmask'd*, 209; T. Barton, *The Conduct of the Paxton-Men*, 278, 288–89, 297, 298; Knouff, "Soldiers and Violence," 172, 188; Silver, *Our Savage Neighbors*, especially 229–32, 253–92; Griffin, *American Leviathan*, especially 152–72; Morgan, *American Slavery, American Freedom*.

12. Treaty of Fort Stanwix, quoted in Reginald Horsman, "American Indian Policy in the Old Northwest, 1783–1812," *William and Mary Quarterly* 18 (January 1961), 38.

13. *Worcester v. Georgia*, 31 U.S. (6 Pet.) 515, 8 L. Ed. 483 (1832); Merrell, "Amerindians," 413–18; Arneil, *John Locke and America*, 194–200; Mehta, *Liberalism and Empire*, especially 117–132, 145–47.

14. For the term "independent commonwealths" (used pejoratively), see, for example, Anon., *The Apology of the Paxton Volunteers*, 193.

Appendix

1. On the strengths and limitations of the sources on Pennsylvania's Indians, see Merrell, " 'I desire.' "

2. *MPCP*, 9:103–4; BF, *A Narrative of the Late Massacres*, 57–58; Eshelman, *Lancaster County Indians*, 386.

3. *MPCP*, 9:103–4; BF, *Narrative*, 57–58; Eshelman, *Lancaster County Indians*, 386.

4. Dowd, *War under Heaven*, 193, 331; C. H. Martin, "Two Delaware Indians who Lived on Farm [*sic*] of Christian Hershey," *Historical Papers and Addresses of the Lancaster County Historical Society* 34 (1930): 219–20; Nolt, "A Spirit of Exclusivity," 10.

5. *MPCP*, 10:255–57; Harper, *Promised Land*, 21, 32, 33.

6. Plumb, *History of Hanover Township*, 480–81; Harvey, *A History of Wilkes-Barré*, 2:640–42; Clark, "Declaration of Lazarus Stewart"; Cavaioli, "A Profile of the Paxton Boys," 88; Downey, *History of Paxton Church*, 31. Stewart's "Declaration," first published in Egle, *History*, 69–70, is of unknown origin and has not been used as a primary source in this book.

7. Godcharles, "Colonel Matthew Smith," citing an obituary from *Kennedy's Gazette*, July 30, 1794; Hindle, "The March of the Paxton Boys," 467; *Lancaster Intelligencer & Journal*, May 16, 1843; Downey, *History of Paxton Church*, 31; Cavaioli, "Profile of the Paxton Boys," 85–86. Cavaioli cites Smith's date of birth as 1734 but agrees with Godcharles on other details. Smith's account, published in 1843, has not been used as a primary source in this work because it is a fabrication.

8. Cavaioli, "Profile of the Paxton Boys," 84–86.

BIBLIOGRAPHY

Primary Sources

Manuscript Collections

American Philosophical Society, Philadelphia
    Franklin correspondence
    Shippen papers
Dauphin County Historical Society, Harrisburg
    Elder collection
Haverford College Library, Haverford, Penna.
    Letters between the Meeting for Sufferings in London and the Meeting for
        Sufferings in Philadelphia, 1757–1815
Historical Society of Pennsylvania, Philadelphia
    Lancaster County papers
    James Logan letterbooks and Logan family papers
    "Journal of Settlement at Wright's Ferry on Susquehanna River" by Rhoda
        Barber, 1830
    Pemberton family papers
    Penn family papers
    Penn manuscripts (Indian affairs, official correspondence)
    Thomas Penn's letters to Richard Peters, 1752–1772
    Pennington papers (Edward Carey Gardner collection)
    Richard Peters papers
    Shippen papers
    Society for the Propagation of the Gospel, letters, 1732–1779
    John Smith correspondence
    Letter of Sally Potts to her sister, Philadelphia, February 9, 1764 (Society collection)
Library Company of Philadelphia
    Print collection
Pennsylvania Historical and Museum Commission, Harrisburg
    Records of the proprietary government of Pennsylvania

Public Record Office of Northern Ireland, Belfast
    Abercorn papers (T.2541)
    Alnwick papers (T.2872)
    G. M. Stewart MSS (T.1442/6)
    Wilmot papers (T.3019)
Stanford University Library, Palo Alto, Calif.
    Jeffery Amherst, Official Papers, British Manuscript Project, Library of
        Congress, microfilm reel 34/40, postscript to item 309, and reel 34/41,
        postscript to item 114 (labeled reels 32 and 33)

Newspapers and Periodicals
    Belfast Newsletter
    Hazard's Register of Pennsylvania
    Lancaster Intelligencer and Journal
    Pennsylvania Gazette
    Pennsylvania Journal

Official Colonial Records
Pennsylvania, Commonwealth of. *Minutes of the Provincial Council of Pennsylvania,
    from the Organization to the Termination of the Proprietary Government.
    Colonial Records of Pennsylvania.* 10 vols. Philadelphia and Harrisburg:
    Theophilus Fenn & Co., Joseph Severns & Co., 1852.
————. *Pennsylvania Archives.* First series, 12 vols. *Volumes I, II, and IV.* Ed.
    Samuel Hazard. Philadelphia: Joseph Severns & Co., 1852–1856.
————. *Pennsylvania Archives.* Second series, 19 vols. *Volumes VII and
    XVIII. Papers Relating to Provincial Affairs.* Ed. John B. Linn and Wm.
    H. Egle. Harrisburg: Lane S. Hart, 1878.
————. *Pennsylvania Archives.* Fourth series, 12 vols. *Volumes II and III. Papers
    of the Governors, 1747–59, 1759–1785.* Ed. George Edward Reed. Harrisburg:
    Wm. Stanley Ray, 1900.
————. *Pennsylvania Archives.* Sixth series, 14 vols. Ed. Thomas Lynch
    Montgomery. *Volume XIV. Early Petitions.* Harrisburg: Harrisburg Publishing
    Company, 1907.
————. *Pennsylvania Archives.* Eighth series, 8 vols. *Volumes VI and VII. Votes of
    the Assembly, October 14, 1756 to January 3, 1764, January 4, 1764 to October
    19, 1770.* Ed. Charles F. Horan. Harrisburg: Harrisburg Publishing Company,
    1907.
Pennsylvania, General Assembly, House of Representatives. *Votes and Proceedings
    of the House of Representatives of the Province of Pennsylvania, met at
    Philadelphia, on the Fourteenth of October, Anno Domini 1755, and Continued
    by Adjournments.* Philadelphia: B. Franklin, 1756.

————. *Votes and Proceedings of the House of Representatives of the Province of Pennsylvania met at Philadelphia, on the Fourteenth of October, anno domini 1763, and Continued by Adjournments*. Philadelphia: B. Franklin, 1764.

Contemporary Pamphlets, Poetry, and Songs

"Agricola." *The Squabble: A Pastoral Eclogue* (Philadelphia: Andrew Steuart, 1764). Reprinted in John Dunbar, ed., *The Paxton Papers*. The Hague: Martinus Nijhoff, 1957.

Anon. *The Address of the People call'd Quakers, In the Province of Pennsylvania, to John Penn, Esquire, Lieutenant-Governor of the said Province, &c.* (Philadelphia: Andrew Steuart, 1764). Reprinted in John Dunbar, ed., *The Paxton Papers*. The Hague: Martinus Nijhoff, 1957.

Anon. *An Answer to the Pamphlet Entituled the Conduct of the Paxton Men, impartially represented: Wherein the ungenerous Spirit of the Author is Manifested, &c. And the spotted Garment pluckt off* (Philadelphia: Anthony Armbruster, 1764). Reprinted in John Dunbar, ed., *The Paxton Papers*. The Hague: Martinus Nijhoff, 1957.

Anon. *The Apology of the Paxton Volunteers addressed to the candid & impartial World* (N.p.: n.p., 1764). Reprinted in John Dunbar, ed., *The Paxton Papers*. The Hague: Martinus Nijhoff, 1957.

Anon. "A Battle! A Battle! A Battle of Squirt, Where no Man is kill'd And no Man is hurt! To the Tune of three Blue Beans, in a Blue Bladder; Rattle Bladder Rattle!" (Philadelphia: Edward Merefield, 1764). Reprinted in John Dunbar, ed., *The Paxton Papers*. The Hague: Martinus Nijhoff, 1957.

Anon. *The Cloven-Foot discovered* (N.p.: n.p., 1764). Reprinted in John Dunbar, ed., *The Paxton Papers*. The Hague: Martinus Nijhoff, 1957.

Anon. *A Dialogue, Between Andrew Trueman, and Thomas Zealot; About the killing the Indians at Cannestogoe and Lancaster* (Philadelphia: Anthony Armbruster, 1764). Reprinted in John Dunbar, ed., *The Paxton Papers*. The Hague: Martinus Nijhoff, 1957.

Anon. *A Dialogue, Containing Some Reflections on the Late Declaration and Remonstrance, Of the Back-Inhabitants of the Province of Pennsylvania. With a Serious and Short Address, to those Presbyterians, who (to Their Dishonor) have too much abetted, and conniv'd at the late Insurrection. By a Member of that Community* (Philadelphia: Andrew Steuart, 1764). Reprinted in John Dunbar, ed., *The Paxton Papers*. The Hague: Martinus Nijhoff, 1957.

Anon. *The [P]axton Boys, A Farce. Translated from the Original French, By a Native of Donegall*. 2nd ed. (Philadelphia: Anthony Armbruster, 1764). Reprinted in John Dunbar, ed., *The Paxton Papers*. The Hague: Martinus Nijhoff, 1957.

Anon. *A Serious Address, to Such of the Inhabitants of Pennsylvania, As have connived at, or do approve of, the late Massacre of the Indians at Lancaster; or the Design of Killing Those Who Are Now in the Barracks at Philadelphia* (Philadelphia:

Andrew Steuart, 1764). Reprinted in John Dunbar, ed., *The Paxton Papers.* The Hague: Martinus Nijhoff, 1957.

Anon. "A Touch on the Times. A New Song. To the tune of Nancy Dawson." Philadelphia(?): n.p., 1764. American Antiquarian Society, Early American Imprints, 1st series, no. 41494 (filmed), 4 pages.

Anon. "True Paxton Boys. A New Song, in High Vogue in Northampton County, in the Province of Pennsylvania (To the tune of Bold Sawyer)." Philadelphia: Printed for the author, 1771. American Antiquarian Society, Early American Imprints, 1st series, no. 12153 (filmed), 1 sheet.

Barton, Thomas. *The Conduct of the Paxton-Men, Impartially represented; The Distresses of the Frontiers, and the Complaints and Sufferings of the People fully stated; and the Methods recommended by the wisest Nations, in such Cases, seriously consider'd; With Some Remarks upon the Narrative, of the Indian-Massacre, lately publish'd* (Philadelphia: Andrew Steuart, 1764). Reprinted in John Dunbar, ed., *The Paxton Papers.* The Hague: Martinus Nijhoff, 1957.

———. *Unanimity and Public Spirit. A Sermon Preached at Carlisle, and some other Episcopal Churches, in the Counties of York and Cumberland, soon after General Braddock's Defeat.* Philadelphia: Franklin and Hall, 1755.

Dawkins, Henry. *The Paxton Expedition. Inscribed to the Author of the Farce, by H. D.* (Philadelphia: n.p., 1764). Reprinted in John Dunbar, ed., *The Paxton Papers.* The Hague: Martinus Nijhoff, 1957.

Dove, David James. *The Quaker Unmask'd; or, Plain Truth: Humbly address'd to the Consideration of all the Freemen of Pennsylvania.* 2nd ed. (Philadelphia: Andrew Steuart, 1764). Reprinted in John Dunbar, ed., *The Paxton Papers.* The Hague: Martinus Nijhoff, 1957.

Dunbar, John R., ed. *The Paxton Papers.* The Hague: Martinus Nijhoff, 1957.

Franklin, Benjamin. *Cool Thoughts on the Present Situation of Our Public Affairs. In a Letter to a Friend in the Country.* Philadelphia: W. Dunlap, 1764.

———. *A Narrative of the Late Massacres, in Lancaster County, of A Number of Indians, Friends of this Province, By Persons unknown. With some Observations on the same* (Philadelphia: Anthony Armbruster, 1764). Reprinted in John Dunbar, ed., *The Paxton Papers.* The Hague: Martinus Nijhoff, 1957.

———. *Observations concerning the Increase of Mankind, Peopling of Countries, &c.* In William Clarke, *Observations on the late and present Conduct of the French, With Regard to their Encroachments upon the British Colonies in North America: Together with Remarks on the Importance of these Colonies to Great Britain.* Boston: S. Kneeland, 1755.

Gymnast, Christopher. *The Paxtionade: A Poem. By Christopher Gymnast, Esqr.; With the Prolegomena and Exercitations of, Scriblerus* (Philadelphia: Anthony Armbruster, 1764). Reprinted in John Dunbar, ed., *The Paxton Papers.* The Hague: Martinus Nijhoff, 1957.

Hunt, Isaac ["Philo-Liberatatis," pseud.]. *A Looking-Glass for Presbyterians. Or a brief Examination of Their Loyalty, Merits, and other Qualifications*

for Government: With some Animadversions on the Quaker unmask'd.
Humbly Address'd to the Consideration of the Loyal Freemen of Pennsylvania
(Philadelphia: Anthony Armbruster, 1764). Reprinted in John Dunbar, ed.,
The Paxton Papers. The Hague: Martinus Nijhoff, 1957.

————. *A Looking-Glass, &c. Numb. II* (N.p.: n.p., 1764). Reprinted in John
Dunbar, ed., *The Paxton Papers.* The Hague: Martinus Nijhoff, 1957.

Hunt, Isaac. *A Humble Attempt at Scurrility: In Imitation of Those Great Masters*
of the ART, the Rev. Dr. S—th; the Rev. Dr. Al———n; the Rev. Mr. Ew-n;
the irreverend D. J. D-ve, and the heroic J—n D————-n, Esq; Being a Full
Answer to the Answer to the Observations on Mr. H———s's Advertisement.
By Jack Retort, Student in Scurrility. Quilsylvania [Philadelphia]: Anthony
Armbruster, 1765.

"Philadelphiensis." *Remarks on the Quaker Unmask'd; Or Plain Truth Found to be*
Plain Falshood. Humbly Address'd to the Candid (Philadelphia: John Morris,
1764). Reprinted in John Dunbar, ed., *The Paxton Papers.* The Hague:
Martinus Nijhoff, 1957.

"Philalethes." *The Quaker Vindicated; or, Observations on A Late Pamphlet,*
Entituled, The Quaker Unmask'd, Or, Plain Truth (Philadelphia: Andrew
Steuart, 1764). Reprinted in John Dunbar, ed., *The Paxton Papers.* The
Hague: Martinus Nijhoff, 1957.

"Philanthropos." *The Quakers Assisting, To Preserve the Lives of the Indians, in the*
Barracks, Vindicated And proved to be consistent with Reason, Agreeable to our
Law, hath an inseperable Connection with the Law of God, and exactly agree-
able with the Principles of the People call'd Quakers (Philadelphia: Anthony
Armbruster, 1764). Reprinted in John Dunbar, ed., *The Paxton Papers.* The
Hague: Martinus Nijhoff, 1957.

————. *The Quakers Assisting, To preserve the Lives of the Indians, in the Barracks,*
vindicated: Shewing wherein, the Author of the Quaker Unmask'd, hath turn'd
King's Evidence; impeached himself, and cleared the Quakers from all the heavy
Charges he hath Published against them. Number II (Philadelphia: Anthony
Armbruster, 1764). Reprinted in John Dunbar, ed., *The Paxton Papers.* The
Hague: Martinus Nijhoff, 1957.

"Philanthropy." *An Answer, to Pamphlet Entituled The Conduct of the Paxton*
Men, impartially represented: Wherein the ungenerous Spirit of the Author is
Manifested, &c. And the spotted Garment pluckt off (Philadelphia: Anthony
Armbruster, 1764). Reprinted in John Dunbar, ed., *The Paxton Papers.* The
Hague: Martinus Nijhoff, 1957.

Read, Charles. *Copy of a Letter from Charles Read, Esq.; To the Hon. John Ladd, Esq;*
and his Associates, Justices of the Peace for the County of Gloucester (Philadelphia:
Andrew Steuart, 1764). Reprinted in John Dunbar, ed., *The Paxton Papers.*
The Hague: Martinus Nijhoff, 1957.

Smith, Matthew, and James Gibson. *A Declaration and Remonstrance of the dis-*
tressed and bleeding Frontier Inhabitants Of the Province of Pennsylvania,

Presented by Them to the Honourable the Governor and Assembly of the Province, Shewing the Causes of Their late Discontent and Uneasiness and the Grievances Under which they have laboured, and which they humbly pray to have redress'd (Philadelphia: William Bradford, 1764). Reprinted in John Dunbar, ed., *The Paxton Papers*. The Hague: Martinus Nijhoff, 1957.

"Well Wisher." *An Historical Account, of the Late Disturbance, between the Inhabitants of the Back Settlements; of Pennsylvania, and the Philadelphians, &. Impartially related by a well Wisher. The Second Edition, may be called a Piracy. I Said Printed at Rome: I meant nothing but Printed in Second-Street, by Andrew Steuars-Stockfish* (Philadelphia: Anthony Armbruster, 1764). Reprinted in John Dunbar, ed., *The Paxton Papers*. The Hague: Martinus Nijhoff, 1957.

"Wiggwag, Timothy." *The Author of Quaker Unmask'd, Strip'd Start Naked, Or the Delineated Presbyterian Play'd Hob With* (Philadelphia: n.p., 1764). Reprinted in John Dunbar, ed., *The Paxton Papers*. The Hague: Martinus Nijhoff, 1957.

Williamson, Hugh ["W. D.," pseud.]. *The Plain Dealer: Or, A few Remarks upon Quaker Politicks, And their Attempts to Change the Government Of Pennsylvania. With Some Observations on the false and abusive Papers which they have lately publish'd. Numb. I. To Be Continued* (Philadelphia: Andrew Steuart, 1764). Reprinted in John Dunbar, ed., *The Paxton Papers*. The Hague: Martinus Nijhoff, 1957.

———. *The Plain Dealer: Or, Remarks on Quaker Politicks in Pennsylvania. Numb. III. To Be Continued. By W. D. Author No. I* (Philadelphia: Andrew Steuart, 1764). Reprinted in John Dunbar, ed., *The Paxton Papers*. The Hague: Martinus Nijhoff, 1957.

Williamson, Hugh. *What is sauce for a Goose is also sauce for a Gander. Being a small Touch in the Lapidary Way. Or Tit for Tat, in your own Way. An Epitaph On a certain great Man. Written by a departed Spirit and now Most humbly inscrib'd to all his dutiful Sons and Children, Who may hereafter chose to distinguish him by the name of A Patriot.* Philadelphia: Anthony Armbruster, 1764.

Contemporary Accounts and Collected Documents

Barton, William, ed. *Memoirs of the Life of David Rittenhouse, LL.D. F.R.S. Late President of the American Philosophical Society, &c., Interspersed with Various Notices of Many Distinguished Men with an Appendix, Containing Sundry Philosophical and Other Papers, Most of Which Have Not Hitherto Been Published.* Philadelphia: Edward Parker, 1813.

Bourdin, H. L., and S. T. Williams, eds. "Crèvecouer on the Susquehanna, 1774–1776." *Yale Review* 14 (1925): 552–84.

Boyd, Julian P., and Robert J. Taylor, eds. *The Susquehannah Company Papers.* 11 vols. Ithaca, N.Y.: Cornell University Press, 1962–1971.

Clark, Martha B., ed. "Declaration of Lazarus Stewart." *Papers of the Lancaster County Historical Society* 14.10 (1910): 301–9.

Davies, John. *A Discovery of the True Causes Why Ireland Was Never Entirely Subdued And Brought Under Obedience of the Crown Until the Beginning of His Majesty's Happy Reign.* Ed. James J. Myers. 1612; Washington, D.C.: Catholic University Press of America, 1988.

Dunn, Mary Maples, and Richard S. Dunn, eds. *The Papers of William Penn.* 4 vols. Philadelphia: University of Pennsylvania Press, 1981–1987.

Foulke, Samuel. "Fragments of a Journal Kept by Samuel Foulke, of Bucks County, While a Member of the Colonial Assembly of Pennsylvania, 1762–3–4." *Pennsylvania Magazine of History and Biography* 5 (1881): 60–73.

Franklin, Benjamin. *The Papers of Benjamin Franklin.* Ed. Leonard W. Labaree. 30 vols. New Haven, Conn.: Yale University Press, 1959–93.

Heckewelder, John. *History, Manners, and Customs of the Indian Nations, Who Once Inhabited Pennsylvania and the Neighbouring States.* 1876; New York: Arno Press, 1971.

———. *A Narrative of the Missions of the United Brethren Among the Delaware and Mohegan Indians, from its Commencement in the Year 1740, to the Close of the Year 1808.* 1820; New York: Arno Press, 1971.

Hooker, Richard J., ed. *The Carolina Backcountry on the Eve of the Revolution: The Journal and Other Writings of Charles Woodmason, Anglican Itinerant.* Chapel Hill: University of North Carolina Press, 1953.

Hunter, William A., ed. "Thomas Barton and the Forbes Expedition." *Pennsylvania Magazine of History and Biography* 95 (October 1971): 431–83.

Jacobs, Wilbur R., ed. *The Paxton Riots and the Frontier Theory.* Chicago: Rand McNally, 1967.

James, Alfred P., ed. *Writings of General John Forbes Relating to his Service in North America.* Menasha, Wisc.: Collegiate Press, 1938.

Locke, John. *Second Treatise of Government.* Edited with an introduction by C. B. McPherson. 1690; Indianapolis, Ind.: Hackett, 1980.

Muhlenberg, H. Melchior. *The Journals of Henry Melchior Muhlenberg. In Three Volumes.* Trans. Theodore G. Tappert and John W. Doberstein. Philadelphia: Muhlenberg Press, 1942–1958.

O'Callaghan, E. B., ed. *Documents Relative to the Colonial History of New York.* 15 vols, 1853–1887. Procured by John Romeyn Brodhead. *Vol. VII.* Albany, N.Y.: Weed, Parsons, 1856.

Post, Christian Frederick. "The Journal of Christian Frederick Post, in his Journey from *Philadelphia* to the *Ohio*, on a Message from the Government of *Pennsylvania* to the *Delaware, Shawanese* and *Mingo* Indians settled there, and formerly in Alliance with the *English.*" In Charles Thomson, *An Enquiry into the Causes of the Alienation of the Delaware and Shawanese Indians from the British Interest.* London: J. Wilkie, 1759.

———. "The second journal of Christian Frederick Post, on a message from the Governor of Pennsylvania, to the Indians on the Ohio, in the latter part of the same year." In Robert Proud, *The History of Pennsylvania, in North America, from the Original Institution and Settlement of that Province*. 2 vols. Vol. 2, part II, Appendix. 1798; Spartanburg, S.C.: Reprint Co., 1967.

Proud, Robert. *The History of Pennsylvania, in North America, from the Original Institution and Settlement of that Province, under the first Proprietor and Governor William Penn, in 1681, till after the Year 1742 ... To Which is Added a Brief Description of the Said Province and of the General State, in Which it Flourished, Principally Between the Years 1760 and 1770*. 2 vols. 1797–1798; Spartanburg, S.C.: Reprint Co., 1967.

Shippen, Joseph. "Military Letters of Joseph Shippen." *Pennsylvania Magazine of History and Biography* 36 (1912): 367–85.

Smith, James. *An Account of the Remarkable Occurrences in the Life and Travels of Col. James Smith, (now a citizen of Bourbon County, Kentucky) during his Captivity with the Indians, in the years 1755, '56, '57, '58, & '59* (Lexington, Ky.: John Bradford, 1799). Reprinted in *Scoowa: James Smith's Captivity Narrative*. Columbus: Ohio Historical Society, 1978.

Smith, William. *A Brief State of the Province of Pennsylvania in Which the Conduct of their Assemblies for Several Years Past is Impartially Examined, and the True cause of the Continual Encroachments of the French Displayed, More Especially the Secret Design of their Late Unwarrantable Invasion and Settlement upon the River Ohio*. 1755; New York: J. Sabin, 1865.

Soderlund, Jean R., ed. *William Penn and the Founding of Pennsylvania, 1680–1684: A Documentary History*. Philadelphia: University of Pennsylvania Press, 1983.

Thomson, Charles. *An Enquiry into the Causes of the Alienation of the Delaware and Shawanese Indians from the British Interest*. London: J. Wilkie, 1759.

Van Doren, Carl, ed. *Letters and Papers of Benjamin Franklin and Richard Jackson, 1753–1785*. Philadelphia: American Philosophical Society, 1947.

Woolman, John. *The Journal of John Woolman, and A Plea for the Poor*. John Greenleaf Whittier edition. Introduction by Frederick B. Tolles. 1961; Gloucester, Mass.: P. Smith, 1971.

Nineteenth-century Histories

Clare, Israel Smith. *A Brief History of Lancaster County*. Lancaster, Penna.: Argus, 1892.

Downey, William W. *History of Paxton Church*. Harrisburg, Penna.: Independent Steam Book and Job Print, 1877.

Egle, William H. *History of the Counties of Dauphin and Lebanon, in the Commonwealth of Pennsylvania: Biographical and Genealogical*. Philadelphia: Everts and Peck, 1883.

Ellis, Franklin, and Samuel Evans. *History of Lancaster County, with Biographical Sketches of Many of its Pioneers and Prominent Men*. Philadelphia: Everts and Peck, 1883.

Gordon, Thomas F. *The History of Pennsylvania, from its Discovery by Europeans to the Declaration of Independence in 1776.* Philadelphia: Carey, Lea & Carey, 1829.

Harris, Alex. *A Biographical History of Lancaster County. Being a History of Early Settlers and Eminent Men of the County; as Also Much Other Unpublished Historical Information Chiefly of a Local Character.* Lancaster, Penna.: Elias Barr & Co., 1872.

Hayden, Horace E., ed. *The Massacre of Wyoming: The Acts of Congress for the Defense of the Wyoming Valley, Pennsylvania, 1776–1778: With the Petitions of the Sufferers by the Massacre of July 3, 1778, for Congressional Aid.* Wilkes-Barré, Penna.: Wyoming Historical and Geological Society, 1895.

Jones, U. J. *History of the Early Settlement of Juniata Valley: Embracing an Account of the Early Pioneers, and the Trials and Privations Incident to the Settlement of the Valley, Predatory Incursions, Massacres, and Abductions by the Indians During the French and Indian Wars, and the War of the Revolution, &c.* Philadelphia: Henry B. Ashmead, 1856.

McAlarney, Mathias W., ed. *History of the Sesqui-Centennial of Paxtang Church. September 18, 1890.* Harrisburg, Penna.: Harrisburg Publishing Company, 1890.

Mombert, J. L. *An Authentic History of Lancaster County in the State of Pennsylvania.* Lancaster, Penna.: J. E. Barr, 1869.

Parkman, Francis. *The Conspiracy of Pontiac and the Indian War after the Conquest of Canada.* 3 vols. Boston: Little, Brown, 1898.

Plumb, Henry Blackman. *History of Hanover Township, Including Sugar Notch, Ashley, and Nanticoke Boroughs, And Also a History of Wyoming Valley in Luzerne County, Pennsylvania.* Wilkes-Barré, Penna.: Robert Baur, 1885.

Rupp, Israel Daniel, ed. *An Account of the Manners of the German Inhabitants of Pennsylvania, Written 1789, by Benjamin Rush, M.D.* Philadelphia: Samuel P. Town, 1875.

———, comp. *The History and Topography of Dauphin, Cumberland, Franklin, Bedford, Adams, and Perry Counties.* Lancaster, Penna.: Gilbert Hills, 1846.

———, comp. *History of Lancaster County.* Lancaster, Penna.: Gilbert Hills, 1844.

The Scotch-Irish in America: Proceedings and Addresses of the Eighth Scotch-Irish Congress, at Harrisburg, PA, June 4–7, 1896. Comprising lectures by John M. Cooper, Samuel Evans, William Henry Egle, A. Boyd Hamilton, Robert McKeen, George Norcross, W. F. Rutherford, and J. W. Simonton. Nashville, Tenn.: Scotch-Irish Society of America, 1897.

Stone, William L. *Border Wars of the American Revolution.* 2 vols. New York: Harper, 1845.

Turner, Frederick Jackson. "The Significance of the Frontier in American History." In *Report of the American Historical Association* (Washington, D.C., 1893): 199–227.

Wallace, B. J. "Insurrection of the Paxton Boys." *Presbyterian Quarterly Review* 8 (1860): 627–77.

Watson, John Fanning. *Annals of Philadelphia*. Philadelphia: E. L. Carey & A. Hart, 1830.

Webster, Richard. *A History of the Presbyterian Church in America*. Philadelphia: J. M. Wilson, 1857.

Wing, Conway P., et al. *History of Cumberland County, Pennsylvania, With Illustrations*. Philadelphia: James D. Scott, 1879.

Select Secondary Literature

Anderson, Fred. *Crucible of War: The Seven Years' War and the Fate of Empire in British North America, 1754–1766*. New York: Vintage, 2000.

———. *The War That Made America: A Short History of the French and Indian War*. New York: Viking, 2005.

Arneil, Barbara. *John Locke and America: The Defence of English Colonialism*. Oxford: Clarendon Press, 1996.

Barr, Daniel P. "'A Road for Warriors': The Western Delawares and the Seven Years War." *Pennsylvania History* 73.1 (2006): 1–36.

Barton, Rose G. "The Rev. Thomas Barton." *Lancaster County Historical Society Papers* 30 (1926): 101–4.

Baumann, Lottie M. "Massacre of Conestoga Indians, 1763: Incidents and Details." *Historical Papers and Addresses of the Lancaster County Historical Society* 18 (1914): 169–85.

Bockelman, Wayne L. "Local Politics in Pre-Revolutionary Lancaster County." *Pennsylvania Magazine of History and Biography* 97 (January 1973): 45–74.

Boyd, Julian P. "Connecticut's Experiment in Expansion: The Susquehannah Company, 1753–1803." *Journal of Economic and Business History* 4 (1931): 36–89.

———. *The Susquehannah Company: Connecticut's Experiment in Expansion*. New Haven, Conn.: Yale University Press, 1935.

Brackbill, Martin H. "The Manor of Conestoga in the Colonial Period." *Papers of the Lancaster County Historical Society* 42.2 (1938): 17–46.

———. "Peter Bezaillion's Road." *Papers of the Lancaster County Historical Society* 43.1 (1939): 1–48.

Bronner, Edwin B. "The Quakers and Non-Violence in Pennsylvania." *Pennsylvania History* 35.1 (1968): 1–22.

Brooks, Joanna. "Held Captive by the Irish: Quaker Captivity Narratives in Frontier Pennsylvania." *New Hibernia Review* 8 (Autumn 2004): 31–46.

Brumwell, Stephen. *White Devil: A True Story of War, Savagery, and Vengeance in Colonial America*. New York: Da Capo Press, 2005.

Butzin, Peter A. "Politics, Presbyterians and the Paxton Riots, 1763–64." *Journal of Presbyterian History* 51 (1973): 70–84.

Buxbaum, Melvin. H. *Benjamin Franklin and the Zealous Presbyterians*. University Park: Penn State University Press, 1975.

Calloway, Colin. *The American Revolution in Indian Country: Crisis and Diversity in Native American Communities*. New York: Cambridge University Press, 1995.

———. *The Scratch of a Pen: 1763 and the Transformation of North America*. New York: Oxford University Press, 2006.

Camenzind, Krista. "From the Holy Experiment to the Paxton Boys: Violence, Manhood, and Race in Pennsylvania during the Seven Years' War." Unpublished Ph.D. dissertation, University of California, San Diego, 2002.

Cavaioli, Frank J. "A Profile of the Paxton Boys: Murderers of the Conestoga Indians." *Journal of the Lancaster County Historical Society* 87 (1983): 74–96.

Cross, Pearson G. "Collective Action in Colonial America: The Structural Determinants of Individual Participation in the Paxton Riots, 1763–64." Unpublished Ph.D. dissertation, Brandeis University, 1997.

Crowley, James E. "The Paxton Disturbance and Ideas of Order in Pennsylvania Politics." *Pennsylvania History* 37.4 (1970): 317–39.

Cummings, Hubertis M. "The Paxton Killings." *Journal of Presbyterian History* 44 (December 1966): 219–43.

Cutcliffe, Stephen H. "Sideling Hill Affair: The Cumberland County Riots of 1765." *Western Pennsylvania Historical Magazine* 59 (January 1976): 39–53.

Davidson, Robert L. *War Comes to Quaker Pennsylvania, 1682–1756*. New York: Columbia University Press, 1957.

Dickson, R. J. *Ulster Emigration to Colonial America, 1718–1775*. London: Routledge and Kegan Paul, 1966.

Dixon, David. *Never Come to Peace Again: Pontiac's Uprising and the Fate of the British Empire in North America*. Norman: University of Oklahoma Press, 2005.

Donnelly, James S., Jr. "Hearts of Oak, Hearts of Steel." *Studia Hibernica* 21 (1981): 7–73.

Dowd, Gregory Evans. *A Spirited Resistance: The North American Indian Struggle for Unity, 1745–1815*. Baltimore: Johns Hopkins University Press, 1992.

———. *War under Heaven: Pontiac, the Indian Nations, and the British Empire*. Baltimore: Johns Hopkins University Press, 2002.

Dunaway, Wayland F. "Pennsylvania as an Early Distribution Center of Population." *Pennsylvania Magazine of History and Biography* 55 (1931): 134–64.

———. *The Scotch-Irish of Colonial Pennsylvania*. Chapel Hill: University of North Carolina Press, 1944.

Dunn, Richard S. "William Penn's Odyssey: From Child of Light to Absentee Landlord." In John Morrill, Paul Slack, and Daniel Woolf, eds., *Public Duty and Private Conscience in Seventeenth Century England: Essays Presented to G. E. Aylmer*. Oxford: Clarendon Press, 1993.

Engels, Jeremy. "'Equipped for Murder': The Paxton Boys and 'the Spirit of Killing all Indians' in Pennsylvania, 1763–1764." *Rhetoric and Public Affairs* 8.3 (2005): 355–82.

Eshelman, H. Frank. *Lancaster County Indians: Annals of the Susquehannocks and other Indian Tribes of the Susquehanna Territory from about the Year 1500 to 1763, the Date of their Extinction.* Lancaster, Penna.: n.p., 1908.

———. "The Political History and Development of Lancaster County's First Twenty Years, 1729–1749." *Lancaster County Historical Society Papers* 20 (1916): 37–68.

Eustace, Nicole. "'Passion is the Gale': Emotion and Power on the Eve of the American Revolution." Unpublished Ph.D. dissertation, University of Pennsylvania, 2001.

Faragher, John Mack. *A Great and Noble Scheme: The Tragic Story of the Expulsion of the French Acadians from Their American Homeland.* New York: Norton, 2005.

Fowler, William M., Jr. *Empires at War: The French and Indian War and the Struggle for North America, 1654–1763.* New York: Walker, 2005.

Frantz, John B., and William Pencak. *Beyond Philadelphia: The American Revolution in the Pennsylvania Hinterlands.* University Park: Penn State University Press, 1998.

Franz, George William. *Paxton: A Study of Community Structure and Mobility in the Colonial Pennsylvania Backcountry.* New York: Garland, 1989.

———. "The Paxton Boys." In Robert Secor, gen. ed., *Pennsylvania 1776.* University Park: Penn State University Press, 1975.

Gleason, J. Philip. "A Scurrilous Colonial Election and Franklin's Reputation." *William and Mary Quarterly*, 3rd Ser., 18 (January 1961): 68–84.

Godcharles, Frederic A. "Colonel Matthew Smith: Soldier and Statesman." *Northumberland County Historical Society Proceedings and Addresses* 12 (March 1, 1942): 35–54.

———. "The Influence of Lancaster County on the Pennsylvania Frontier." *Lancaster County Historical Society Papers* 14 (1920): 77–82.

Graymont, Barbara. *The Iroquois in the American Revolution.* Syracuse, N.Y.: Syracuse University Press, 1972.

Green, E. R. R. "Scotch-Irish Emigration: An Imperial Problem, 1636–1776." *Western Pennsylvania History Magazine* 35 (1952): 193–209.

———. "The 'Strange Humors' That Drove the Scotch-Irish to America, 1729." *William and Mary Quarterly*, 3rd series, 12 (January 1955): 113–23.

Griffin, Patrick. *American Leviathan: Empire, Nation, and Revolutionary Frontier.* New York: Hill and Wang, 2007.

———. *The People with No Name: Ireland's Ulster Scots, America's Scots Irish, and the Creation of a British Atlantic World, 1689–1764.* Princeton, N.J.: Princeton University Press, 2001.

Hanna, Charles A. *The Scotch-Irish or the Scot in North Britain, North Ireland, and North America*. 1902; Baltimore: Genealogical Publishing Co., 1968.

Hanna, William S. *Benjamin Franklin and Pennsylvania Politics*. Stanford: Stanford University Press, 1964.

Harper, Steven C. *Promised Land: Penn's Holy Experiment, the Walking Purchase, and the Dispossession of the Delawares, 1600–1763*. Bethlehem, Penna.: Lehigh University Press, 2006.

Harvey, Oscar Jewell. *A History of Wilkes-Barré, Luzerne County, Pennsylvania, from its First Beginnings to the Present Time; Including Chapters of Newly-Discovered early Wyoming Valley History, Together with Many Biographical Sketches and Much Genealogical Material*. 6 vols. Wilkes-Barré, Penna.: Raeder Press, 1909–1930.

Hinderaker, Eric. *Elusive Empires: Constructing Colonialism in the Ohio Valley, 1673–1800*. Cambridge: Cambridge University Press, 1997.

Hinderaker, Eric, and Peter Mancall. *At the Edge of Empire: The Backcountry in British North America*. Baltimore: Johns Hopkins University Press, 2003.

Hindle, Brooke. "The March of the Paxton Boys." *William and Mary Quarterly*, 3rd ser., 3 (October 1946): 461–86.

Hunter, William A. *Forts on the Pennsylvania Frontier, 1753–1758*. Harrisburg: Pennsylvania Historical and Museum Commission, 1960.

———. "Victory at Kittanning." *Pennsylvania History* 23.3 (1956): 376–407.

Hutson, James H. "Benjamin Franklin and Pennsylvania Politics, 1751–1755: A Reappraisal." *Pennsylvania Magazine of History and Biography* 93 (July 1969): 303–71.

———. "The Campaign to Make Pennsylvania a Royal Province, 1764–1770," part I. *Pennsylvania Magazine of History and Biography* 94 (October 1970): 427–63.

———. "The Campaign to Make Pennsylvania a Royal Province, 1764–1770," part II. *Pennsylvania Magazine of History and Biography* 95 (January 1971): 28–49.

———. "An Investigation of the Inarticulate: Philadelphia's White Oaks." *William and Mary Quarterly*, 3rd ser., 28 (January 1971): 3–26.

———. *Pennsylvania Politics, 1746–1770: The Movement for Royal Government and Its Consequences*. Princeton, N.J.: Princeton University Press, 1972.

Jacobs, Wilbur. *Dispossessing the American Indian: Indians and Whites on the Colonial Frontier*. New York: Charles Scribner's Sons, 1972.

———. "The Indian Frontier of 1763." *Western Pennsylvania History Magazine* 34 (1951): 185–98.

———. *Wilderness Politics and Indian Gifts: The Northern Colonial Frontier, 1748–1763*. Lincoln: University of Nebraska Press, 1950.

Jennings, Francis. *The Ambiguous Iroquois Empire: The Covenant Chain Confederation of Indian Tribes with English Colonies from Its Beginnings to the Lancaster Treaty of 1744*. New York: Norton, 1984.

———. *The American Indian and the American Revolution*. Chicago: Newberry Library, 1983.

———. "The Constitutional Evolution of the Covenant Chain." *Proceedings of the American Philosophical Society* 115 (April 1971): 88–96.

———. "The Delaware Interregnum." *Pennsylvania Magazine of History and Biography* 89 (April 1965): 174–98.

———. *Empire of Fortune: Crowns, Colonies, and Tribes in the Seven Years War in America*. New York: Norton, 1988.

———. "Glory, Death, and Transfiguration: The Susquehannock Indians in the Seventeenth Century." *Proceedings of the American Philosophical Society* 112 (January 1968): 15–53.

———. "Incident at Tulpehocken." *Pennsylvania History* 35.4 (1968): 335–55.

———. "The Indians' Revolution." In Alfred E. Young, ed., *The American Revolution: Explorations in the History of American Radicalism*. De Kalb: Northern Illinois University Press, 1976.

———. "The Indian Trade of the Susquehanna Valley." *Proceedings of the American Philosophical Society* 110 (December 1966): 406–24.

———. *The Invasion of America: Indians, Colonialism, and the Cant of Conquest*. New York: Norton, 1984.

———. "The Scandalous Indian Policy of William Penn's Sons: Deeds and Documents of the Walking Purchase." *Pennsylvania History* 37.1 (1970): 19–39.

———. "A Vanishing Indian: Francis Parkman Versus His Sources." *Pennsylvania Magazine of History and Biography* 87 (July 1963): 306–23.

———. "Virgin Land and Savage People." *American Quarterly* 23 (October 1971): 519–41.

Jones, Maldwyn A. "The Scotch-Irish in British America." In Bernard Bailyn and Philip D. Morgan, eds., *Strangers within the Realm: Cultural Margins of the First British Empire*. Chapel Hill: University of North Carolina Press, 1991.

Kelker, Luther R. *History of Dauphin County, Pennsylvania*. 3 vols. New York: Lewis, 1907.

Ketcham, Ralph L. "Conscience, War, and Politics in Pennsylvania, 1755–1757." *William and Mary Quarterly*, 3rd ser., 20 (July 1963): 416–39.

King, J. W. "Colonel John Armstrong." *Western Pennsylvania Historical Magazine* 10 (July 1927): 129–45.

Klein, H. M. J., ed. *Lancaster County, A History*. 4 vols. New York: Lewis, 1924.

Klein, Randolph Shipley. *Portrait of an Early American Family: The Shippens of Pennsylvania across Five Generations*. Philadelphia: University of Pennsylvania Press, 1975.

Klett, Guy S. *Presbyterians in Colonial Pennsylvania*. Philadelphia: University of Pennsylvania Press, 1937.

———. "Scotch-Irish Presbyterians Pioneering along the Susquehanna River." *Pennsylvania History* 20.2 (1953): 165–79.

Knouff, Gregory T. "Soldiers and Violence on the Pennsylvania Frontier." In John B. Frantz and William Pencak, eds., *Beyond Philadelphia: The American Revolution in the Pennsylvania Hinterlands*. University Park: Penn State University Press, 1998.

Landsman, Ned. "James Logan and the Atlantic Enlightenment." Stenton, www.stenton.org/research/landsman_enlightenment.cfm (accessed July 3, 2006).

———. "Presbyterians, Evangelicals, and the Educational Culture of the Middle Colonies." *Pennsylvania History* 64, special supplementary issue (Summer 1997): 168–82.

Lemisch, Jesse, and John K. Alexander. "The White Oaks, Jack Tar, and the Concept of the 'Inarticulate'... With a Rebuttal by James H. Hutson." *William and Mary Quarterly*, 3rd ser., 29 (January 1972): 109–42.

Lemon, James T. *The Best Poor Man's Country: A Geographical Study of Southeastern Pennsylvania*. Baltimore: Johns Hopkins University Press, 1972.

Leyburn, James G. *The Scotch-Irish: A Social History*. Chapel Hill: University of North Carolina Press, 1962.

Lincoln, Charles H. "Representation in the Pennsylvania Assembly Prior to the Revolution." *Pennsylvania Magazine of History and Biography* 23 (1899): 23–34.

———. *The Revolutionary Movement in Pennsylvania, 1760–1776*. Philadelphia: University of Pennsylvania Press, 1901.

Lockhart, Audrey. *Some Aspects of Emigration from Ireland to the North American Colonies between 1660 and 1775*. New York: Arno Press, 1976.

Maier, Pauline. "Popular Uprisings and Civil Authority in Eighteenth-Century America." *William and Mary Quarterly*, 3rd ser., 27 (January 1970): 3–35.

Mancall, Peter C. "The Revolutionary War and the Indians of the Upper Susquehanna Valley." *American Indian Culture and Resource Journal* 12.1 (1988): 39–58.

———. *Valley of Opportunity: Economic Culture along the Upper Susquehanna, 1700–1800*. Ithaca, N.Y.: Cornell University Press, 1991.

Marietta, Jack D. "Conscience, the Quaker Community and the French and Indian War." *Pennsylvania Magazine of History and Biography* 95 (January 1971): 3–27.

Marshall, Peter. "The West and the Amerindians, 1756–1776." In Jack P. Greene and J. R. Pole, eds., *Blackwell Companions to American History: A Companion to the American Revolution*. Malden, Mass.: Blackwell, 2000.

Marston, Daniel. *The French-Indian War*. Oxford: Osprey, 2002.

Martin, James Kirby. "The Return of the Paxton Boys and the Historical State of the Pennsylvania Frontier, 1764–1774." *Pennsylvania History* 38.2 (1971): 117–33.

Mayer, Holly A. "From Forts to Families: Following the Army into Western Pennsylvania, 1758–1776." *Pennsylvania Magazine of History and Biography* 130 (January 2006): 5–44.

Mayer, Peter, ed. *The Pacifist Conscience.* Chicago: Henry Regnery, 1967.

McBride, Ian. *The Siege of Derry in Ulster Protestant Mythology.* Dublin: Four Courts Press, 1997.

McConnell, Michael. *A Country Between: The Upper Ohio Valley and Its Peoples, 1724–1774.* Lincoln: University of Nebraska Press, 1992.

McConville, Brendan. *Those Daring Disturbers of the Peace: The Struggle for Property and Power in Early New Jersey.* Ithaca, N.Y.: Cornell University Press, 1999.

Mehta, Uday Singh. *Liberalism and Empire: A Study in Nineteenth-Century British Liberal Thought.* Chicago: University of Chicago Press, 1999.

Merrell, James H. "Amerindians and the New Republic." In Jack Greene and J. R. Pole, eds., *Blackwell Companions to American History: A Companion to the American Revolution.* Malden, Mass.: Blackwell, 2000.

———. " 'I desire that all I have said . . . may be taken down aright': Revisiting Teedyuscung's 1756 Treaty Council Speeches." *William and Mary Quarterly* 63 (October 2006): 777–826.

———. *Into the American Woods: Negotiators on the Pennsylvania Frontier.* New York: Norton, 1999.

Merritt, Jane T. *At the Crossroads: Indians and Empire on the Mid-Atlantic Frontier, 1700–1763.* Chapel Hill: University of North Carolina Press, 2003.

Miller, Jay. "The Delaware as Women: A Symbolic Solution." *American Ethnologist* 1 (August 1974): 507–14.

Miller, Kerby A., et al., eds. *Irish Immigrants in the Land of Canaan: Letters and Memoirs from Colonial and Revolutionary America, 1675–1815.* New York: Oxford University Press, 2003.

Morgan, Edmund S. *American Slavery, American Freedom: The Ordeal of Colonial Virginia.* New York: Norton, 1976.

———. *Benjamin Franklin.* New Haven, Conn.: Yale University Press, 2002.

Moyer, Paul. " 'A Dangerous Combination of Villains': Pennsylvania's Wild Yankees and the Social Context of Agrarian Resistance in Early America." *Pennsylvania History* 73.1 (2006): 37–68.

———. *Wild Yankees: The Struggle for Independence along Pennsylvania's Revolutionary Frontier, 1760–1820.* Ithaca, N.Y.: Cornell University Press, 2007.

Murphy, Raymond E. *Pennsylvania: A Regional Geography.* Harrisburg: Pennsylvania Book Service, 1937.

Myers, James P. "Pennsylvania's Awakening: The Kittanning Raid of 1756." *Pennsylvania History* 66.3 (1999): 399–420.

———. "The Rev. Thomas Barton's Authorship of *The Conduct of the Paxton Men Impartially Represented* (1764)." *Pennsylvania History* 61.2 (1994): 155–83.

Nolt, Steven M. "A Spirit of Exclusivity: The Progress of Religious Conflict in Colonial Pennsylvania." *Pennsylvania Mennonite Heritage* (April 1996): 2–16.

Olson, Alison. "The Pamphlet War over the Paxton Boys." *Pennsylvania Magazine of History and Biography* 123 (January/April 1999): 31–55.

O'Toole, Fintan. *White Savage: William Johnson and the Invention of America.* New York: Farrar, Straus and Giroux, 2005.

Ousterhout, Anne M. "Frontier Vengeance: Connecticut Yankees vs. Pennamites in the Wyoming Valley." *Pennsylvania History* 62.3 (1995): 330–63.

———. *A State Divided: Opposition in Pennsylvania to the American Revolution.* Westport, Conn.: Greenwood Press, 1987.

Peckham, Howard. *Pontiac and the Indian Uprising.* Princeton, N.J.: Princeton University Press, 1947.

Pencak, William A., and Daniel K. Richter, eds. *Friends and Enemies in Penn's Woods: Indians, Colonists, and the Racial Construction of Pennsylvania.* University Park: Penn State University Press, 2004.

Richter, Daniel K. *Facing East from Indian Country: A Native History of Early America.* Cambridge, Mass.: Harvard University Press, 2001.

———. "A Framework for Pennsylvania Indian History." *Pennsylvania History* 57.3 (1990): 236–61.

———. *The Ordeal of the Longhouse: The Peoples of the Iroquois League in the Era of European Colonization.* Chapel Hill: University of North Carolina Press, 1992.

———. "War and Culture: The Iroquois Experience." *William and Mary Quarterly*, 3rd ser., 40 (October 1983): 528–59.

———. "Whose Indian History?" *William and Mary Quarterly*, 3rd ser., 50 (April 1993): 379–93.

Ries, Linda A. "The Rage of Opposing Government: The Stump Affair of 1768." *Cumberland County History* 1 (Summer 1984): 21–45.

Rowe, G. S. "The Frederick Stump Affair, 1768, and Its Challenge to Legal Historians of Early Pennsylvania." *Pennsylvania History* 49.4 (1982): 259–88.

Russell, Marvin F. "Thomas Barton and Pennsylvania's Colonial Frontier." *Pennsylvania History* 46.4 (1979): 313–34.

Schock, Edwin T., Jr. "The 'Cloven Foot' Rediscovered: The Historiography of the Conestoga Massacre through Three Centuries of Scholarship." *Journal of the Lancaster County Historical Society* 96.3 (1994): 99–112.

Sharpless, Isaac. "A Pennsylvania Episode." *Bulletin of the Friends Historical Society of Philadelphia* 1 (February 1907): 70–74.

Shepherd, William R. *History of Proprietary Government in Pennsylvania.* New York: Columbia University Press, 1896.

———. "The Land System of Provincial Pennsylvania." In *Annual Report of the American Historical Association for the year 1895* (Washington, D.C., 1896): 117–25.

Shirk, Willis L., Jr. "Wright's Ferry: A Glimpse into the Susquehanna Backcountry." *Pennsylvania Magazine of History and Biography* 120 (January/April 1996): 61–87.

Shoemaker, Nancy. *A Strange Likeness: Becoming Red and White in Eighteenth-Century America*. New York: Oxford University Press, 2004.

Silver, Peter. "Indian Hating and the Rise of Whiteness in Provincial Pennsylvania." Unpublished Ph.D. dissertation, Yale University, 2001.

———. *Our Savage Neighbors: How Indian War Transformed Early America*. New York: Norton, 2008.

Sipe, C. Hale. *The Indian Wars of Pennsylvania*. 2 vols. 1929; Bowie, Md.: Heritage Books, 2000.

Slaughter, Thomas P. "Crowds in Eighteenth-Century America: Reflections and New Directions." *Pennsylvania Magazine of History and Biography* 115 (January 1991): 3–34.

———. "Interpersonal Violence in a Rural Setting: Lancaster County in the Eighteenth Century." *Pennsylvania History* 58.2 (1991): 98–123.

Sloan, David. "The Paxton Riots: A Study of Violence and Passive Resistance in Colonial Pennsylvania." Unpublished Ph.D. dissertation, University of California at Santa Barbara, 1970.

———. "'A Time of Sifting and Winnowing': The Paxton Riots and Quaker Non-violence in Pennsylvania." *Quaker History* 66 (1977): 3–22.

Smolenski, John. "Friends and Strangers: Religion, Diversity, and the Ordering of Public Life in Colonial Pennsylvania, 1681–1764." Unpublished Ph.D. dissertation, University of Pennsylvania, 2001.

Speck, Frank G. "The Delaware Indians as Women: Were the Original Pennsylvanians Politically Emasculated?" *Pennsylvania Magazine of History and Biography* 70 (October 1946): 377–89.

Stanley, George F. G. "The Six Nations and the American Revolution." *Ontario History* 56 (1964): 217–32.

Stefon, Frederick J. "The Wyoming Valley." In John B. Frantz and William Pencak, eds., *Beyond Philadelphia: The American Revolution in the Pennsylvania Hinterlands*. University Park: Penn State University Press, 1998.

Stephenson, R. S. "Pennsylvania Provincial Soldiers in the Seven Years' War." *Pennsylvania History* 62.2 (1995): 196–212.

Stillé, Charles J. "The Attitudes of the Quakers during the Provincial Wars." *Pennsylvania Magazine of History and Biography* 10 (1886): 283–315.

Stotz, Charles Morse. *Outposts of the War for Empire. The French and English in Western Pennsylvania: Their Armies, Their Forts, Their People, 1749–1764*. Pittsburgh, Penna.: University of Pittsburgh Press, 1985.

Taylor, Robert J. "Trial at Trenton." *William and Mary Quarterly*, 3rd ser., 26 (1969): 521–47.

Thayer, Theodore. "The Friendly Association." *Pennsylvania Magazine of History and Biography* 67 (October 1943): 356–76.

———. *Israel Pemberton, King of the Quakers*. Philadelphia: Historical Society of Pennsylvania, 1943.

———. *Pennsylvania Politics and the Growth of Democracy, 1740–1776*. Harrisburg: Pennsylvania Historical and Museum Commission, 1953.

———. "The Quaker Party of Pennsylvania, 1755–1765." *Pennsylvania Magazine of History and Biography* 71 (January 1947): 19–43.

Tolles, Frederick B. *James Logan and the Culture of Provincial Pennsylvania*. Boston: Little, Brown, 1957.

———. *Meeting House and Counting House: The Quaker Merchants of Colonial Philadelphia, 1682–1763*. Chapel Hill: University of North Carolina Press, 1948.

———. "Nonviolent Contact: The Quakers and the Indians." *Proceedings of the American Philosophical Society* 57 (April 1963): 93–101.

Treese, Lorett. *The Storm Gathering: The Penn Family and the American Revolution*. University Park: Penn State University Press, 1992.

Trinterud, Leonard. *The Forming of an American Tradition: A Re-examination of Colonial Presbyterianism*. Philadelphia: Westminster Press, 1949.

Tully, Alan W. *Forming American Politics: Ideals, Interests, and Institutions in Colonial New York and Pennsylvania*. Baltimore: Johns Hopkins University Press, 1994.

Turner, Frederick Jackson. "The Old West." *Proceedings of the State Historical Society of Wisconsin*, 56 (1908): 184–233.

Van Every, Dale. *Forth to the Wilderness: The First American Frontier, 1754–1774*. New York: William Morrow, 1961.

Vaughan, Alden T. "Frontier Banditti and the Indians: The Paxton Boys' Legacy, 1763–1775." *Pennsylvania History* 51.1 (1984): 1–29.

———. "Philadelphia under Siege." *American History* 33 (February 1999): 26–33.

Wallace, Anthony F. C. *King of the Delawares: Teedyuscung, 1700–1763*. 1949; Syracuse, N.Y.: Syracuse University Press, 1990.

———. "Women, Land and Society: Three Aspects of Aboriginal Delaware Life." *Pennsylvania Archaeologist* 17 (1947): 1–35.

Wallace, Helen B. *Historic Paxton: Her Days and Her Ways, 1722–1913*. Harrisburg: Privately printed, 1913.

Ward, Matthew C. "An Army of Servants: The Pennsylvania Regiment During the Seven Years' War." *Pennsylvania Magazine of History and Biography* 119 (January/April 1995): 75–93.

———. *Breaking the Backcountry: The Seven Years' War in Virginia and Pennsylvania, 1754–1765*. Pittsburgh, Penna.: University of Pittsburgh Press, 2003.

Warden, G. B. "The Proprietary Group in Pennsylvania, 1754–1764." *William and Mary Quarterly*, 3rd ser., 21 (July 1964): 367–89.

Webster, Eleanor M. "Insurrection at Fort Loudon in 1765: Rebellion or Preservation of Peace?" *Western Pennsylvania Historical Magazine* 47 (April 1964): 125–39.

Weslager, C. A. *The Delaware Indians: A History.* New Brunswick, N.J.: Rutgers University Press, 1972.

―――. "The Delaware Indians as Women." *Journal of the Washington Academy of Sciences* 24 (December 1944): 381–88.

Westerkamp, M. J. *Triumph of the Laity: Scots-Irish Piety and the Great Awakening, 1625–1760.* New York: Oxford University Press, 1988.

White, Richard. *The Middle Ground: Indians, Empires, and Republics in the Great Lakes Region, 1650–1815.* New York: Cambridge University Press, 1991.

Windhausen, John D. "Quaker Pacifism and the Image of Isaac Norris, II." *Pennsylvania History* 34.4 (1967): 346–60.

Woceck, M. S. *Trade in Strangers: The Beginnings of Mass Migration to North America.* University Park: Penn State University Press, 1999.

Wood, Ellen Meiksins. *The Origin of Capitalism: A Longer View.* London: Verso, 2002.

Wood, J. H., Jr. *Conestoga Crossroads: Lancaster, Pennsylvania, 1730–1790.* Harrisburg: Pennsylvania Historical and Museum Commission, 1979.

―――. "The Town Proprietors of Lancaster, 1730–1790." *Pennsylvania Magazine of History and Biography* 96 (July 1972): 346–68.

Worner, W. F. "The Church of England in Lancaster County." *Papers of the Lancaster County Historical Society* 41.2–3 (1937): 25–92.

Young, A. H. "Thomas Barton: A Pennsylvania Loyalist." *Ontario Historical Society Papers and Records* 30 (1934): 33–42.

INDEX

Note: Page numbers in *italics* refer to illustrations.

British policy: and French and Indian War, 65–70, 86, 97–100, 118; and imperialism, 52, 53, 65–68, 109; toward Indians, 102; and Post's peace missions, 100–104, 107–11; and smallpox dissemination, 121–22

Broadly, Paul, 88

Brycelius, Paul, 161–62

Bucks County, 33, 34, *35*

Burd, James, 79, 91, 103, 104, 121

Bushy Run, *98*, 124

Butler, John, 228, 229, 230

Butler, Zebulon, 220, 226, 227, 229

Calvinists, 25

Canassatego, 47–49, 50, 84, 90

Canyase, 85–86

Captain Bull, 107, 128, 134, 221

Cartlidge, John, 22

Catholics, 3, 25, 186

Cayuga Indians: and American Revolution, 228; and Conestoga Indiantown, 43; and France, 58; and land sales of Iroquois, 42; and Philadelphia conferences, 43; and threat of war, 123

Chagrea (Jegrea), 134, 137, 179

Chambersburg, *13*, 107–8

Charles I, King of England, 186

Charles II, King of England, 2

Cherokee Indians, 232–33

Chester County, 33, 34, *35*

Chew, Benjamin, 162, 195, 217

Civility (Tagotolessa), 21–22, 41, 43, 45

Clause, Daniel, 60, 84

Clayton, Asher, 120, 128, 144, 225

Colden, Cadwallader, 148

College of New Jersey (later Princeton University), 189

Committees of Correspondence, 227

Conduct of the Paxton-Men, Impartially Represented (Barton), 174, 175, 181

Conestoga Indians: covenant with Onas, 2, 41, 43–45, 132, 134–35, 136; evidence against, 137, 163–64, 179, 182–83; and Iroquois confederacy, 45; and John Penn, 132; origins of name, 11; and pamphlet war, 174, 176, 179; at Paxton meeting, 92; and proprietary government, 43; protection of Indiantown survivors, 136, 138–39, 140–43, 180; settlers' suspicions of, 133, 134; and squatters, 51; and treaty of 1701, 11–14, 15, 21, 42; and William Penn, 2, 11–14, 15, 43, 134–35, 136. *See also* massacres of Conestoga Indians

Conestoga Indiantown: commitment to remain at, 134–35; and Conestoga Township, 34; founding of, 12; and French and Indian War, 92; location of, *13, 35, 52*; massacre at, 1–2, 135–36, 137–39; ownership of, 5, 42, 43, 209; and settlers, 21; and William Penn, 14

Conestoga Manor, 21, 32–33, 43, 209–10

Conestoga Township, 34

Congregationalists, 174, 187

Connecticut: and Lydius deed of 1754, 59–61; settlers from, 116–17, 218, 219–21, 223, 225, 226–27, 228–29. *See also* Susquehannah Company

Connoodaghtoh, 11, 12, 14–15, 92

Conoys, 12–13

Cool Thoughts on the Present Situation of Our Public Affairs (Franklin), 197–98

counties of Pennsylvania, 33–36, *35*

Covenant Chain, 12, 42, 55, 57–58, 84

Cox, John, 88

Craig's Settlement, *13*, 49

Cresap's War, 24

Croghan, George: and Easton conferences, 94, 96, 105; and Fort Cumberland, 67; and Paxton meeting, 92, 93; on potential for Indian war, 117; and squatters, 51; and Stump affair, 215

Cromwell, Oliver, 186, 187

Cumberland Boys, 120, 125, 143

Cumberland County, *35*, 36, *52*, 88, 119

Dawkins, Henry, *172, 173*

De Haas, John Philip, 221–22

Delaware George, 103

Delaware Indians: and Albany Congress, 58; and British imperialism, 67–68; and Denny, 97; displacement of, 15–17, 20; and Easton conferences, 84–85, 89–90, 93–97, 105–7, 115–17; and Edge Hill ambush, 124; and Fort Stanwix Treaty, 217–18; and French alliance, 61, 70, 101, 101, 108; and French and Indian War, 6, 58, 71, 74, 83, 86; and Iroquois confederacy, 17, 44, 45, 52–53, 93, 115–16; leadership of, 6, 49, 52–53, 54 (*see also* Teedyuscung); and Lydius deed of 1754, 219; and Ohio country, 106–7; origins of name, 16; and Pontiac's War, 117, 118–19, 121, 122, 130; and Post's peace missions, 100–104, 107–11; raids on settlements, 70–71, 74–75, 83, 86; and Sassoonan's nephews, 49, 52–53; and settlers' encroachment, 50; settlers' suspicions of, 133; at Shackamaxon, 15, 17, *18*; and status as women, 48, 70, 71, 85–86, 94, 110; and